ESSENTIALS
of
New Testament
GREEK
REVISED

A STUDENT'S GUIDE
STEVEN L. COX

B&H
ACADEMIC

Nashville, Tennessee

Design and Typesetting by
Steven L. Cox
Cordova, TN 38088

978-0-8054-2029-6

Dewey Decimal Classification: 225.48
Subject Heading: Greek Language \ Bible. New Testament

15 16 17 18 19 20 21 22   18 17 16 15 14 13

to Vivian,
my wife, companion, and friend
Proverbs 31:10-31

TABLE OF CONTENTS

PREFACE

    This workbook is designed to enhance the study of *Essentials to New Testament Greek,* revised edition, by Ray Summers and Thomas Sawyer. Teachers will find it a helpful classroom tool. Students pursuing independent studies will also benefit from these exercises because they are closely keyed to the textbook.

    Most Greek workbooks concentrate almost solely on translation skills. This workbook not only seeks to build translation skills but also to enhance understanding of Greek grammar and syntax. The exercises build an understanding of why a passage is translated in a particular way. Together with the exercises are questions concerning the grammar in the exercises. From chapter to chapter, users review and drill vocabulary and conjugation, eventually arriving at mastery of the language.

    Each lesson in the workbook begins with questions over the corresponding lesson in the textbook. Each sentence in the textbook exercises is listed, together with questions regarding the grammar and syntax of these sentences. Some lessons include paradigms under the sentences, and users fill in spaces by conjugating or locating Greek words. Other questions deal with the significance of verb tense, mood, and voice. Questions concerning a word's function in the sentence are numerically coded to the corresponding section in the textbook. This allows users to confirm their answers and encourages them to review points of grammar. The answer key at the end of the workbook is designed to help users refine their initial translations; it must not be used as a crutch or shortcut.

    I wish to express my own gratitude to Broadman & Holman Publishes, particularly to Stephen Bond, Trent Butler, Leonard Goss, John Landers, and Tim Grubbs. Gary and Trina Fulton helped answer typesetting questions. I am endebted to fellow teachers of New Testament Greek, including David Phillips, Ken Easley, Dale Ellenberg, Chuck Quarrels, and Thomas Sawyer. My students at Mid-America Baptist Theological Seminary have tested this material in the classroom. Special thanks are in order to Randy Gibson, Stephen Kearfott, Brian Rainey, Michael Wilson, and Danny Wright.

    Finally, I thank my children Dana and Bryan and my daughter-in-law Kathie. I must also mention my three grandchildren: Reagan Lynn, David Steven, Jonathan Bryan. Most of all, I thank my wife, Vivian, for her patience; her encouragement has made it possible to complete this project.

Steven L. Cox
Revised
October, 1999

ABBREVIATIONS

1 pl.	first plural	ind. rel. prn.	indefinite relative pronoun
2 pl.	second plural	indic.	indicative
3 pl.	third plural	inf.	infinitive
1PP	first personal pronoun	inst.	instrumental
2PP	second personal pronoun	int. prn.	interrogative pronoun
3PP	third personal pronoun	loc.	locative
1 sg.	first singular	masc.	masculine
2 sg.	second singular	N/A	not applicable
3 sg.	third singular	neut.	neuter
1st	first	neg. prn.	negative pronoun
2nd	second	nom.	nominative
3rd	third	obj.	object
abl.	ablative	opt.	optative
acc.	accusative	part.	participle
act.	active	pass.	passive
adj.	adjective	perf.	perfect
adv.	adverb	pl.	plural
aor.	aorist	plperf.	pluperfect
conj.	conjunction	pos. adj.	possessive adjective
dat.	dative	pres.	present
dep.	deponent	pn.	predicate nominative
descrip.	descriptive	prep.	preposition
do	direct object	rfx. prn.	reflexive pronoun
fem.	feminine	rel. prn.	relative pronoun
fut.	future	s.	subject
gen.	genitive	sing.	singular
imp.	imperfect	subj.	subjunctive
imper.	imperative	v.	verb
impers.	impersonal	voc.	vocative
ind. prn.	indefinite pronoun		

LESSON 1: The Letters and Sounds of Greek

1.1.a The student should write the alphabet on separate cards in order to enhance memory. Index cards measuring 3" by 5" are recommended. The student should write all the vocabulary words on separate cards, beginning with lesson two.

1.1.b Write the letters of the Greek alphabet, in both the upper and lower cases. Write the upper case letters on the left side of the column and the lower case on the right side.

1.	6.	11.	16.	21.
2.	7.	12.	17.	22.
3.	8.	13.	18.	23.
4.	9.	14.	19.	24.
5.	10.	15.	20.	

1.1.c Both the Erasmian and Modern pronunciation systems are listed in Appendix A.

1.1.d When ___ is followed by γ, κ, or χ it is pronounced like an English n.

1.1.e What is the difference between the sigma forms σ and ς? (1.1)

1.2.a α ε ι κ ν ο π σ τ υ ω are written on the lower line. Practice writing these letters below.

1.2.b γ η μ ρ ς χ are written on the lower line, and they extend below the lower line. Practice writing these letters below.

1.2.c δ θ λ are written on the lower line, and they extend above the imaginary middle line. Practice writing these letters below.

_____

- -

_____

1.2.d β ζ ξ φ ψ are written on and below the lower line, and they extend above the imaginary middle line. Practice writing these letters below.

_____

- -

_____

1.2.e Explain the use of capital letters in the Greek language. Write the Greek alphabet in capital letters.

_____

- -

_____

_____

_____

- -

_____

1.2.f Note the similarity of Greek and English letters.

1.3.a List the seven Greek vowels. ___ ___ ___ ___ ___ ___ ___ Of these ___ and ___ are always short in pronunciation; ___ and ___ are always long; ___, ___, and ___ may be long or short.

1.3.b A **close** vowel is pronounced with the mouth closed. ι and υ are **close** vowels. An **open** vowel is a vowel that is pronounced with the mouth open. α, ε, η, ο, and ω are **open** vowels.

1.4.a What is a diphthong?

1.4.b List the common diphthongs and their transliterations.

a.   c.   e.   g.

b.   d.   f.

1.4.c Diphthongs are formed by the combination of an open vowel followed by a closed vowel, with the exception of υι.

1.4.d The two irregular diphthongs are ____ and ____. These two diphthongs are pronounced by sounding the two letters very close together rather than giving each one a distinct sound. Two examples are, au and ou .

1.4.e What is an iota subscript? When is the iota subscript used (with what vowels in order to form a diphthong)? The iota subscript diphthongs are: ___, ___, and ___. The iota subscripts are transliterated as ___ ___ and ___. Note that the iota subscript does not affect the pronunciation.

1.5 There are ___ consonants in the Greek language. What are the three classes of consonants in the Greek language? _____ _____ _____.

1.5.a ___, ___, ___, and ___ are liquid consonants. Why are these consonants called liquid consonants?

1.5.b.1. How are mutes properly pronounced?

1.5.b.2 Categorize how labials, dentals, and palatals are sounded.

_____ are pronounced with the teeth and the tongue.

_____ are pronounced with the back of the throat.

_____ are pronounced by using the lips.

1.5.b.3 _____ refers to the way in which the lips, teeth, tongue, and throat are used to form sound; whereas, _____ refers to how smoothly or roughly you pronounce the letter.

1.5.b.4 Review the mute consonants according to their correct classification.

1.5.c ___, ___, ___, and ___ are sibilant consonants. What is the significance of sibilant consonants?

1.5.c.1 List the compound consonants. Why are they called compound consonants?

1.6 EXERCISES:

1.6.a Review the names of the letters of the Greek alphabet.

1.6.b Write the alphabet on the following lines a minimum of two times before proceeding to the next letter. Begin with the lower case letters and go through the alphabet before attempting to write the upper case letters.

_____

- -

_____

_____

- -

_____

_____

- -

_____

1.6.c Pronounce aloud each Greek letter and diphthong a minimum of five times. See 1.1 and 1.4 of the textbook.

1.6.d Write the following Greek words and their transliterations.

GREEK WORD	TRANSLITERATION	DEFINITION
1.		John
2.		Peter
3.		Philip
4.		Gabriel
5.		Paul
6.		Timothy
7.		Titus
8.		James

LESSON 2: Pronunciation and Accents

2.1.a What syllable of the Greek word is to be stressed? (See also 2.7 of the textbook.)

2.1.b What is the value of the definite article with the noun in a lexicon or a sentence?

2.2.a True/False: The exact way in which some Greek letters were pronounced in the New Testament era is certain.

2.2.b One of the major arguments in favor of using modern pronunciation is its present day use. The argument that *koine* Greek may have sounded similar to modern Greek is demonstrated by the various textual variants of the Greek New Testament. o and ω, in many textual variants, are the basis of such discrepancy. Often manuscripts were copied when a person would dictate to scribes, and the scribes wrote what they heard. In the case of o and ω (which are pronounced identically in modern Greek), one letter could easily be confused for the other, especially when either letter would be appropriate.

2.2.c What are the two values of the Erasmian system of pronunciation?

2.3.a Greek has two breathing marks. ___ represents the smooth breathing mark, and ___ represents the rough breathing mark.

2.3.b Every Greek word beginning with a _____ or a _____ must have a breathing mark, and words that have an initial ___ must have a rough breathing mark.

2.3.c The breathing mark is placed over the single _____ which begins a word or over the second _____ of a diphthong which begins a word.

2.3.d How does each of the breathing marks affect the pronunciation of a given word?

2.4 List the punctuation marks used in the Greek language by name and by letter.

1.   3.

2.   4.

2.5.a What is the purpose of an apostrophe in a Greek sentence?

2.5.b _____ occurs when a word ending with a short vowel drops the short vowel when followed by a word beginning with a vowel.

2.5.c When two words appear together and elision occurs, how does this affect the pronunciation of these words?

2.5.d _____ involves the contraction of vowels, diphthongs, or a combination of the two at the end of one word and the beginning of a second word, causing the merger of the two vowels into one.

2.5.e A(n) _____ (') is placed over the contracted vowel of crasis in order to retain the breathing mark of the second word.

2.5.f _____ (¨) appears over the second of two vowels standing together to show that the vowels are pronounced separately and do not form a diphthong.

2.6.a.1 How can you determine the number of syllables in a word?

2.6.a.2 There are no specific rules for dividing Greek words into syllables. Name two general rules that may be followed?

2.6.b.1 What are the names for each of the last three syllables of a word? Demonstrate the names of the last three syllables of ἀδελφός below.

2.7.a List the three accent marks by name and by letter.

1.   2.   3.

2.7.b Fill in the blank with the appropriate answer.

1. The _____ accent represents the rising voice.

2. The _____ accent represents the falling voice.

3. The _____ accent represents both the rising and falling voice.

4. The _____ accent can stand on any one of the last three syllables, and it will stand on long or short syllables.

5. The _____ accent can stand on the ultima only; however, it can stand on long or short syllables.

6. The _____ accent can stand on long syllables only and will occur only on the penult and ultima.

2.7.c The fourth syllable from the end is rarely accented.

2.7.d Where is the breathing mark placed when it stands on the same syllable as does the accent?

2.8 EXERCISES:

2.8.a Write the transliterations, in syllables, of the following words. Review the pronunciation of these words. (1.1 and 1.4)

Word	Transliteration	Word	Transliteration
λύ εις		εἰ ρή νη	
λύ ου σι(ν)		ἡ με ρῶν	
λαμ βά νο μεν		υἱ ός	
φέ ρω		ἤ γα γον	
ταῦ τα		ἀγ γε λί α	
ἐρ χό με θα		ἅ γι ος	
θά να τος		κα θα ρί ζω	
δῶ ρον		ποι οῦ μεν	
ἱ ε ροῦ		ψεύ δο μαι	

2.8.b Write the vocabulary of this lesson and then divide each of these words into syllables. Transliterate each word and practice the pronunciation of each word. (1.1 and 1.4)

	VOCABULARY	SYLLABLES	TRANSLITERATION
1.			
2.			
3.			
4.			
5.			
6.			
7.			
8.			
9.			
10.			

Lesson 3: Verbs—Present Active Indicative

_____

3.1 Be sure to master the vocabulary before attempting the exercises in each lesson.

3.2.1 Greek verbs, like the verbs of other languages, have _____, _____, _____, _____, and _____. Sawyer listed five pertinent components of the verb. The lexical form of a verb is essential and is considered as the sixth component in this workbook.

3.2.2 What form is the lexical form of a verb?

3.2.3 The six components of the identification of a verb are described below.

3.2.3.a.1 _____ is defined in English as the quality of the verb which has to do with time. In Greek, however, there are two characteristics in the manner of action that must be considered: the time of the action and the kind of action.

3.2.3.a.2 There are three possibilities as to the time of action: _____, _____, or _____. As to the kind of action, there are also three possibilities: _____, _____ or _____.

3.2.3.a.3 Write the name of the appropriate kind of action with its definition.

_____ action describes the action as having been completed with the result of the action continuing. (--------·|-------->) or (————·|·--------)

_____ action is expressed with the aorist tense and does not specify the kind of action. (---------) or (————) or (·).

_____ action implies a continuation of action. (-----------) or (————>).

3.2.3.b _____ is the quality of verbs which indicates the relationship of the subject to the action. The _____ VOICE means the subject is doing the action, i.e., "he is loosing." The _____ VOICE means the subject is the recipient of the action or is being acted upon, i.e., "he is being loosed." The _____ VOICE expresses the action returning to the subject.

3.2.3.c.1 _____ is the quality of verbs which indicates the relation of the action to reality.

3.2.3.c.2 What does the mood of a verb reveal?

3.2.3.c.3 The _____ mood is that mood which confirms the reality of the action from the perspective of the speaker.

3.2.3.c.4 The _____, _____, and _____, are the three potential moods. (See lessons 24 and 25 and the paradigm at the back of the textbook.)

3.2.3.d _____ is the quality of verbs which indicates whether the subject is speaking "I see," is being spoken to "you see," or is being spoken of "he, she, or it sees."

3.2.3.e _____ is the quality of verbs which indicates whether the subject is **SINGULAR** "I am loosing" (first person singular) or **PLURAL** "We are loosing" (first person plural).

3.2.3.f The *lexical form* of a word is the purest or most basic form of a word. In nouns, adjectives, and pronouns the lexical form is the nominative singular form. The declining of nouns, adjectives, and pronouns will be discussed in subsequent lessons.

3.3 In the Greek language no _____ _____ is needed because this is included in the inflected or personal ending of the verb. The use of subject pronouns is a special use that will be discussed in lessons seven, nine, and ten.

3.3.a Note that the rule of the accent of verbs is *recessive*. This means that the accent will move as near to the beginning of the word as possible. If the ultima has a short syllable, the antepenult (the third syllable from the end of the word) will be accented; however, if the ultima has a long syllable, the penult (the second syllable from the end of the word) will be accented.

3.3.b What is an infinitive? What is unique about the ending of an infinitive?

3.3.c.1 The _____ of the verb remains constant or unchanged as verb endings change according to person and number. The **PRESENT STEM** of the verb may be obtained by removing the ____ from the first person singular or lexical form. The conjugation of any regular present active indicative verb may be formed by finding the stem and then adding the personal endings: -ω, -εις, -ει, -ομεν, -ετε, and -ουσι(ν). These **PERSONAL ENDINGS** were connected to the **STEM** by the **VARIABLE VOWELS**: ο before an ending beginning with μ or ν and ε before other endings. The primary active endings -ω, -εις, -ει, and -ουσι(ν) are examples where the variable vowel and the personal endings have become inseparably contracted through the development of the Greek language. ω and ουσι(ν) have the connecting vowel ο whereas εις and ει have ε. The student, therefore, should be concerned only with the verb stem and the verb ending of present active indicative verbs.

3.3.c.2 Conjugate the verbs of lessons two and three in their present active indicative forms, in a separate notebook. This discipline should be continued with verbs in subsequent lessons.

3.3.d The _____ _____ indicates linear or progressive action at the present time, i.e., "he looses" or "he is loosing."

3.3.e There is no distinction between the _____ _____ _____ and the second person plural in modern English, though in Greek these two are distinct.

3.3.f The movable ν frequently is added to third singular and plural verbs that are followed by words beginning with a vowel/diphthong, or at the end of a sentence or clause.

3.4 EXERCISES:

3.4.a Translate the following verbs from Greek to English:

1.   ἄγει -

        ἀκούει -

        βλέπει -

        ἔχει -

   a. What is the stem of each of these verbs? (3.3.c)

   b. What does the -ει ending reveal about the subject of these verbs? (3.3)

2.   ἐγείρομεν -

        γινώσκομεν -

        γράφομεν -

        λαμβάνομεν -

   a. What is the function of ο in these verbs? (See 3.3.c.1 of the workbook.)

   b. Why are these verbs accented on the antepenult? (3.3.a)

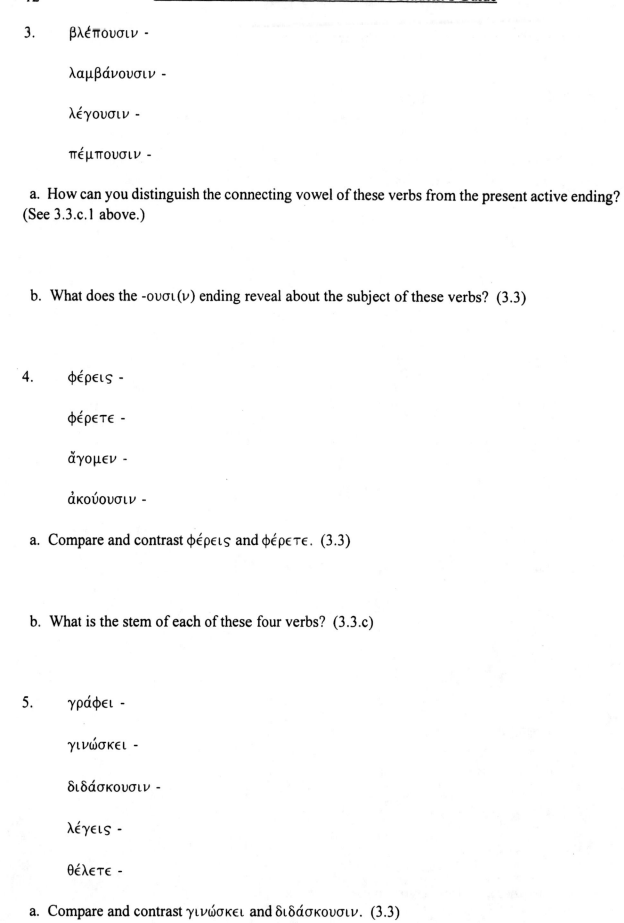

3.   βλέπουσιν -

        λαμβάνουσιν -

        λέγουσιν -

        πέμπουσιν -

a. How can you distinguish the connecting vowel of these verbs from the present active ending? (See 3.3.c.1 above.)

b. What does the -ουσι(ν) ending reveal about the subject of these verbs? (3.3)

4.   φέρεις -

        φέρετε -

        ἄγομεν -

        ἀκούουσιν -

a. Compare and contrast φέρεις and φέρετε. (3.3)

b. What is the stem of each of these four verbs? (3.3.c)

5.   γράφει -

        γινώσκει -

        διδάσκουσιν -

        λέγεις -

        θέλετε -

a. Compare and contrast γινώσκει and διδάσκουσιν. (3.3)

b. Why is γινώσκει the correct accent and γίνωσκει not the correct accent? (See section 3.3.a of the workbook.)

3.4.b Translate, dissect, and parse the following verbs. (See 3.1, 3.3, and section 3.3.c.1 of the workbook.)

1. γινώσκεις   PART OF SPEECH: STEM:

    TENSE: PERSON: ENDING:

    VOICE: NUMBER: CONNECTING VOWEL:
                                            SEE 3.3.c.1 ABOVE.

    MOOD: LEXICAL FORM: SUBJECT:

2. ἔχομεν   PART OF SPEECH: STEM:

    TENSE: PERSON: ENDING:

    VOICE: NUMBER: CONNECTING VOWEL:

    MOOD: LEXICAL FORM: SUBJECT:

3. ἄγουσιν   PART OF SPEECH: STEM:

    TENSE: PERSON: ENDING:

    VOICE: NUMBER: CONNECTING VOWEL:

    MOOD: LEXICAL FORM: SUBJECT:

4. πέμπει   PART OF SPEECH: STEM:

    TENSE: PERSON: ENDING:

    VOICE: NUMBER: CONNECTING VOWEL:

    MOOD: LEXICAL FORM: SUBJECT:

5. ἐγείρει

PART OF SPEECH: STEM:

TENSE: PERSON: ENDING:

VOICE: NUMBER: CONNECTING VOWEL:

MOOD: LEXICAL FORM: SUBJECT:

6. ἀκούομεν

PART OF SPEECH: STEM:

TENSE: PERSON: ENDING:

VOICE: NUMBER: CONNECTING VOWEL:

MOOD: LEXICAL FORM: SUBJECT:

7. ἔχετε

PART OF SPEECH: STEM:

TENSE: PERSON: ENDING:

VOICE: NUMBER: CONNECTING VOWEL:

MOOD: LEXICAL FORM: SUBJECT:

8. φέρουσιν

PART OF SPEECH: STEM:

TENSE: PERSON: ENDING:

VOICE: NUMBER: CONNECTING VOWEL:

MOOD: LEXICAL FORM: SUBJECT:

9. ἀκούω

PART OF SPEECH: STEM:

TENSE: PERSON: ENDING:

VOICE: NUMBER: CONNECTING VOWEL:

MOOD: LEXICAL FORM: SUBJECT:

10.   διδάσκεις   PART OF SPEECH: STEM:

          TENSE: PERSON: ENDING:

          VOICE: NUMBER: CONNECTING VOWEL:

          MOOD: LEXICAL FORM: SUBJECT:

Lesson 4: Nouns–Second Declension

4.1. The conjunction καί, is indeclinable and its use will be discussed in lesson 13. For now, know that καί is a simple connecting word used to join two or more clauses, phrases, or words.

4.2.a _____ is a convenient way of grouping nouns according to their endings. It has no effect on the translation.

4.2.b There are three declensions in the Greek language. *Inflection* is the change in form of a word by the addition of suffixes or prefixes to the stem in order to show its relation to other words.

4.2.c The largest number of nouns in Greek are nouns of the _____ declension nouns.

4.2.d The second declension contains mainly _____ and _____ nouns. ___ is the predominant vowel sound of the second declension.

4.3.a In Greek the _____ _____, which corresponds to the English "the," is declined as is the noun, but there is no _____ _____ in the Greek language corresponding to the English "a."

4.3.b How is the indefinite idea expressed in Greek?

4.3.c The definite articles ὁ and οἱ are called proclitics. They are not accented and are pronounced very closely with the word which follows. (9.6.a) The Greek article is used to point out particular identity. This is referred to as the **ARTICULAR USE** of a noun or other substantive. (30.3) When no definite article is used with the noun or substantive, it is called the **ANARTHROUS USE**. (30.5) The **ANARTHROUS USE** of nouns or substantives is used to indicate quality and essence. For the present time the student should concentrate on the use of the definite article. The significance of the anarthrous construction will be discussed in lesson 30.

4.3.d Why does Sawyer insist that the student master the forms of the definite article?

4.3.e The masculine forms of the definite article are used with all masculine nouns, and the neuter forms of the definite article are used with all neuter nouns, regardless of the _____.

4.3.f The _____ case does not have a definite article because the case of direct address does not call for the use of an article.

4.4.a A noun is a word that designates a _____, _____, or _____. A Greek noun is identified by listing the nominative singular form (or lexical form), followed by the appropriate definite article in the nominative singular.

4.4.b The student should concentrate on six points in the location of nouns: case, gender, number, position in the sentence (i.e., subject, indirect object, direct object, etc.), lexical form (the nominative singular form of the given noun), and the declension.

4.4.c Normally the definite article will _____ the noun.

4.5.a Case has to do with the function of the noun in relation to the _____ or to other parts of the sentence. Greek nouns have _____ inflected forms, or _____ forms when the vocative form is different from the nominative. There are _____ distinctive case functional ideas covered by these forms. (Note that some introductions to New Testament Greek do not treat the genitive and ablative or dative, locative, and instrumental as distinctive case functions.)

4.5.b One may locate the stem of a second declension noun by removing the final ος of the nominative singular masculine noun or the final ον of the nominative singular neuter noun.

4.5.c Write the name of each case with its definition with.

_____ This case is the case of location or position. The form of this case is identical to the dative. This case is adverbial in translation.

_____ This case is the case of direct address. This case always takes the same form as the nominative in the plural. The masculine singular form of this case varies in inflection from the nominative; however, in the neuter gender the form remains the same as the nominative.

_____ This case, which is also the third inflected form of the dative, is the case which expresses means. This case expresses the means by which the action is carried out.

_____ This case is the case of separation. It uses the same form as a genitive; however, the function is distinct.

_____ This case is one of designation, or the naming case. Its primary use is that of the subject of a sentence or clause.

_____ This case is the case of description. It is used to attribute quality to the word it modifies. Quite frequently this case expresses possession, either possessor or object possessed. Normally this case immediately follows the substantive that it modifies.

_____ This case is limited to the object. It marks the limit or the end of the action. The most common use of this case is that of the direct object.

_____ This case expresses interest. Its most frequent use (but not the only one) is to express the indirect object of a verb.

4.6.a Gender defines whether a noun or substantive is _____, _____, or _____. (Remember this is based on the noun/substantive ending, and even more so the nominative singular ending.) The determination of the gender of some words (in the English to Greek translation) must be learned as a part of the lexical study.

4.6.b *Number* defines whether a given noun is singular or plural.

4.7.a Why is word order not essential in Greek to determine the function of a word in a sentence?

4.7.b What is the significance of word order in Greek?

4.7.c The _____ _____ should be the guide to determine the use of a word in a Greek sentence. (See also 7.5)

4.8.a A review of the accenting of second declension nouns:

   A second declension noun with an acute accent on the antepenult will be accented like ἄνθρωπος.

   A second declension noun with an acute accent on the penult will be accented like λόγος.

   A second declension noun with a circumflex accent on the penult will be accented like δοῦλος.

   A second declension noun with an acute accent on the ultima will be accented like υἱός. This last rule of accent is the result of a special declension rule of accent: **An acute accent on the ultima in the nominative singular of second declension nouns usually changes to circumflex when the ultima becomes long except in the accusative plural.**

4.8.b Neuter nouns of the second declension differ from masculine nouns in the _____ _____ and the _____ and _____ _____. The principles of accent are the same. The final (α) in second declension neuter nouns is always short.

4.9 EXERCISES:

1. ὁ ἄνθρωπος γινώσκει τὸν νόμον.

a. Locate ἄνθρωπος. (4.1, 4.5.a, and 4.8.a)

PART OF SPEECH: FUNCTION IN THE SENTENCE:

CASE: GENDER: DECLENSION:

NUMBER: LEXICAL FORM:

b. Why is νόμον the direct object in this sentence? (4.1, 4.5.g, and 4.8.a)

2. ὁ δοῦλος φέρει δῶρον.

a. Locate ὁ. (4.1 and 4.3 and 4.3.c of the workbook)

PART OF SPEECH: FUNCTION IN THE SENTENCE:

CASE: GENDER: DECLENSION:

NUMBER: LEXICAL FORM:

b. Why is δῶρον not used with a definite article in this sentence? (4.3)

3. ὁ ἀπόστολος λέγει λόγον.

a. Is ὁ ἀπόστολος translated "an apostle" or "the apostle" in this sentence? On what do you base your answer? (4.1 and 4.3)

b. Parse λέγει. (3.1 and 3.3)

PART OF SPEECH: TENSE: PERSON:

SUBJECT: VOICE: NUMBER:

STEM: MOOD: LEXICAL FORM:

4. ἔχεις τὸν καρπόν.

a. Parse ἔχεις. (3.1 and 3.3)

PART OF SPEECH: TENSE: PERSON:

SUBJECT: VOICE: NUMBER:

STEM: MOOD: LEXICAL FORM:

b. How can you be sure of the subject when there is no nominative in the sentence? (3.3)

c. How can you be sure whether καρπόν is masculine or neuter in gender? (4.1, 4.3, 4.4, and 4.6)

5. οἱ ἀδελφοὶ ἀκούουσιν τοὺς λόγους τοῦ ἀγγέλου.

a. Parse ἀκούουσιν. (3.1 and 3.3)

PART OF SPEECH: TENSE: PERSON:

SUBJECT: VOICE: NUMBER:

STEM: MOOD: LEXICAL FORM:

b. Is τοῦ ἀγγέλου genitive or ablative? How can you be sure? (2.1, 4.5.b, 4.8.a and 7.5)

6. πέμπετε δῶρα τῷ ἱερῷ.

a. Dissect and parse πέμπετε. (3.1 and 3.3 and 3.3.c.1 of the workbook)

PART OF SPEECH: STEM:

TENSE: PERSON: ENDING:

VOICE: NUMBER: CONNECTING VOWEL:

MOOD: LEXICAL FORM: SUBJECT:

b. Locate δῶρα. (4.1 and 4.8.b)

PART OF SPEECH: FUNCTION IN THE SENTENCE:

CASE: GENDER: DECLENSION:

NUMBER: LEXICAL FORM:

c. Is ἱερῷ dative, locative, or instrumental? How can you be sure? (4.1, 4.5.d, 4.8.b, and 7.5)

7. βλέπομεν τοὺς οἴκους τῶν ἀδελφῶν.

a. Dissect and parse βλέπομεν. (3.1 and 3.3)

PART OF SPEECH: STEM:

TENSE: PERSON: ENDING:

VOICE: NUMBER: CONNECTING VOWEL:

MOOD: LEXICAL FORM: SUBJECT:

b. Is οἴκους the indirect or direct object in this sentence? How can you be sure? (4.1, 4.5.g, and 4.8.a)

8. οἱ υἱοὶ τῶν ἀνθρώπων ἄγουσιν τοὺς δούλους.

a. What is the subject of ἄγουσιν? How can you be sure? (4.1, 4.5.a, and 4.8.a)

b. What is the function of τῶν ἀνθρώπων in this sentence? (4.1, 4.5.b, and 4.8.a)

c. Locate δούλους. (4.1, 4.5.g, and 4.8.a)

PART OF SPEECH: FUNCTION IN THE SENTENCE:

CASE: GENDER: DECLENSION:

NUMBER: LEXICAL FORM:

9. λαμβάνω δῶρα καρπῶν καὶ ἄρτου.

a. Is the subject of λαμβάνω expressed in this sentence? How can you identify the subject of λαμβάνω in this sentence? (3.3)

b. Parse λαμβάνω. (3.1 and 3.3)

PART OF SPEECH: TENSE: PERSON:

SUBJECT: VOICE: NUMBER:

STEM: MOOD: LEXICAL FORM:

c. Are καρπῶν and ἄρτου genitive or ablative? What are they descriptive of? (2.1, 4.1, 4.5.b, and 4.8.a)

10. γράφομεν τοῖς ἀδελφοῖς.

a. Does γράφομεν express linear, undefined, or perfected action? Explain the significance of this action. (3.3.d)

b. How can you determine the gender of ἀδελφοῖς since τοῖς is both masculine and neuter dative/locative/instrumental plural? (4.1, 4.6, and 4.8.a)

11. βλέπω τὸν κύριον τῷ οἴκῳ.

a. Why is a nominative noun not necessary in this sentence? (3.3)

b. What case is κύριον in this sentence? (4.1 and 4.8.a) What is the significance of this case? (4.5.g)

12. οἱ ἀπόστολοι γινώσκουσιν τὸν νόμον καὶ διδάσκουσιν τοὺς ἀνθρώπους.

a. Locate ἀπόστολοι. (4.1 and 4.8.a)

PART OF SPEECH: FUNCTION IN THE SENTENCE:

CASE: GENDER: DECLENSION:

NUMBER: LEXICAL FORM:

b. What function does νόμον serve in this sentence? (4.1, 4.5.g, and 4.8.a) What about ἀνθρώπους? (4.5.g and 4.8.a)

c. Does διδάσκουσιν express progressive or perfected action? Explain. (3.2 and 3.3.d)

13. οἱ ἄνθρωποι βλέπουσιν ἀποστόλους τῷ ἱερῷ καὶ τῷ οἴκῳ.

a. Why is the movable ν expected in the phrase βλέπουσιν ἀποστόλους? (3.3.f)

b. Locate ἀποστόλους. (4.1 and 4.8.a)

PART OF SPEECH: FUNCION IN THE SENTENCE:

CASE: GENDER: DECLENSION:

NUMBER: LEXICAL FORM:

c. Are ἱερῷ and οἴκῳ dative, locative, or instrumental? How can you be sure? (4.1, 4.5.e, 4.8.a and b, and 7.5)

14. ὁ ἄγγελος λέγει λόγους θανάτου τοῖς ἀνθρώποις καὶ τοῖς υἱοῖς.

a. Parse λέγει. (3.1 and 3.3)

PART OF SPEECH: TENSE: PERSON:

SUBJECT: VOICE: NUMBER:

STEM: MOOD: LEXICAL FORM:

b. Locate τοῖς as used in this sentence. (4.1 and 4.3 and 4.3.c of the workbook)

CASE: PART OF SPEECH:

NUMBER: FUNCTION IN THE SENTENCE:

GENDER: LEXICAL FORM:

15. ὁ ὄχλος θέλει βλέπειν τὸν κύριον.

a. What part of speech is βλέπειν? What is the significance of this part of speech? (3.3.b)

b. What case is κύριον? What is the function of κύριον? (4.1, 4.5.g, and 4.8.a)

16. οἱ υἱοὶ φέρουσιν λίθους τῷ οἴκῳ.

 a. How can you be sure that υἱοὶ is nominative plural masculine rather than vocative plural masculine? (4.1, 4.3, 4.5.h, 4.8.a, and 7.5)

 b. Is οἴκῳ dative, locative, or instrumental? What is the significance and function of this case in this sentence? (4.1, 4.5.d, and 4.8.a)

Lesson 5: Nouns—First Declension

5.1 Supplemental vocabulary.

αὐτός, -ή, -ό - he, she, it (9.1 and 9.2)
ἀφίημι- I forgive (29.1)
ἀποστέλλω - I send (7.1)
ἐάν - if This is a conditional particle that
   is used to negate the verb (usually
   subjunctive) that immediately follows. (24.1)

λαλέω -I speak (26.1)
μή - not This is a negative particle that is
   usually used with the subjunctive
   mood. (21.1)

5.2.a Most first declension nouns are _____, but a few are _____.

5.2.b The first declension nouns with the article ____ are feminine. All first declension nouns ending with ____ or ____ in the nominative singular are feminine.

5.2.c The first declension nouns with the article ____ are masculine. First declension nouns whose nominative singular ends with ____ or ας are masculine. (See your textbook, chapter 5, page 23, footnote 1.)

5.2.d The first declension is noted for the dominance of the ___ sound.

5.2.e The stem of a first declension noun is found by removing the first declension ending of the nominative singular form of a given word. Once the stem is located, the noun endings for all cases may be found by removing the stem.

5.3.a The first declension has _____ main sets of endings. The student should be mindful that the _____ of the noun, not the declension, determines the articles used.

5.3.b Remember that the vocative case does not have a definite article. (See 4.3.f of the workbook.)

5.4.a The textbook lists four of the five systems of inflected endings in the singular of the first declension. The _____ _____ are the same in all systems of the first declension.

5.4.b The _____ _____ determines the system of declining the noun.

5.4.c How does one locate the stem of a first declension noun?

5.4.d Three of the first declension systems are _____ and one of the first declension systems is _____.

5.4.e.a.1 When the first declension noun stem ends in ε, ι, or ρ, the predominant vowel will be a _____, which is retained throughout the word.

5.4.e.a.2 When the first declension noun stem ends in σ, λλ, or one of the double consonants (ζ, ξ, or ψ), the nominative singular ends in a _____ which changes into the second and third inflected forms in the singular.

5.4.e.a.3 When the first declension noun stem ends in any letter other than ε, ι, ρ, σ, λλ, or one of the double consonants (ζ, ξ, or ψ), the nominative singular will end in ___, which remains throughout the singular.

5.4.e.b A few masculine nouns have _____ _____ endings. They have a _____ definite article and are modified by _____ adjectives.

5.5 EXERCISES:

1. ὁ ἀπόστολος διδάσκει παραβολὴν τοῖς ἀνθρώποις.

    a. Dissect and parse διδάσκει. (3.1 and 3.3)

PART OF SPEECH: STEM:

TENSE: PERSON: ENDING:

VOICE: NUMBER: CONNECTING VOWEL:

MOOD: LEXICAL FORM: SUBJECT:

    b. Why is παραβολὴν translated "a parable" rather than "the parable"? (4.3, 5.1, and 5.4.a)

    c. ἀνθρώποις could be translated either dative, locative, or instrumental. What is the significance of the dative translation? (4.1, 4.5.d, and 4.8.a)

2. βλέπει ὁ μαθητὴς τὸν προφήτην τῇ ἐκκλησίᾳ.

a. Why does μαθητὴς have a masculine article though the word is not a second declension noun? (5.1 and 5.4.b)

b. Explain the function προφήτην has in this sentence. (4.3, 4.5.g, 5.1, and 5.4.b)

c. Locate ἐκκλησίᾳ. (5.1 and 5.4.a.1)

PART OF SPEECH: FUNCTION IN THE SENTENCE:

CASE: GENDER: DECLENSION:

NUMBER: LEXICAL FORM:

3. οἱ υἱοὶ τῶν ἀνθρώπων γινώσκουσιν ἀγάπην καὶ ἀλήθειαν καὶ τὰς γραφάς.

a. ἀνθρώπων could be either masculine, feminine or neuter based on its ending. In what gender is this word and what is the significance of this use? (4.1, 4.5.b, and 4.8.a)

b. What case is ἀγάπην in? What case is ἀλήθειαν in? What case is γραφάς in? (4.5.g) Why are the endings of these words so radically different? (5.1, 5.3, and 5.4.a)

c. The various uses of καὶ will be discussed in lesson 13. What part of speech is καὶ? (4.1)

4. Ἐὰν (if) ταῖς γλώσσαις τῶν ἀνθρώπων λαλῶ (I speak) καὶ τῶν ἀγγέλων, ἀγάπην δὲ (but) μὴ (not) ἔχω, . . . (1 Cor. 13:1)

a. Is γλώσσαις dative, locative, or instrumental? (5.1, 5.5.a.1, 4.5.f, and 7.5) Context within the sentence is the best guide in determining case when case endings are identical.

b. λαλῶ is a present active subjunctive, with the subjunctive mood expressing a condition. The subjunctive mood will be discussed in lesson 24.

c. μὴ is used to negate the verbs in moods other than those in the indicative. (See 5.1 in the workbook and 9.5 and 21.1 of the textbook.)

5. ὁ προφήτης διδάσκει εἰρήνην καὶ ἀλήθειαν.

a. Is ὁ προφήτης best translated as "a prophet" or "the prophet"? On what do you base your decision? (4.3, 5.1, and 5.4.b)

b. Dissect and parse διδάσκει. (3.1 and 3.3)

PART OF SPEECH: STEM:

TENSE: PERSON: ENDING:

VOICE: NUMBER: CONNECTING VOWEL:

MOOD: LEXICAL FORM: SUBJECT:

c. Locate εἰρήνην. (5.1 and 5.4.a.1)

PART OF SPEECH: FUNCTION IN THE SENTENCE:

CASE: GENDER: DECLENSION:

NUMBER: LEXICAL FORM:

6. γινώσκει ὁ μαθητὴς ἁμαρτίαν καὶ λέγει λόγους τῆς βασιλείας.

a. What is the subject of γινώσκει? How about λέγει? (3.3)

b. The various uses of καὶ will be discussed in lesson 13. What part of speech is καὶ? (4.1)

c. How can you be sure that βασιλείας is genitive/ablative singular feminine rather than accusative plural feminine? (5.1, 5.3, 5.4.a.1, and 7.5)

7. ὁ ἀπόστολος γράφει τοῦ οἴκου τῇ ἐκκλησίᾳ.

a. Note the identical stem γραφ- in the words γράφει and γραφήν. Contrast these two words. (3.1, 3.3, 5.1, and 5.4.a.3)

b. Is οἴκου genitive singular masculine or ablative singular masculine? (4.1, 4.5.c, and 4.8.a) How can you be sure? (7.5)

c. Is τῇ ἐκκλησίᾳ dative, locative, or instrumental? Explain the significance of this case. (4.5.d, 5.1, 5.4.a, and 7.5)

8. οἱ υἱοὶ γινώσκουσιν τὴν ἐντολὴν καὶ λέγουσιν παραβολὴν τῷ ὄχλῳ.

a. Dissect and parse γινώσκουσιν. (3.1 and 3.3)

PART OF SPEECH: STEM:

TENSE: PERSON: ENDING:

VOICE: NUMBER: CONNECTING VOWEL:

MOOD: LEXICAL FORM: SUBJECT:

b. In this sentence ἐντολὴν follows γινώσκουσιν and παραβολὴν follows λέγουσιν. What case are these nouns in? (5.1 and 5.4.a.3) What is the significance of this case? (4.5.g)

c. Is ὄχλῳ dative, locative, or instrumental? (4.1, 4.5.d, 4.8.a, and 7.5) What is the significance of these three named cases? (4.5.d-f)

9. θέλουσιν λέγειν τὴν ἀλήθειαν τῆς ἐντολῆς.

  a. What part of speech is λέγειν? What is the significance of this part of speech? (3.3)

  b. Why is the ending of ἀλήθειαν -αν and the article is τὴν? Why is the word not spelled ἀληθείην? (5.1, 5.3, and 5.4.a.1)

  c. ἐντολῆς could be either genitive or ablative. In what case is this word used in this sentence and what is the significance of this use? (5.1, 4.5.b, and 5.4.a.3)

10. τὸν κύριον βλέπει ὁ ἄγγελος καὶ γινώσκει τὴν ἡμέραν εἰρήνης.

  a. What is the subject of γινώσκει? On what do you base your answer? (See 3.1 and 3.3 of the textbook and 3.3.a of the workbook.)

  b. Why are τὸν and τὴν both accusative singular definite articles and spelled differently? (4.3 and 5.3)

  c. Locate εἰρήνης. (5.1 and 5.4.a.3)

PART OF SPEECH: FUNCTION IN THE SENTENCE:

CASE: GENDER: DECLENSION:

NUMBER: LEXICAL FORM:

11. ἀκούετε τὴν διδαχὴν τοῦ μαθητοῦ καὶ γινώσκετε τὴν δόξαν τῆς βασιλείας.

a. Dissect and parse ἀκούετε. (3.1 and 3.3)

PART OF SPEECH: STEM:

TENSE: PERSON: ENDING:

VOICE: NUMBER: CONNECTING VOWEL:

MOOD: LEXICAL FORM: SUBJECT:

b. Why is the ending of δόξαν -αν and the article is τὴν? Why is the word not spelled δόξην? (5.1, 5.3, and 5.4.a.2)

12. οἱ προφῆται λέγουσιν λόγους ἀληθείας ὄχλοις ἀνθρώπων.

a. Locate προφῆται. (5.1 and 5.4.b)

PART OF SPEECH: FUNCTION IN THE SENTENCE:

CASE: GENDER: DECLENSION:

NUMBER: LEXICAL FORM:

b. Is ἀληθείας genitive singular feminine, ablative singular feminine, or accusative plural feminine? (5.1 and 5.4.a) How can you be sure? (See 4.7.c of the workbook and 7.5 of the textbook.)

c. Is ὄχλοις dative, locative, or instrumental? (4.5.d) How can you be sure? (See 4.7.c of the workbook and 7.5 of the textbook.)

13. ἄγεις τοὺς υἱοὺς καὶ λέγεις παραβολὴν τῶν γραφῶν.

a. What is the subject of ἄγεις? How about λέγεις? How can you be sure? (3.3)

b. Dissect and parse λέγεις. (3.1 and 3.3)

PART OF SPEECH: STEM:

TENSE: PERSON: ENDING:

VOICE: NUMBER: CONNECTING VOWEL:

MOOD: LEXICAL FORM: SUBJECT:

c. Locate γραφῶν. (5.1 and 5.4.a.3)

PART OF SPEECH: FUNCTION IN THE SENTENCE:

CASE: GENDER: DECLENSION:

NUMBER: LEXICAL FORM:

14. γινώσκουσιν οἱ μαθηταὶ τῶν προφητῶν τὰς ἐντολὰς τοῦ κυρίου.

a. Why does μαθηταὶ have a masculine definite article though this is a first declension noun? (5.1 and 5.4.b)

b. Is προφητῶν masculine, feminine, or neuter in gender? How can you be sure? (5.1 and 5.3.b)

c. Is ἐντολὰς genitive singular feminine, ablative singular feminine, or accusative plural feminine? How can you be sure? (5.1, 5.3, and 5.1.a.3)

d. Is τοῦ κυρίου genitive or ablative case? How are these two words translated in the case you chose? How would these words be translated in the case that you did not choose? (4.1, 4.5.b, and 4.8.a)

15. ἐξουσίαν ἔχει ὁ υἱὸς τοῦ ἀνθρώπου ἀφιέναι (to forgive) ἁμαρτίας (Mark 2:10).

   a. What effect does the word order of this sentence have on its translation? Why? (4.7)

   b. What part of speech is ἀφιέναι? What is the significance of this part of speech? (3.3)

   c. Is ἁμαρτίας genitive singular feminine, ablative singular feminine, or accusative plural feminine? How can you be sure? (5.1, 5.4.a, and 7.5)

16. ὁ κύριος διδάσκει τὴν ἐκκλησίαν ἀγάπῃ.

   a. How can you be sure that κύριος is the subject of διδάσκει? (4.1, 4.3, 4.5.a, and 4.8.a)

   b. Parse διδάσκει. (3.1 and 3.3)

PART OF SPEECH: TENSE: PERSON:

SUBJECT: VOICE: NUMBER:

STEM: MOOD: LEXICAL FORM:

   c. Is ἀγάπῃ dative, locative, or instrumental? (4.5.f, 5.1, and 5.4.a.3) How can you be sure? (See 4.7.c of the workbook and 7.5 of the textbook.) What is the significance of this case? (4.5.f)

LESSON 6: Adjectives of the First and Second Declension

6.1.a Supplemental vocabulary.

ἀλλά - but (12.1)

ἀποκάλυψις, εως, ἡ - revelation

δέ - but (9.1

εἰμί - I am (9.1)

εὐαγγέλιον, τό - gospel, good
  news (10.1)

θεός, ὁ - God, a god (7.1)

οὐ, οὐκ - not (9.1)

παλαιός, -ά -όν - old (28.1)

σύ - you (9.1 and 9.2)

ψαλμός, ὁ - hymn

6.1.b ἀγαθός, -ή, -ον in general denotes essential goodness, as in character, whereas καλός, -ή, -όν is non-essential goodness such as "attractive, good looking, or suitable."

6.1.c The mastery of the Greek adjective, like the definite article, provides an excellent opportunity for the reinforcement of the learning of the first and second declension noun endings, since adjectives have the same endings as used in the declension of the nouns. (See sections 4.3, 4.8.a and b, 5.3, and 5.4.a and b.)

6.1.d Adjectives may be distinguished in the vocabulary in that they are listed in the nominative singular masculine form with the feminine and neuter endings immediately following (i.e., ἄλλος, -η, -o). (See 6.2.)

6.2.a Adjectives are accented according to the rule of noun accent; that is, the accent remains on the same syllable as far as the general rules of accent will permit.

6.2.b Adjectives, like nouns, have _____, _____, and _____. When an adjective is used to modify a noun, it must agree with the noun in case, number, and gender.

6.3.a _____ and _____ adjectives follow the endings of the second declension; whereas, _____ adjectives follow those of the first declension.

6.3.b The fact that determines the ending of an adjective modifying a noun is the _____ and not the _____ of the noun.

6.3.c In the sentence βλέπω τὸν πιστὸν ἀδελφόν, "I see the faithful brother," the form of the adjective πιστός must be in the _____ case (πιστόν) in order to agree with ἀδελφόν.

6.3.d The nominative singular ending of feminine adjectives is _____ after ε, ι, ρ; however, any other stem ending the feminine singular ending will have ___.

6.3.e Note the first and second declension forms of the adjective ἀγαθός, -ή, -όν and δίκαιος, -α, -ον.

6.4.a.1 The _____ use of the adjective attributes a quality to the noun modified. List the two ways the author illustrates this use. Write the English translation of the these Greek examples.

  1.

  2.

6.4.a.2 In the attributive use of adjectives, the definite article usually _____ the adjective. (6.4.a)

6.4.a.3 ὁ ἀγαθὸς λόγος and ὁ λόγος ὁ ἀγαθὸς are equivalent expressions, but they are not identical. The English translation does not demonstrate the difference; however, in ὁ ἀγαθὸς λόγος, the adjective is stressed and more prominent; and in ὁ λόγος ὁ ἀγαθὸς, emphasis is distributed more equally (Dana nad Mantey, pp. 151-152).

6.4.b.1 The _____ use of the adjective makes an assertion or statement about the noun. List the two positions where the author illustrates this use. Write the English translation of the these Greek examples.

  1.

  2.

6.4.b.2 The predicate use when the article usually preceding the noun and not the adjective. A second identifying factor is that the predicate adjective is always in the *nominative* case.

6.4.b.3 The distinction between the attributive and the predicative adjective is much more important in Greek than in English. Later it will be observed that some of the most important and characteristic elements are based on this distinction.

6.4.b.4 A noun combined with a predicate adjective constitutes a complete sentence. The verbs of being ("is" and "are") are implied in this construction. Whenever the predicate verb is implied, the student should place the English interpretation in parenthesis ( ) to advise the reader that the verbs of being are implied and not literally present in the text.

6.4.c.1 The _____ use of the adjective has the adjective functioning as a noun. This type adjective may take on the form and use of any case.

6.4.c.2 The substantive use of the adjective is similar to the attributive use in that the substantive adjective attributes characteristics to an unexpressed noun in the same way the attributive adjective modifies an expressed noun.

6.4.c.3 The student should observe that no specific noun can be supplied by the substantive adjective, unless it is clearly implied by the context of the clause or sentence. Some unexpressed noun, identified by the gender and number of the adjective, must be understood. Note that the implied noun should be placed in parenthesis ( ). When a collective or general sense is intended, including both men and women, the _____ _____ is used.

6.4.c.4 The definite _____ can also be used substantively. (30.3)

6.4.d Occasionally the _____ _____ of certain adjectives is used adverbially.

6.5 EXERCISES:

1. ὁ ἀγαπητὸς μαθητὴς ἀκούει τοὺς ἀγαθοὺς λόγους.

  a. How can you be certain that ἀγαπητὸς modifies μαθητὴς and ἀγαθοὺς modifies λόγους? (6.1, 6.2, and 6.3)

  b. Are the two adjectives ἀγαπητὸς and ἀγαθοὺς attributive, predicative, or substantive? On what do you base your answer? (6.1, 6.3, and 6.4.a)

2. ἄγει τὸν μόνον υἱὸν τῷ μικρῷ οἴκῳ.

  a. How is μόνον used in this sentence? On what do you base your answer? (6.1, 6.3, and 6.4.a)

  b. Locate οἴκῳ. (4.1 and 4.8.a)

PART OF SPEECH   FUNCTION IN THE SENTENCE:

CASE: GENDER: DECLENSION:

NUMBER: LEXICAL FORM:

3. Ἅγιος ἅγιος ἅγιος κύριος ὁ θεός . . . (Rev. 4:8)

  a. Transliterate this sentence. (1.1 and 1.4)

  b. What is the significance of the case, number, and gender of the appearances of ἅγιος? (6.2)

4. κακὴ ἁμαρτία καὶ ἡ βασιλεία ἀγαθή.

  a. Are κακὴ and ἀγαθή functioning as attributive, predicative, or substantive adjectives? What is the primary indicator? (6.1, 6.3, and 6.4.b)

  b. What part of speech is καὶ? What is its function in this sentence? (See 4.1 of the textbook and 4.1 of the workbook.)

5. βλέπομεν τὸν κακὸν καρπὸν καὶ τὸν καλὸν ἄρτον.

  a. Dissect and parse βλέπομεν. (2.1 and 3.3)

PART OF SPEECH: STEM:

TENSE: PERSON: ENDING:

VOICE: NUMBER: CONNECTING VOWEL:

MOOD: LEXICAL FORM: SUBJECT:

  b. What case are the adjectives κακὸν and καλὸν in? (6.3)

c. What is the function of καρπὸν and ἄρτον in the sentence? (4.5.g and 6.3)

6. ἀγαπητοί, οὐκ (not) ἐντολὴν καινὴν γράφω ὑμῖν (to you) ἀλλ᾽ (but) ἐντολὴν παλαιὰν (old) . . . (1 John 2:7)

a. What case, number, and gender is ἀγαπητοί in the above sentence? What is the significance of this case? (4.5.h, 4.8.a, 6.1, 6.3, and 6.4.c)

b. ἀλλά is listed as a supplemental vocabulary word in 6.1.a of the workbook. The form ἀλλά 'used in this sentence is the enclitic form ἀλλ᾽. An enclitic is a word which (whenever possible) looses its accent and is pronounced with the preceding word. (See also 9.6.b)

c. Dissect and parse γράφω. (3.1 and 3.3)

PART OF SPEECH: STEM:

TENSE: PERSON: ENDING:

VOICE: NUMBER: CONNECTING VOWEL:

MOOD: LEXICAL FORM: SUBJECT:

7. οἱ προφῆται λέγουσιν καινοὺς λόγους ἀληθείας τοῖς πιστοῖς.

a. Locate προφῆται. (5.1 and 5.4.b)

PART OF SPEECH: FUNCTION IN THE SENTENCE:

CASE: GENDER: DECLENSION:

NUMBER: LEXICAL FORM:

b. Is ἀληθείας genitive singular feminine, ablative singular feminine, or accusative plural feminine? (5.1 and 5.4.a.1) How can you be sure? (See 4.7.c of the workbook and 7.5 of the textbook.)

c. Is τοῖς πιστοῖς "the faithful" men or women as used in this sentence? On what do you base your answer? (6.1, 6.3, and 6.4.c)

8. ὁ ἀπόστολος γινώσκει τοὺς δικαίους καὶ τὰς δικαίας.

  a. Compare and contrast δικαίους and δικαίας? (6.1 and 6.3)

  b. Does γινώσκει express progressive or perfected action? Explain. (3.2 and 3.3.d)

9. αἱ ἡμέραι πονηραί εἰσιν (are) (Eph. 5:16).

  a. In what use is the adjective πονηραί in the phrase αἱ ἡμέραι πονηραί? What is the significance of this use? (6.1, 6.3, and 6.4.b)

  b. Is the verb of being εἰσιν (is) necessary in this sentence? Why or why not? (6.4.b, 9.1, and 9.4)

10. τοὺς νεκροὺς ὁ θεὸς ἐγείρει ταῖς ἐσχάταις ἡμέραις.

  a. What is the subject of ἐγείρει? On what do you base your answer? (3.3, 4.8.a, 7.1, and 7.5)

  b. Parse ἐγείρει. (3.1 and 3.3)

PART OF SPEECH: TENSE: PERSON:

SUBJECT: VOICE: NUMBER:

STEM: MOOD: LEXICAL FORM:

c. Is ἡμέραις dative, locative, or instrumental? (5.1 and 5.4.a.1) What is the significance of this case? (4.5.e)

11. πιστὸς δὲ (but) ὁ θεός (1 Cor. 10:13).

a. δὲ is a postpositive conjunction, which means that it appears as the second or third word of a clause or sentence, but it is translated as the first word of a clause or sentence. (See 9.1 and 9.5)

b. Why is there no need for a verb in this sentence? (6.4.b)

12. ὁ υἱὸς τοῦ ἀνθρώπου ἔχει δικαίους φέρειν τὴν ἀλήθειαν τοῖς ἀνθρώποις.

a. What factors confirm that υἱὸς is the subject of ἔχει? (4.1, 4.5.a, 4.8.a, and 7.5)

b. Is ἀνθρώπου genitive or ablative in case? (4.1 and 4.8.a) How can you be sure? (7.5)

c. What part of speech is φέρειν? What is the significance of this part of speech? (3.1 and 3.3)

13. ἀγαθὸς ὁ ἀδελφὸς καὶ διδάσκει τοὺς πιστοὺς τῇ ἐκκλησίᾳ.

a. Are the adjectives ἀγαθὸς and πιστοὺς attributive, predicate, or substantive? On what do you base your answer? (6.1, 6.3, and 6.4.b and c)

b. What is the subject of διδάσκει? (3.1 and 3.3)

c. Why is the position of the article important in translating the adjective? (6.4.b)

14. ὁ δίκαιος μαθητὴς γράφει ἄλλην παραβολήν ὅλῃ τῇ ἐκκλησίᾳ.

a. Explain the agreement of elements of the attributive phrase ὁ δίκαιος μαθητὴς. (4.1, 5.1, 5.4.b, 6.1, 6.2, 6.3, and 6.4.a)

b. Is ἐκκλησίᾳ dative, locative, or instrumental? (5.1 and 5.4.a.1) What is the significance of this case? (4.5.d)

15. ὁ ἕτερος ἄνθρωπος ἔχει τὸν μόνον κάλον υἱόν.

a. What is the difference between ἄλλος and ἕτερος? (6.1)

b. ὁ ἕτερος ἄνθρωπος could be just as well stated (in Greek) as _____. (6.4.a)

c. What factors identify υἱόν as accusative singular masculine? (4.1, 4.3, and 4.8.a)

16. πιστὴ ἡ διδαχὴ καὶ ὁ νόμος δίκαιος.

a. How can you be certain that πιστὴ modifies διδαχὴ and δίκαιος modifes νόμος? In what uses are these adjectives in relation to the respective nouns? (6.1, 6.2, 6.3, and 6.4.b)

b. Locate νόμος. (4.1 and 4.8.a)

PART OF SPEECH: FUNCTION IN THE SENTENCE:

CASE: GENDER: DECLENSION:

NUMBER: LEXICAL FORM:

17. ἕκαστος ψαλμὸν (hymn) ἔχει, διδαχὴν ἔχει, ἀποκάλυψιν (revelation) ἔχει, γλῶσσαν ἔχει (1 Cor. 14:26).

  a. Is ἕκαστος in the attributive, predicative, or substantive use in this sentence? (6.1, 6.3, and 6.4.c) What is the function of ἕκαστος in this sentence? (4.5.a)

  b. Notice the four occurrences of ἔχει in this sentence and the three occurrences of ἅγιος in sentence three above. This is a classic example of **paranomasia**, where a word or word stem is repeated in close proximity.

  c. Note that ἀποκάλυψιν is an accusative singular feminine third declension noun. See lesson 18.2 for the declension of ἀποκάλυψις.

18. οἱ κακοὶ ἄνθρωποι λέγουσιν ἕτερον εὐαγγέλιον (gospel).

  a. How can you be sure that the adjective κακοὶ is in the attributive use in the phrase οἱ κακοὶ ἄνθρωποι. (6.1, 6.3, and 6.4.a)

  b. Why is the movable ν expected in the phrase λέγουσιν ἕτερον? (3.3.f)

  c. What is the function of εὐαγγέλιον in this sentence? (See 4.5.g, 4.8.b, and 10.1 of the text book and 6.1.a of the workbook.)

LESSON 7: The Greek Sentence

7.1 Supplemental vocabulary.

δικαιοσύνη, ἡ - righteousness (24.1)   ἐν - in (prep) (8.1)
ἐγώ - I (9.1 and 9.2)   πνεῦμα, πνεύματος, τό - spirit (19.1)
εἰμι - I am (9.1 and 9.4)   χαρα, ἡ - joy (10.1

7.2.a _____ is word formation. This is based on the study of prefixes and suffixes of words in order to translate them into Greek.

7.2.b _____ is the orderly arrangement of words and their relation to one another to convey a meaning in a sentence.

7.2.c In the event that a given word has more than one meaning, how do you translate the word within a sentence?

7.3.a A _____ is an independent clause and may also contain other clauses, phrases, and various kinds of structures. (Dana and Mantey define clauses as having "two pivotal points of syntax, the noun and the verb." See Dana and Mantey, p. 269).

7.3.b A _____ and a _____ constitute the most elementary form of a sentence.

7.3.c In Greek one word sentences do occur. How do you know the subject of a verb if there is no noun or any other substantive in the sentence?

7.4.a.1 Many Greek sentences are simple statements with a _____ and a _____.

7.4.a.2 Occasionally Greek sentences have proper nouns that are accompanied by the _____ that is left untranslated for a more proper communication.

7.4.b.1 A sentence with a _____ _____ has a linking verb connecting the subject to a substantive in the predicate (which is also in the nominative case).

7.4.b.2 In a sentence with a predicate nominative, the _____ is accompanied by the article, regardless of its location in the sentence.

7.4.c.1 Some sentences have a direct object and/or indirect object with the former being in the _____ case and the latter being in the _____ case.

7.4.c.2 Remember that modifiers such as definite articles and adjectives must agree with the noun that they modify in _____, _____, and _____.

7.4.d.1 A _____ sentence has two or more independent clauses joined by a coordinating conjunction.

7.4.d.2 A _____ sentence has a main or independent clause and one or more dependent clauses.

7.5 Review Sawyer's eight points in translating a Greek sentence. **This is one of the most important exercises that will prepare you for the proper translation of Greek sentences.**

7.6 Review the elements for proper translation of languages including: the four parties of translation, the three stages of translation, and the two extremes many translators fall for.

7.7 EXERCISES:

1. οἱ ἀδελφοὶ πρῶτοι καὶ οἱ δοῦλοι ἔσχατοι.

  a. In what use is the adjective πρῶτοι in the phrase οἱ ἀδελφοὶ πρῶτοι? What about ἔσχατοι in the phrase οἱ δοῦλοι ἔσχατοι? What is the significance of this use? (6.1, 6.3, 6.4.b)

  b. How can this be a complete sentence when there is no verb present? (See 9.4 of the textbook and 6.4.b.3 of the workbook.) Is this a point of accidence or syntax? Explain. (7.2)

  c. Locate ἔσχατοι. (6.1 and 6.3)

PART OF SPEECH: FUNCTION IN THE SENTENCE:

CASE: GENDER: DECLENSION:

NUMBER: LEXICAL FORM:

2. γινώσκομεν τὰς παραβολὰς τῆς βασιλείας καὶ τὰς διδαχὰς τῶν ἐκλησιῶν.

a. Parse γινώσκομεν. (3.1 and 3.3)

PART OF SPEECH: TENSE: PERSON:

SUBJECT: VOICE: NUMBER

STEM: MOOD: LEXICAL FORM:

b. Is παραβολὰς genitive singular feminine, ablative singular feminine, or accusative plural feminine? What about διδαχὰς? (5.1 and 5.4.a) How can you be sure of your answer? (See 4.7.c of the workbook and 7.5 of the textbook.

3. οἱ μαθηταὶ γράφουσιν γραφὰς ἀγάπης, εἰρήνης, καὶ ἀληθείας τοῖς ἄνθρώποις.

a. Why does the first declension noun μαθηταὶ have a masculine article? (5.1, 5.3, and 5.4.b)

b. If γραφὰς is accusative plural feminine, how can you assume that ἀληθείας is genitive singular feminine since there is no definite article present? (5.1, 5.4.a.1, 7.1, and 7.5)

c. Is ἄνθρώποις dative, locative, or instrumental? How can you be sure? (4.1, 4.5.d, 4.8.a, and 7.5)

4. κεφαλὴ δὲ (and) τοῦ Χριστοῦ ὁ θεός (1 Cor. 11:3).

a. Note that the use of the article ὁ designates θεός as the subject. κεφαλὴ is anarthrous (no article) and is the compliment. Why is a verb not necessary in this sentence? (6.4.b)

b. Transliterate this sentence. (1.1 and 1.4)

5. λύει ἐκκλησίας τοῦ θεοῦ πονηροῖς λόγοις.

a. In what use is the adjective πονηροῖς in this sentence? What is the significance of this use? (6.1, 6.3, and 6.4.a)

b. Is λόγοις dative, locative, or instrumental? How can you be sure? (2.1, 4.5.f, and 7.5)

6. ὁ προφήτης ἄγει τοὺς ἀνθρώπους, καὶ μέλλει λέγειν λόγους τῆς βασιλείας τοῦ θεοῦ.

a. Locate ἀνθρώπους (4.1 and 4.8.a)

PART OF SPEECH: FUNCTION IN THE SENTENCE:

CASE: GENDER: DECLENSION:

NUMBER: LEXICAL FORM:

b. What is the subject of μέλλει? On what do you base your answer? (See 3.1, 3.3, and 7.1 of the textbook and 3.3.a of the workbook.)

c. Why is the ending of βασιλείας -ας and the article is τῆς? Why is the word not spelled βασιλείης? (5.1, 5.3, and 5.4.a.2)

7. δικαιοσύνη (righteousness) καὶ εἰρήνη καὶ χαρὰ (joy) ἐν πνεύματι (Spirit) (Rom. 14:17).

a. What part of speech is καί? How is καί used in this sentence? (4.1 and 13.4.a)

b. πνεύματι is a locative singular neuter third declension noun. (See 19.1 and 19.3.b.)

8. λαμβάνουσιν ἄρτον καὶ καρποὺς τῶν οἴκων καὶ φέρουσιν δῶρα τοῖς ὄχλοις.

    a. Compare the accidence of ἄρτον and καρποὺς as much as possible. (4.1 and 4.8.a)

    b. Is οἴκων genitive or ablative? What is the significance of this case? (4.1, 4.5.c, and 4.8.a)

9. ὁ θεὸς πέμπει ἀποστόλους τοῖς Ἰουδαίοις καὶ κρίνει ὅλον τὸν κόσμον.

    a. Is θεὸς translated "God" or "the God"? On what do you base your answer? Why is θεὸς likely the subject of the sentence? (4.3, 4.8.a, 7.1, 7.4.b, and 7.5)

    b. Is Ἰουδαίοις inclusive of the male gender only? Why or why not? (6.3, 6.4.c, and 7.1)

    c. Locate κόσμον. (4.8.a and 7.1)

PART OF SPEECH: FUNCTION IN THE SENTENCE:

CASE: GENDER: DECLENSION:

NUMBER: LEXICAL FORM:

10. Ἐγώ (I) εἰμι (am) ἡ ὁδὸς καὶ ἡ ἀλήθεια καὶ ἡ ζωή (John 14:6).

    a. Ἐγώ is the subject of the verb εἰμι. This verb requires a predicate nominative rather than an object to complete the meaning. (See 9.4.)

    b. Why does the second declension noun ὁδὸς have a feminine article? (7.1 and 5.3)

11. ἄνθρωποι λύουσιν τὰς καλὰς ἐκκλησίας καὶ τοὺς καινοὺς οἴκους.

   a. Dissect and parse λύουσιν. (3.1 and 3.3)

PART OF SPEECH: STEM:

TENSE: PERSON: ENDING:

VOICE: NUMBER: CONNECTING VOWEL:

MOOD: LEXICAL FORM: SUBJECT:

   b. How can you be sure that καλὰς modifies ἐκκλησίας? What about καινοὺς modifying οἴκους? What is the significance of this use? (6.1, 6.2, 6.3, and 6.4.a)

   c. Is this a compound sentence? Why or why not? (See 7.4.d of the textbook and 7.4.d.1 of the workbook)

12. διδάσκει τὰς γραφὰς τῷ λαῷ καὶ εὑρίσκει τὴν ἀλήθειαν.

   a. What is the subject of διδάσκει? How can you be sure? (3.1 and 3.3)

   b. Is λαῷ dative, locative, or instrumental? (4.8.a and 7.1) How can you be sure? What is the case function of λαῷ in this sentence? (4.5.d and 7.5)

   c. Locate ἀλήθειαν. (5.1, and 5.4.a.1)

PART OF SPEECH: FUNCTION IN THE SENTENCE:

CASE: GENDER: DECLENSION:

NUMBER: LEXICAL FORM:

13. συνάγομεν βαπτίζειν τῇ ἐκκλησίᾳ.

   a. Parse συνάγομεν. (3.3 and 7.1)

PART OF SPEECH: TENSE: PERSON:

SUBJECT: VOICE: NUMBER:

STEM: MOOD: LEXICAL FORM:

   b. Is βαπτίζειν a verb form, a noun, or an adjective? Explain. (3.3 and 7.1)

   c. Is ἐκκλησίᾳ dative, locative, or instrumental? (5.1 and 5.4.a.1) How can you be sure? Based on the case, what is the use of ἐκκλησίᾳ in the above sentence? (4.5.e and 7.5)

14. οἱ πρεσβύτεροι ἄγουσιν τοὺς ἁμαρτωλοὺς τῇ ἀληθείᾳ.

   a. Is οἱ translated in this sentence? Why or why not? (7.1 and 7.4.a)

   b. What is the function of τοὺς ἁμαρτωλοὺς in this sentence? What is the significance of this function? (4.5.g, 4.8.a, and 7.1)

   c. Locate ἀληθείᾳ. (5.1 and 5.4.a.1)

PART OF SPEECH: FUNCTION IN THE SENTENCE:

CASE: GENDER: DECLENSION:

NUMBER: LEXICAL FORM:

15. ἀποστέλλει ὁ κύριος τοὺς μαθητὰς τῷ κόσμῳ λέγειν τοῖς λαοῖς.

a. Locate μαθητάς. (5.1 and 5.4.b)

PART OF SPEECH: FUNCTION IN THE SENTENCE:

CASE: GENDER: DECLENSION:

NUMBER: LEXICAL FORM:

b. The infinitive is used to express purpose in this sentence. (See Sawyer 31.4.a and Dana and Mantey, p. 214.)

c. Is λαοῖς dative, locative, or instrumental? How can you be sure? Based on this case, how is this word used in this sentence? (4.1, 4.5.d, and 7.5)

16. ὁ λαὸς συνάγει χαίρειν τῷ ἱερῷ.

a. Dissect and parse συνάγει. (3.3 and 7.1)

PART OF SPEECH: STEM:

TENSE: PERSON: ENDING:

VOICE: NUMBER: CONNECTING VOWEL:

MOOD: LEXICAL FORM: SUBJECT:

b. Identify fully the word χαίρειν. (3.3 and 7.1)

c. Is ἱερῷ dative, locative, or instrumental? (4.1 and 4.8.b) How can you be sure? Based on this case, how is this word used in this sentence? (4.5.e and 7.5)

17. πάλιν ἐντολὴν καινὴν γράφω ὑμῖν (to you). (1 John 2:8).

a. What part of speech is πάλιν? (7.1)

b. Parse γράψω. (3.1 and 3.3)

PART OF SPEECH: TENSE: PERSON:

SUBJECT: VOICE: NUMBER:

STEM: MOOD: LEXICAL FORM:

c. ὑμῖν is the dative/locative/instrumental form of σύ. (9.2)

18. ὁ θεὸς ἀγάπη ἐστίν (is), καὶ ὁ μένων (the one abiding) ἐν (in) τῇ ἀγάπῃ ἐν τῷ θεῷ μένει καὶ ὁ θεὸς ἐν αὐτῷ (him) μένει (1 John 4:16).

a. What is the subject of ἐστίν (Present Indicative 3rd singular verb of being)? On what do you base your answer? (5.1, 7.1, and 7.5)

b. μένων is a present active participle that is nominative singular masculine. μένων is used substantively in this sentence. (7.1, 20.2, and 20.7.b.2)

c. List the occurrences of paranomasia in this sentence. (See lesson six, sentence 17.b of the workbook.) Is this a point of accidence or syntax? Explain. (7.2)

LESSON 8: Prepositions

8.1.a Note that εἰς, ἐκ and ἐν are proclitics: they are so closely associated with the following word that they have no accent of their own and are pronounced as a part of that word. (9.6.a)

8.1.b Supplemental vocabulary.

ἅμα - together with (adv.)   ἔξω - outside of (24.1)
ἀποθνήσκω - I die (13.1)   Ἰησοῦς, ὁ - Jesus (12.1)
ζάω - I live (26.1)   ποιέω - I do, make (26.1)
διάβολος, ὁ - devil (20.1)   σάββατον, τό - Sabbath (22.1)
διδάσκαλος, ὁ - teacher (10.1)   ὥστε - so (22.1)

8.2.a Prepositions show _____ and _____ of action.

8.2.b The definite article may act substantively not only for a noun, but also a preposition. Prepositions have a variety of meanings which only the _____ will reveal. (See 7.5 and 8.4)

8.3.a A _____ is a word which is used to help substantives express their case function. Its position normally is immediately before the substantive with which it is associated.

8.3.b _____ _____ can also function as prepositions. For a more detailed description see 12.1.b of the workbook.

8.3.c Prepositions do not govern cases. The substantive that is used with the preposition is best described as the object of the preposition, according to modern linguistics. Prepositions developed in language to clarify the relation of the verb to the noun and to mark the _____ and _____ of the action expressed by the verb.

8.4 Only the basic meanings of prepositions appear in the vocabulary; however, in the translating of texts, other possible meanings occur. What three principles govern the correct translation of a preposition?

8.5.a Many prepositions drop the final short vowel when they appear before a word beginning with a vowel. This is called _____. (See also 2.5 of the textbook.) A(n) _____ is added to show the loss of a vowel.

8.5.b Prepositions that experience elision also experience change in the remaining final consonant if it is a _____ consonant.

8.6.a One of the predominant uses of the preposition is its combination with a(n) _____ to form compound verbs. This use is for emphasis.

8.6.b What redundant feature takes place when a verb compounded by a preposition appears in a sentence? (Note that the preposition is not repeated in the translation.)

8.7 EXERCISES:

1. ὁ ἀπόστολος διδάσκει ἐν τῇ ἐκκλησίᾳ.

a. Locate ἀπόστολος. (4.1, 4.3, and 4.8.a)

PART OF SPEECH: FUNCTION IN THE SENTENCE:

CASE: GENDER: DECLENSION:

NUMBER: LEXICAL FORM:

b. Is ἐκκλησίᾳ dative, locative, or instrumental?) How can you be sure? (7.5, 8.1, and 8.4) What is the significance of this case? (4.5.e, 5.1, and 5.4.a.1

2. ὁ μαθητὴς λέγει παραβολὴν περὶ τῆς βασιλείας.

a. The word μαθητὴς appears to be genitive singular feminine or ablative singular and has a nominative singular masculine definite article preceding it. Why? (4.3, 5.1, and 5.4.b)

b. Is βασιλείας genitive singular feminine, ablative singular feminine, or accusative plural feminine? (5.1, 5.4.a.3, 7.5, 8.1, and 8.4) What is the significance of the case function that the preposition expresses? (4.5.b)

3. ἄρτον σὺν καρποῖς φέρουσιν ἐκ τοῦ οἴκου καὶ πρὸς τοὺς ἀνθρώπους.

a. Dissect and parse φέρουσιν. (3.1 and 3.3)

PART OF SPEECH: STEM:

TENSE: PERSON: ENDING:

VOICE: NUMBER: CONNECTING VOWEL:

MOOD: LEXICAL FORM: SUBJECT:

b. What case does the use of ἐκ call for in this verse? (8.1) Does ἐκ portray description or separation in this sentence? (4.5.c and 8.4)

c. Is ἀνθρώπους classed as the object of the preposition πρός? Why or why not? (See 4.1, 4.8.a, 8.1, and 8.4 of the textbook and 8.3.d of the workbook.)

4. Χριστὸς ἀπέθανεν (died) ὑπὲρ τῶν ἁμαρτιῶν ἡμῶν (our) κατὰ τὰς γραφάς (1 Cor. 15:3).

a. Parse ἀπέθανεν. (13.1 and 16.2)

PART OF SPEECH: **VERB**   TENSE: **2 aor.**   PERSON: **3rd**
STEM: ἀποθαν-   VOICE: **dep.**   NUMBER: **sing.**
SUBJECT: Χριστὸς   MOOD: **indic.**   LEXICAL FORM: ἀποθνήσκω

b. Locate ἡμῶν. (9.1 and 9.2)

PART OF SPEECH: **1PP**   FUNCTION IN THE SENTENCE: **descrip. of** ἁμαρτιῶν
CASE: **gen.**   GENDER: **N/A**   DECLENSION: **N/A**
NUMBER: **pl.**   LEXICAL FORM: ἐγώ

c. Is γραφάς genitive singular feminine, ablative singular feminine, or accusative plural feminine? (5.1 and 5.4.a.1) On what do you base your answer? (8.1 and 8.4)

5. λαμβάνομεν ἀγαθὰς διδαχὰς ἀπὸ τοῦ πιστοῦ ἀδελφοῦ.

a. Dissect and parse λαμβάνομεν. (3.1. and 3.3)

PART OF SPEECH: STEM:

TENSE: PERSON: ENDING:

VOICE: NUMBER: CONNECTING VOWEL:

MOOD: LEXICAL FORM: SUBJECT:

b. Is the above use of the two adjectives a matter of accidence or syntax? Explain. (7.2)

c. Is ἀπὸ used with the genitive or the ablative case? (8.1 and 8.4) What is the significance of this use? (4.5.c)

6. εἰρήνην ἔχομεν πρὸς τὸν θεὸν διὰ τοῦ κυρίου ἡμῶν (our) Ἰησοῦ (Jesus) Χριστοῦ (Rom. 5:1).

a. Why is it not necessary for the subject of ἔχομεν to be stated in this sentence? (3.3)

b. What is the significance of πρὸς in relation to ἔχομεν and τὸν θεόν? (8.1 and 8.4)

c. How is διὰ translated in this sentence? On what do you base your answer? (8.1, 7.5, and 8.4)

7. διὰ τῶν γραφῶν τῶν μαθητῶν γινώσκομεν τὴν ἀλήθειαν.

a. What is the relationship of γραφῶν to the preposition διὰ? (See 8.3.d of the workbook.)

b. Is γραφῶν genitive or ablative? (4.5.b, 5.1, 7.5, 8.1, and 8.4) What about μαθητῶν? What gender is μαθητῶν? (5.1)

c. Why does the noun ἀλήθειαν end with αν and has τὴν as its definite article? (5.1, 5.3, and 5.4.a.1)

8. τοὺς μαθητὰς ὁ ἀδελφὸς πέμπει ἐκ τῶν οἴκων καὶ εἰς τὴν ἐκκλησίαν.

a. Is μαθητὰς genitive singular feminine, ablative singular feminine, accusative plural feminine, or accusative plural masculine? How can you be sure? (5.1, 5.4.b, 7.5, 8.1, and 8.4)

b. Parse πέμπει. (3.1 and 3.3)

PART OF SPEECH: TENSE: PERSON:

STEM: VOICE: NUMBER:

SUBJECT: MOOD: LEXICAL FORM:

c. Does ἐκ express description or separation? What case is this emphasis associated with? (4.5.c, 8.1, and 8.4)

9. ὁ κύριος λέγει παραβολὴν ἐν λόγοις ἀγάπης.

a. What elements identify κύριος as the subject of λέγει? (4.1, 4.5.a, 4.8.a, and 7.5)

b. Is λόγοις dative, locative, or instrumental? (2.1, 4.5.f, and 4.8.a) How can you be sure? (7.5, 8.1, and 8.4)

10. Οὐκ (not) ἐπ᾿ ἄρτῳ μόνῳ ζήσεται (will live) ὁ ἄνθρωπος (Matt. 4:4).

   a. Explain the spelling of ἐπί in this sentence. (2.5 and 8.1)

   b. Note that this sentence is not arranged like a typical English sentence. Explain this common Greek phenomenon. (7.5)

   c. Parse ζήσεται. (14.2 and 26.1)

PART OF SPEECH: **VERB**	TENSE: **fut.**	PERSON: **3rd**
STEM: ζη-	VOICE: **mid.**	NUMBER: **sing.**
SUBJECT: ἄνθρωπος	MOOD: **indic.**	LEXICAL FORM: ζάω

11. οἱ πιστοὶ προφῆται ἄγουσιν τοὺς δικαίους μαθητὰς τοῦ κυρίου πρὸς τὸ ἱερόν.

   a. Is πιστοὶ in the attributive, predicative, or substantive use in this sentence? What is the significance of this use? (6.1, 6.3, and 6.4.a)

   b. How can you be sure that μαθητὰς is masculine in gender? (4.3, 5.1, 5.4.b, and 6.2)

   c. What case is τοῦ κυρίου in? (4.1 and 4.8.a) Does τοῦ κυρίου express description or separation? (4.5.b and 4.8.a)

12. ὁ ἄνθρωπος λέγει ἀγαθὸν λόγον τῷ μαθητῇ καὶ ἄγει τοὺς υἱοὺς εἰς τὸν οἶκον.

   a. Is this sentence a compound or a complex sentence? Explain. (7.4.d)

b. What part of speech is καί? (4.1) How is καί used in this sentence? (13.3)

c. How do you determine the meaning of εἰς in this sentence since there are three possible meanings? (7.5, 8.1, 8.4) Why does εἰς not have an accent? (See 8.1.a of the workbook.)

13. ὥστε (so) κύριός ἐστιν (is) ὁ υἱὸς τοῦ ἀνθρώπου καὶ τοῦ σαββάτου (Sabbath) (Mark 2:28).

a. Note the use of the adverb ὥστε in this sentence. (See 12.1.d of the workbook.)

b. ἐστιν is a present active indicative third singular form of the verb εἰμί. ἐστιν is an enclitic, which means that it attaches itself to the preceding word with the result it loses its accent under certain conditions. What is the subject of ἐστιν in this sentence? How can you be sure? (4.8.a, 7.5, 9.1, and 9.4)

c. What noun does τοῦ ἀνθρώπου describe? What about τοῦ σαββάτου? (See "genitive" 4.5.c of the workbook.)

14. λαμβάνομεν καλὸν καρπὸν ἀντὶ κακοῦ καρποῦ.

a. How can you be sure of the use of καλὸν and κακοῦ since there is no definite article present with these adjectives? (6.1, 6.3, 6.4.a, and 7.5)

b. Does ἀντὶ express description or separation? Explain. (4.5.b, 8.1, and 8.4)

15. ἀπὸ τοῦ ἱεροῦ, διὰ τοῦ οἴκου, πρὸς τὴν ἐκκλησίαν, ὁ ἄνθρωπος ἄγει τοὺς υἱούς.

a. List the prepositions and the cases in which they are used in this sentence. (7.5, 8.1, and 8.4)

b. Locate ἐκκλησίαν. (5.1 and 5.4.a.1)

PART OF SPEECH: FUNCTION IN THE SENTENCE:

CASE: GENDER: DECLENSION:

NUMBER: LEXICAL FORM:

c. In what case is υἱούς? What is the significance of this case? (4.1, 4.5.g, and 4.8.a)

16. ὁ ποιῶν (the one practicing) τὴν ἁμαρτίαν ἐκ τοῦ διαβόλου (devil) ἐστίν (is) (1 John 3:8).

a. ποιῶν is a nominative singular masculine present active participle that is substantive in use. (See 20.2 and 26.1.)

b. How can you be sure that ἁμαρτίαν is accusative singular feminine? (5.1, 5.3, 5.4.a.1, and 7.5)

c. What does the definite article τοῦ reveal about the noun διαβόλου? (See 4.3 and 4.8.a of the textbook and 8.1.b of the workbook.)

17. ἀπὸ τοῦ πιστοῦ ἀγγέλου ἀκούουσιν λόγους ἀγάπης.

a. Locate ἀγγέλου. (2.1 and 4.8.a)

PART OF SPEECH: FUNCTION IN THE SENTENCE:

CASE: GENDER: DECLENSION:

NUMBER: LEXICAL FORM:

b. What is the subject of ἀκούουσιν? How can you be sure? (2.1 and 3.3)

c. Is ἀγάπης properly translated "of love," "from love," "of the love," or "from the love?" Explain. (4.5.b, 5.1, 5.4.a.3, and 7.5)

18. λέγει τὴν ἀλήθειαν ἐν ἀγάπῃ, καὶ ἄγει τοὺς υἱοὺς εἰς τὴν βασιλείαν εἰρήνης.

a. In what case is ἀγάπη? (4.5.f, 5.1, and 5.4.a.3) On what do you base your answer? (7.5, 8.1, and 8.4)

b. Why is υἱούς and not βασιλείαν the direct object of ἄγει? (See 4.1, 4.5.g, 4.8.a, 5.1, 5.4.a.1, 8.1, and 8.4 of the textbook and 8.3.d of the workbook.)

c. Is εἰρήνης genitive singular feminine or ablative singular feminine? (5.1, 5.4.a.3, and 7.5) What is the significance of this case? (4.5.b)

19. οὐκ (not) ἔστιν (is) μαθητὴς ὑπὲρ τὸν διδάσκαλον (teacher) (Matt. 10:24).

a. What is the subject of ἔστιν? On what do you base your answer? (5.1, 5.4.b, and 9.4)

b. Locate διδάσκαλον. (4.8.a and 10.1 of the textbook and 8.1.b of the workbook)

PART OF SPEECH: FUNCTION IN THE SENTENCE:

CASE: GENDER: DECLENSION:

NUMBER: LEXICAL FORM:

20. φέρει ὁ Χριστὸς ἀγάπην ἀπὸ τοῦ θεοῦ πρὸς τοὺς υἱοὺς τῶν ἀνθρώπων.

a. What effect does the order of the subject and verb, φέρει ὁ Χριστὸς, have on the translation of this sentence? Explain. (4.7)

b. Is θεοῦ genitive singular masculine or ablative singular masculine? (4.8.a and 7.1) On what do you base your answer? (7.5, 8.1, and 8.4)

c. How can you be sure of the gender of ἀνθρώπων? (4.1, 4.3, 4.6, and 4.8.a)

LESSON 9: Personal Pronouns and Enclitics

9.1.a Supplemental vocabulary.

Ἀπολλῶς - Apollos
ἀσθενέω - I am sick
βαίνω - I go
Γάϊος - Gaius
Κηφᾶς - Cephas

ὅς - who, which, what (rel. prn.) (27.1)
ὅτι - that (10.1)
πιστεύω - I believe (10.1)
προσκαλέομαι - I call to, invite
τις, τι - anyone, someone (ind. prn.)
   (27.1)

9.1.b The combination of μέν . . . δέ is frequently employed to present contrast with μέν often being left untranslated and δέ translated as "but."

9.2.a Review the declension of the first, second, and third personal pronouns.

9.2.b Note that the unemphatic forms of the first personal pronouns (μου, μοι, and με) are **enclitic**; that is, they have no accent of their own and are pronounced with the word that precedes them. The emphatic forms (ἐμοῦ, ἐμοί, and ἐμέ) are used when emphasis is desired.

9.2.c The unemphatic forms of the second personal pronouns (σου, σοι, and σε) are also enclitic. The emphatic forms (σοῦ, σοί, and σέ) are used when emphasis is desired.

9.3.a.1 What is the function of personal pronouns? How are they used in comparison with English?

9.3.a.2 The _____ is the noun or substantive for which a pronoun stands.

9.3.a.3 A pronoun agrees with its antecedent in _____ and _____. Its _____ is determined by its use in the sentence.

9.3.b Personal pronouns are not used in the _____ case as subjects of verbs unless emphasis is placed upon them.

9.3.c.1 When αὐτός is in the _____ use, whether in the nominative or another case, it is translated "same."

9.3.c.2 When αὐτός is in the _____ use, it is intensive and should be translated "him-self."

9.3.c.3 Another intensive use of the personal pronoun is with a pronoun or _____ _____ of a verb.

9.3.d The _____ (unemphatic) forms of the personal pronoun are used in the genitive case to express possession.

9.3.e After _____ the emphatic forms of the personal pronouns are ordinarily used.

9.4.a All forms of εἰμί are enclitic except _____ and the _____ _____.

9.4.b Why the does εἰμί verb forms not have voice?

9.4.c The εἰμί forms _____ and _____ take a movable ν.

9.4.d εἰμί verbs take a **predicate nominative** rather than an object to complete their meaning. εἰμί verbs never take a(n) _____ _____; therefore, the accusative case is not used.

9.4.e The predicate nominative is in the _____ case to agree with the subject since it completes the meaning of the subject.

9.4.f Explain why Greek does not require the verb of being (εἰμί) to be included in a sentence. How does this affect the order of the words in the sentence? (6.4.b)

9.5 Greek _____ are words that do not properly belong to any other category such as noun, verb, or adjective. Particles are usually used for _____, transition from one idea to another, or to express the negative.

9.5.a In this lesson's vocabulary ἀμήν, δέ, and οὐ (οὐκ, οὐχ) are particles, though _____ in some contexts is a conjunction. ἀμήν is _____, δέ is _____, and οὐ is _____.

9.5.b δέ is **postpositive**. Postpositives are words which cannot stand first in a clause or a sentence. The normal position of these words is second in a clause or sentence, although sometimes they appear as the third word.

9.5.c ___, ____, and ____are negative particles that are usually placed immediately in front of the word they negate.

9.6 Several Greek words are accented with an adjoining word. These words are called _____ and _____ because they are accented and pronounced with words that either precede or follow them.

9.6.a.1 A(n) _____ is so closely associated with the following word that it has no accent of its own and is pronounced as a part of that word.

9.6.a.2 Review the proclitic forms that you have studied up to this point: definite articles, particles, and prepositions.

9.6.a.3 TRUE/FALSE: A **proclitic** does alter the accent of adjacent words.

9.6.b.1 A(n) _____ attaches itself to the preceding word with the result that the _____ loses its accent under certain conditions. Often the preceding _____ has its accent altered.

9.6.b.2 Review the enclitic forms that you have studied up to this point: personal pronouns, particles, and verb forms.

9.7 EXERCISES:

1. οἱ μαθηταί σου διδάσκουσιν τὴν ἐκκλησίαν καὶ ἄγουσιν τοὺς ἀδελφοὺς αὐτῶν εἰς αὐτήν.

   a. Is this sentence a compound sentence or a complex sentence? Explain the significance of the choice that you made. (7.4.d)

   b. Why is σου not accented in this sentence? Is σου emphatic or unemphatic in character? On what do you base your answer? (9.1, 9.2, and 9.3.d) What special classification does the unaccented form of σου fall under? How can you be sure? (9.6.b)

   c. What is the antecedent of αὐτῶν? How about αὐτήν? How can you be sure? (7.5, 9.1, 9.2, and 9.3.a)

2. ἀσθενεῖ (is sick) τις (any) ἐν ὑμῖν; προσκαλεσάσθω (let him call) τοὺς πρεσβυτέρους τῆς ἐκκλησίας (Jas. 5:14).

a. τις is a nominative singular masculine indefinite pronoun. (See 27.1 and 27.3.c.)

b. Parse προσκαλεσάσθω. (9.1.1 and 25.2)

PART OF SPEECH: **VERB**	TENSE: **1 aor.**	PERSON: **3rd**
SUBJECT: **(3rd sing.)**	VOICE: **act.**	NUMBER: **sing.**
STEM: προσκαλε-	MOOD: **imper.**	LEXICAL FORM: προσκαλέομαι

c. Is ἐκκλησίας genitive singular feminine, ablative singular feminine, or accusative plural feminine? (5.1 and 5.4.a.1) How can you be sure? (See 4.7.c of the workbook and 7.5 of the textbook.)

3. τοὺς υἱούς μου διδάσκω καὶ δοξάζομεν τὸν θεόν.

a. What is the antecedent of μου? (3.3, 9.1, 9.2, and 9.3.a) How can you be sure? (7.5)

b. What part of speech is καὶ? How is καὶ used in this sentence? (4.1 and 13.3.a)

c. Is τὸν θεόν translated "God" or "the God"? On what do you base your answer? (4.3, 4.8.a, 7.1, 7.4.b, and 7.5)

4. διὰ σοῦ ὁ θεὸς ἄγει τὰ τέκνα εἰς τὴν βασιλείαν αὐτοῦ καὶ δι᾽ αὐτῶν τοὺς ἄλλους.

a. Why is τέκνα not the subject of the verb ἄγει? (3.3, 4.8.b, 7.5, and 9.1) There are exceptions to this rule. (See 13.3.)

b. Why is the preposition διά in the form of δι᾽ in this sentence? (2.5 and 8.1)

c. What use is the adjective ἄλλους in this sentence? What is the significance of this use? (6.1 and 6.4.c)

5. ὁ πρεσβύτερος Γαΐῳ (Gaius) τῷ ἀγαπητῷ, ὅν (whom) ἐγὼ ἀγαπῶ (I love) ἐν ἀληθείᾳ (3 John 1).

a. What does the diacritical mark (¨) signify in the word Γαΐῳ? What is the significance of this mark? (2.5)

b. ὅν is an accusative singular masculine relative pronoun. (27.1 and 27.3.a) What is its function in the phrase ὅν ἐγὼ ἀγαπῶ ἐν ἀληθείᾳ? What is the significance of this function? (4.5.g)

c. What is the significance of the presence of ἐγὼ in this sentence? (9.1, 9.2, and 9.3.b)

6. ἐγώ εἰμι δοῦλος, σὺ δὲ εἶ μαθητής.

a. Why is δοῦλος in the nominative case rather than the accusative case? (2.1, 4.8.a, and 9.4)

b. Locate σύ. (9.1 and 9.2)

CASE: PART OF SPEECH:

NUMBER: FUNCTION IN THE SENTENCE:

GENDER: LEXICAL FORM:

c. δέ is translated into English as the first word of the second phrase of this sentence. Why is δέ the second word in the Greek phrase σὺ δὲ εἶ μαθητής? (9.1 and 9.5)

7. ἕκαστος ὑμῶν λέγει, Ἐγὼ μέν εἰμι Παύλου, Ἐγὼ δὲ Ἀπολλῶ (Apollos), Ἐγὼ δὲ Κηφᾶ (Cephas), Ἐγὼ δε Χριστοῦ (1 Cor. 1:12).

a. Is ἕκαστος in the attributive, predicative, or substantive use? On what do you base your answer? What is the significance of this use? (See 6.3, 6.4.c, and 7.5 of the textbook and 9.1.a of the workbook.)

b. Parse εἰμι. (9.1, and 9.4)

PART OF SPEECH: TENSE: PERSON:

SUBJECT: VOICE: **NO VOICE**   NUMBER:

STEM: MOOD: LEXICAL FORM:

c. Why are there no verbs in the phrases Ἐγὼ δὲ Ἀπολλῶ (Apollos), Ἐγὼ δὲ Κηφᾶ (Cephas), Ἐγὼ δε Χριστου? (9.4)

8. προφῆται τοῦ θεοῦ ἐστὲ καὶ ἄγγελοι ἀγάπης.

a. What role do προφῆται and ἄγγελοι play in relation to ἐστὲ? (2.1, 4.8.a, 5.1, and 5.4.b) Why are these two nouns not in the accusative case? (9.4)

b. Parse ἐστὲ. (9.1 and 9.4)

PART OF SPEECH: TENSE: PERSON:

SUBJECT: VOICE: **NO VOICE**   NUMBER:

STEM: MOOD: LEXICAL FORM:

c. Locate ἀγάπης. (5.1 and 5.4.a.3)

PART OF SPEECH: FUNCTION IN THE SENTENCE:

CASE: GENDER: DECLENSION:

NUMBER: LEXICAL FORM:

9. ὁ μὲν κύριος πιστός ἐστιν, οἱ δὲ ὄχλοι εἰσὶν πονηροί.

a. What use is the adjective πιστός in? How about πονηροί? (6.1 and 6.4.b) Are the verbs ἐστιν and εἰσὶν necessary in this sentence? Why or why not? (6.4.b and 9.4)

b. How can you be sure that ὄχλοι is the subject of εἰσὶν and that πονηροί is a predicate nominative? (4.1, 4.8.a, 6.1, 6.3, 6.4.b, and 7.5)

c. Why does ἐστιν have a movable ν in this sentence? (3.3.f and 9.4)

10. ὁ ἀδεφός μου ἀναβαίνει πρὸς τὸν οἶκον κἀγὼ διδάσκω αὐτόν.

a. Why is μου not accented? (9.1, 9.2, and 9.6.b)

b. What did κἀγὼ come from? (9.1)

c. Dissect and parse διδάσκω. (3.1, and 3.3)

PART OF SPEECH: AUGMENT: STEM:

TENSE: PERSON: ENDING:

VOICE: NUMBER: CONNECTING VOWEL:

MOOD: LEXICAL FORM: SUBJECT:

11. ὁ Πέτρος λέγει αὐτῷ, Σὺ εἶ ὁ Χριστός (Mark 8:29).

a. Note that λέγει is a present tense verb that is commonly translated as past tense in this sentence. According to Dana and Mantey, "the present tense is thus employed when a past event is viewed with the vividness of a present occurrence" (Dana and Mantey, p. 185). This phenomenon is known as the **historical present**. (3.1 and 3.3)

b. Is Σὺ necessary in the phrase Σὺ εἶ ὁ Χριστός? What is the significance of the presence of Σὺ in this phrase? (9.1, 9.2, and 9.3.b)

c. Why is it impossible for Χριστός to be the subject of εἶ? (4.8.a, 7.1, 7.5, 9.2, and 9.4)

12. γινώσκομεν τὴν ὁδόν, καὶ ἄγομεν ὑμᾶς εἰς τὴν ἐκκλησίαν.

a. Transliterate this sentence. (1.1 and 1.4)

b. Why does the second declension noun ὁδόν have a feminine article? (4.3, 4.8.a, 5.3, and 7.1)

c. Why does ἐκκλησίαν have a different ending than its article τὴν? (5.1, 5.3, and 5.4.a)

13. εἶπεν (said) αὐτοῖς ὁ Ἰησοῦς, Ἐγώ εἰμι ὁ ἄρτος τῆς ζωῆς (John 6:35).

a. Parse εἶπεν. (3.1, 16.1, and 16.2)

PART OF SPEECH: **VERB**	TENSE: **2 aor.**	PERSON: **3rd**
SUBJECT: Ἰησοῦς	VOICE: **act.**	NUMBER: **sing.**
STEM: εἰπ-	MOOD: **indic.**	LEXICAL FORM: λέγω

b. Why is the subject of εἶπεν the last word in the phrase rather than preceding the verb? (4.7 and 7.5)

c. How can you be sure that ἄρτος is <u>not</u> the subject of εἰμι though the definite article ὁ is used with this noun? (3.2, 4.1, 4.8.a, 7.5, and 9.4)

14. κἀγὼ δέ σοι λέγω ὅτι (that) σὺ εἶ Πέτρος (Matt. 16:18).

a. What did κἀγὼ come from? (9.1) What is its function in this sentence? (7.5, 9.2, and 9.3.b)

b. δέ is translated into English as the first word of the second phrase of this sentence. Why is δέ the second word in the Greek phrase κἀγὼ δέ σοι λέγω? (9.1 and 9.5)

c. Note that ὅτι is a subordinating conjunction which means that the clause that it introduces, σὺ εἶ Πέτρος is dependent on the previous clause κἀγὼ δέ σοι λέγω. (See 13.1 and 13.3.a)

15. οἱ ἀδελποί μού εἰσιν ἐν τῷ ὄχλῳ καὶ ἐσθίουσιν ἄρτον.

a. Locate ἀδελποί. (2.1 and 4.8.a)

PART OF SPEECH: FUNCTION IN THE SENTENCE:

CASE: GENDER: DECLENSION:

NUMBER: LEXICAL FORM:

b. What is unusual about μού being accented in this sentence? (9.1 and 9.3.d)

c. Is ὄχλῳ dative, locative, or instrumental? (4.1, 4.5.e, and 4.8.a) How can you be sure? (7.5)

16. οἱ μαθηταὶ τοῦ κυρίου ἄγουσιν τὰ τέκνα αὐτῶν εἰς τὴν βασιλείαν αὐτοῦ.

    a. Dissect and parse ἄγουσιν. (2.1 and 3.3)

PART OF SPEECH: AUGMENT: STEM:

TENSE: PERSON: ENDING:

VOICE: NUMBER: CONNECTING VOWEL:

MOOD: LEXICAL FORM: SUBJECT:

    b. What is the antecedent of αὐτῶν? What about αὐτοῦ? How can you be sure? (9.1, 9.2, and 9.3.a)

17. ἐσμὲν τέκνα θεοῦ (Rom. 8:16).

    a. Locate τέκνα. (4.8.b and 9.1)

PART OF SPEECH: FUNCTION IN THE SENTENCE:

CASE: GENDER: DECLENSION:

NUMBER: LEXICAL FORM:

    b. Is θεοῦ genitive or ablative in case? (4.5.b, 4.8.a, 7.1) How can you be sure?

18. αὐτὸς φέρει τὰ δῶρά μου καὶ τὰ δῶρα αὐτοῦ πρὸς τὸ ἱερόν.

    a. Are the two uses of δῶρα in this sentence nominative plural neuter or accusative plural neuter? (4.1 and 4.8.b) How can you be sure? (7.5) What is the significance of the case of δῶρα in this sentence? (4.5.g)

b. Is πρὸς best translated in this sentence as "for," "at," or "to/toward?" (8.1) How can you be sure? (7.5 and 8.4)

19. Ἐγὼ οὐκ εἰμὶ ὁ Χριστός (John 1:20).

a. What is the subject of εἰμὶ? (9.2 and 9.4) How can you be sure? (7.5 and 9.4)

b. What is the significance of οὐκ in this sentence? (9.1 and 9.5)

c. Locate ὁ. (4.1 and 4.3)

CASE: PART OF SPEECH

NUMBER: FUNCTION IN THE SENTENCE:

GENDER: LEXICAL FORM:

20. ἀμὴν ἀμὴν λέγω ὑμῖν ὅτι (that) ὁ τὸν λόγον μου ἀκούων (the one hearing) καὶ πιστεύων (believing) . . . ἔχει ζωὴν . . . (John 5:24).

a. The definite article ὁ is used substantively in this sentence. (See 30.3) What is the significance of this use? (6.4.c and 30.3)

b. What is the function of ζωὴν in this sentence? (4.5.g, 5.4.a.3, and 7.1)

c. ἀκούων and πιστεύων are both nominative singular masculine present active participles that are in the substantive use. (See 2.12, 10.1, and 20.7.b)

LESSON 10: Demonstrative Pronouns

10.1.a Supplemental vocabulary.

ἐξέρχομαι - I go out of (11.1)   περιπατέω - I walk (26.1)
θυρωρός, ὁ - doorkeeper   πρόβατον, τό - sheep
κατάρα, ἡ - curse   χάρις, ἡ - grace (18.1)

10.1.b Note the conjunctions γάρ and ὅτι. γάρ is _____, which means that it normally appears as the second word of a sentence or clause, but is translated as the first word of the given clause or sentence. Occasionally γάρ stands as the third word of a sentence or clause, and on some rare occasions in classical Greek, γάρ appears as the eighth word. ὅτι is used with the infinitive to express direct discourse.

10.2 Demonstrative pronouns modify nouns (both expressed or implied) by specifying the noun as either "this" or "that" (singular) and "these" or "those" (plural). Demonstrative pronouns, like adjectives, when they modify a noun must agree with the noun in case, number, and gender.

10.2.a.1 οὗτος, αὕτη, and τοῦτο are the three nominative singular forms (masculine, feminine, and neuter, respectively) of the _____ _____, pointing to a person or thing near at hand ("this" and "these" plural). ἐκεῖνος, ἐκείνη, and ἐκεῖνο are the three nominative singular forms (masculine, feminine, and neuter, respectively) of the _____ _____, pointing to a person or thing farther removed ("that" and "those" plural).

10.2.a.2 Note the nominative singular neuter endings of the near (τοῦτο) and far (ἐκεῖνο) demonstratives. These demonstrative forms have the ending ____ appended to the stem, whereas the nominative singular neuter adjective has _____ appended to the stem. (6.1 and 6.3)

10.2.a.3 The endings of οὗτος follow the first and second declension of nouns except for the variation in the _____ and _____ singular neuter.

10.2.a.4 Where there is an α or η in the ending of the demonstrative, the stem will be _____, and where there is an "o" sounding vowel in the ending, the stem will be _____.

10.2.b The forms of ἐκεῖνος are more regular and follow the first and second declension nouns, except in the nominative and accusative singular neuter where the ____ is absent.

10.3.a Demonstrative pronouns are often used as _____ and stand alone. Remember to place the implied noun in parenthesis ( ) in order to indicate that this word is not a literal part of the Greek text.

10.3.b.1 Demonstrative pronouns are frequently used with _____ having a force similar to that of an adjective when it modifies a noun.

10.3.b.2 Demonstrative pronouns never appear with the article immediately preceding them (i.e., ὁ οὗτος ἄνθρωπος or ὁ ἐκεῖνος ἄνθρωπος), but they often appear to be in the predicate use (i.e., οὗτος ὁ ἄνθρωπος or ἐκεῖνος ὁ ἄνθρωπος). Usually this use of the demonstrative pronoun is translated as attributive.

10.3.b.3 The noun modified by the demonstrative pronoun is always rendered so specific by the pronoun as to require the definite article. "This son" is οὗτος ὁ υἱός and not οὗτος υἱός.

10.4 In the Greek language the neuter plural subject may take a _____ verb. This phenomenon is called *skema atticum* by grammarians. In other instances, the neuter plural subject has a plural verb, as one might expect.

10.5 EXERCISES:

1. τούτῳ ὁ θυρωρὸς (doorkeeper) ἀνοίγει, καὶ τὰ πρόβατα (sheep) τῆς φωνῆς (voice) αὐτοῦ ἀκούει (John 10:3).

a. Parse the verb ἀνοίγει. (3.3 and 10.1)

PART OF SPEECH: TENSE: PERSON:

SUBJECT: VOICE: NUMBER:

STEM: MOOD: LEXICAL FORM:

b. The student should be aware that some verbs take their objects in a case other than the accusative. ἀκούω usually takes its object in the genitive or accusative cases. (11.6)

c. πρόβατα is the plural subject of ἀκούει (a singular ending verb). Explain this phenomenon. (See 10.4 of the textbook and 10.4 of the workbook.)

2. ἁμαρτάνει ἐν τῇ καρδίᾳ αὐτοῦ καὶ οὐ γινώσκει χαράν.

a. Is ἐν used with the locative or instrumental case in this sentence? State the reason why you translate the preposition in this case? (7.5, 8.1, and 8.4)

b. Why is χαράν not the subject of γινώσκει? (18.1 and 18.2)

c. What is the antecedent of αὐτοῦ? How can you be sure? (3.3, 7.5, 9.1, 9.2, and 9.3.a)

3. ταύτην τὴν παραβολὴν ἀκούομεν περὶ τῆς ἐκκλησίας.

a. ταύτην τὴν παραβολὴν has ταύτην in the _____ use. Why is this phrase not translated "this is the parable"? (10.1, 10.2, and 10.3.b)

b. Why are the words ταύτην τὴν παραβολὴν in the same case, number, and gender? (See above 10.2.b.3.) What case, number, and gender are these words in? (5.1, 5.4.a.3, 10.1, and 10.2.a)

c. Is περὶ used with the genitive or accusative case in this sentence? Explain your translation of περὶ in this sentence. (8.1 and 8.4)

4. εἰς τὸν αὐτὸν τόπον ἄγομεν τούτους τοὺς ἁμαρτωλοὺς καὶ ἐκεῖνα τὰ τέκνα.

a. τὸν αὐτὸν τόπον has αὐτὸν in the _____ use modifying the noun _____ and meaning _____. (9.1, 9.2, and 9.3.c.1)

b. Dissect and parse the verb ἄγομεν. (2.1 and 3.3)

PART OF SPEECH: AUGMENT: **NONE**   STEM:

TENSE: PERSON: ENDING:

VOICE: NUMBER: CONNECTING VOWEL:

MOOD: LEXICAL FORM: SUBJECT:

c. Why does this sentence have the demonstrative pronoun forms τούτους and ἐκεῖνα with different endings and yet in the same use? (10.1 and 10.2)

5. οὗτος ἀκούει τὸ εὐαγγέλιον τοῦ κυρίου αὐτοῦ καὶ κηρύσσει (preaches) αὐτὸ τῷ λαῷ.

a. What is the difference between οὗτος and αὐτοῦ? How are they translated differently? (9.1, 9.2, 10.1, and 10.2.a)

b. Locate εὐαγγέλιον. (5.1 and 5.4.a.1)

PART OF SPEECH: FUNCTION IN THE SENTENCE:

CASE: GENDER: DECLENSION:

NUMBER: LEXICAL FORM:

c. What is the case function of τῷ λαῷ in this sentence? (4.5.d, 4.8.a, and 7.1)

6. ἄνθρωπος τοῦ κόσμου οὗτός ἐστιν, ἐκεῖνος δέ ἐστιν ἄνθρωπος τῆς βασιλείας τοῦ Χριστοῦ.

a. Why is ἐστιν not accented in this sentence? (9.1, 9.4, and 9.6)

b. Why is the conjunction δέ the second word in the phrase ἐκεῖνος δέ ἐστιν ἄνθρωπος? (9.1 and 9.5)

c. Other than being nouns, why is the phrase τῆς βασιλείας τοῦ Χριστοῦ not in attributive use? (4.8.a, 5.1, 5.4.a.1, 6.4.a, and 7.1)

7. ὁ κύριος αὐτὸς λέγει λόγους χαρᾶς καὶ αὐτὸς λαμβάνω τούτους εἰς τὴν καρδίαν μου.

a. What is the use of αὐτὸς in the phrase ὁ κύριος αὐτὸς λέγει? On what do you base your answer? (9.1, 9.2, and 9.3.c)

b. αὐτὸς λαμβάνω τούτους has τούτους in the _____ use serving as _____ to λαμβάνω and meaning _____. (4.5.g, 10.1, 10.2.a, and 10.3.a)

c. Why does μου not have an accent? (9.1, 9.2, and 9.6.b)

8. ἐκεῖνοι οἱ ἄγγελοί εἰσιν μαθηταὶ τοῦ αὐτοῦ διδασκάλου καὶ κηρύσσουσιν περὶ τῶν παιδίων.

a. What use is ἐκεῖνοι in the phrase ἐκεῖνοι οἱ ἄγγελοί and how is this phrase translated? (10.1, 10.2, and 10.3.b)

b. How is αὐτοῦ used in this sentence? (9.1, 9.2, and 9.3.c)

c. How is περὶ translated in this sentence? On what do you base your answer? (7.5, 8.1, and 8.4)

9. ἐν τούτῳ πιστεύομεν ὅτι ἀπὸ θεοῦ ἐξῆλθες (you came) (John 16:30).

a. Locate τούτῳ. (10.1 and 10.2.a)

CASE: PART OF SPEECH:

NUMBER: FUNCTION IN THE SENTENCE:

GENDER: LEXICAL FORM:

b. Dissect and parse the verb ἐξῆλθες. (11.1 and 16.2)

PART OF SPEECH: **VERB**   AUGMENT: ε to η   STEM: ἐξελθ-
TENSE: **2 aor.**   PERSON: **sec.**   ENDING: -ες
VOICE: **dep.**   NUMBER: **sing.**   CONNECTING VOWEL:
                                                 contracted in the ending
MOOD: **indic.**   LEXICAL FORM: ἐξέρχομαι   SUBJECT: **(2nd sing.)**

c. Does ἀπὸ express possession or separation? With what case is ἀπὸ used? (8.1 and 8.4)

10. Χριστός ἐστιν κύριος τοῦ κόσμου καὶ φέρει ἀγάπην καὶ εἰρήνην καὶ χαρὰν πρὸς αὐτόν.

a. How is πρὸς translated in this sentence? How can you be sure? (7.5, 8.1, and 8.4)

b. What is the antecedent of αὐτόν? What point of grammar confirms the antecedent of αὐτόν? (7.5, 9.1, 9.2, and 9.3.a)

11. Οὗτός ἐστιν ὁ υἱός μου ὁ ἀγαπητός. (Matt. 3:17).

a. How is Οὗτός used in this sentence? What is the significance of this use? (9.4, 10.1, 10.2, and 10.3.a)

  b. In what use is the adjective ἀγαπητός? What word does ἀγαπητός modify and what is the significance of this use? (6.1, 6.3, and 6.4.a)

  c. In what other way could the phrase ὁ υἱός μου ὁ ἀγαπητός be written? (6.1, 6.3, and 6.4.a)

12. οὗτος γάρ ἐστιν ὁ νόμος καὶ οἱ προφῆται (Matt. 7:12).

  a. What is the subject of ἐστιν? (9.4, 10.1, and 10.2) What rule of grammar does this appear to break? (7.5)

  b. Why does προφῆται have an apparent feminine ending, yet it is used with the masculine definite article οἱ? (4.3, 5.1, and 5.4.b)

13. ἁμαρτάνεις, καὶ ὁ ἀδελφός σου ἀνοίγει τὴν ὁδὸν εἰρήνης καὶ χαρὰς πρός σου.

  a. Parse the verb ἁμαρτάνεις. (3.3 and 10.1)

PART OF SPEECH:	TENSE:	PERSON:
SUBJECT:	VOICE:	NUMBER:
STEM:	MOOD:	LEXICAL FORM:

  b. Why does the noun ὁδὸν use a feminine definite article τὴν? (5.3 and 7.1)

  c. Is πρός translated as "for, for the sake of," "at, on, near," or "to, toward, with, at" in this sentence? On what do you base your answer? (7.5, 8.1, and 8.4)

14. αὐτὸς ἀναβαίνει πρὸς τὸ ἱερὸν ὅτι ἔχει ἁμαρτίαν ἐν τῇ καρδίᾳ αὐτοῦ.

   a. Is τὸ ἱερὸν nominative singular neuter, accusative singular neuter, or accusative singular masculine? How can you be sure? (4.1, 4.3, 4.8.b, 7.5, 8.1, and 8.4)

   b. How is ὅτι is best translated in this sentence? (10.1) On what do you base your translation? (7.5)

   c. Is ἐν translated as "in" or "by" in this sentence? On what do you base your answer? (8.1 and 8.4)

15. ἐκεῖνος γινώσκει εἰρήνην καὶ χαράν, οὗτος δὲ γινώσκει ἁμαρτίαν ὅτι οὐκ ἀκούει τὴν ἐπαγγελίαν τοῦ θεοῦ.

   a. What use is ἐκεῖνος and οὗτος in respectively and how should these words be translated? (10.1, 10.2, and 10.3.a)

   b. How does οὐκ affect ἀκούει? (9.1 and 9.5)

   c. Locate θεοῦ. (4.8.a and 7.1)

PART OF SPEECH: FUNCTION IN THE SENTENCE:

CASE: GENDER: DECLENSION:

NUMBER: LEXICAL FORM:

16. ὁ Χριστὸς κεθαλὴ τῆς ἐκκλησίας (Eph. 5:23).

a. What is the verb in this sentence? On what do you base your answer? (9.4)

b. What is the function of κεθαλὴ in this sentence? What is the significance of this function? (5.4.a.3, 7.1, and 9.4)

c. Why is the ending of ἐκκλησίας different than its definite article? (5.1, 5.3, and 5.4.a.1)

17. ὅσοι γὰρ ἐξ ἔργων νόμου εἰσίν, ὑπὸ κατάραν (curse) εἰσίν (Gal. 3:10).

a. Locate ὅσοι. (6.3 and 10.1)

CASE: PART OF SPEECH:

NUMBER: FUNCTION IN THE SENTENCE:

GENDER: LEXICAL FORM:

b. Why is ἐκ spelled ἐξ in this sentence? (8.1)

18. βάλλει (He throws) τὸ ἱμάτιον αὐτοῦ ἐπὶ τοῦ λίθου.

a. What is the subject of βάλλει? How can you be sure? (3.3 and 7.5)

b. What is the function of ἱμάτιον in this sentence? What is the significance of this function? (4.5.g, 4.8.b, and 10.1)

c. In what case is λίθου? (4.1, 4.5.b, and 4.8.a) On what do you base your answer? (7.5, 8.1, and 8.4)

19. καὶ αὕτη ἐστὶν ἡ ἀγάπη, ἵνα (that) περιπατῶμεν (we might walk) κατὰ τὰς ἐντολὰς αὐτοῦ (2 John 6).

a. Why must the verb of being be present in the phrase αὕτη ἐστὶν ἡ ἀγάπη? (10.3.b)

b. Note ἵνα is a subordinating conjunction that introduces a dependent clause. (13.3.a and 24.1)

c. Dissect and parse περιπατῶμεν. (See 10.1.a of the workbook and 24.3.c.1, 26.1, and 26.5 of the textbook.)

PART OF SPEECH: **VERB**   AUGMENT: **N/A**   STEM: περιπατ-
TENSE: **PRESENT**   PERSON: **FIRST**   ENDING: -μεν
VOICE: **act.**   NUMBER: **pl.**   CONNECTING VOWEL: -ω-
MOOD: **subj.**   LEXICAL FORM: περιπατέω   SUBJECT: **(1st pl.)**

20. οὐ γάρ ἐστε ὑπὸ νόμον ἀλλὰ ὑπὸ χάριν (grace) (Rom. 6:14).

a. Why is the negative particle spelled οὐ rather than οὐκ? (9.1) What is the significance of the placement of οὐ in this sentence? (9.5)

b. Why is γάρ the second word of the clause, yet it is translated as the first word of the clause. (See 9.5 and 10.1 of the textbook and 10.1.b of the workbook.)

c. Locate χάριν. (18.1 and 18.4)

PART OF SPEECH: **NOUN**   FUNCTION IN THE SENTENCE: **obj.** of ὑπὸ
CASE: **acc.**   GENDER: **fem.**   DECLENSION: **3rd**
NUMBER: **sing.**   LEXICAL FORM: χάρις

LESSON 11: Present Middle and Passive Indicative

11.1.a Supplemental vocabulary:

δικαιοσύνη, ἡ - righteousness (24.1)
Ἰησοῦς, ὁ - Jesus (12.1)
ὅς, ἥ, ὅ - who, which, what (27.1)
ὅταν - when, whenever (20.1)
τίθημι - I lay down (29.1)

τίς, τί - why, who, what (27.1)
τρίτος, -η, ον - third (31.1)
χείρων, χείρονος, ὁ, ἡ - worse than
ψυχή, ἡ - life (25.1)

11.1.b The student should be aware of the combination of prepositions with the verb ἔρχομαι. The primary meaning of ἔρχομαι is "I come, I go." This definition of ἔρχομαι is not radically changed by the addition of the preposition. Prepositions mark the direction and position of the action expressed by the verb. Almost all prepositions may be prefixed to a verb, which modifies or intensifies the meaning in some way. All prepositions drop their final vowel before a word beginning with a vowel, with the exception of περί or πρό.

ἀπό (from, away) + ἔρχομαι (I go) = ἀπ- + ἔρχομαι = ἀπέρχομαι

διά (through) + ἔρχομαι (I go) = δι + ἔρχομαι = διέρχομαι

εἰς (into) + ἔρχομαι (I go) = εἰς + ἔρχομαι = εἰσέρχομαι

ἐκ (ἐξ before a word beginning with a vowel) (out of) + ἔρχομαι (I go) = ἐξ + ἔρχομαι =
  ἐξέρχομαι

κατά (down) + ἔρχομαι (I go) = κατ + ἔρχομαι = κατέρχομαι

σύν (with, together) + ἔρχομαι (I go) = συν + ἔρχομαι = συνέρχομαι

11.2.a English has two voices: the active and the passive. Greek, however, has three voices. These are the active, the middle, and the passive voices.

11.2.b The _____ voice has the subject performing the action.

11.2.c The _____ voice has the subject as participating in the action, either directly or indirectly, and yet the action is also upon the subject itself (usually expressed with reflexive pronouns).

11.2.d The _____ voice depicts the subject as being acted upon by another agent.

11.3.a The passive forms are the same as the middle forms in the **present**, **imperfect**, and **perfect** tenses.

11.3.b In tenses where the forms of the middle and passive are the same, the _____ of the sentence will indicate whether a form should be translated as middle or passive.

11.3.c The conjugation of any present middle/passive indicative verb may be formed by finding the stem and then adding the variable vowel ___ or ___, then adding the middle/passive personal endings ____, ____, ____, ____, ____, and _____. (In the second person singular, an exception to the middle/passive personal endings is the result of a vowel contraction, resulting in the different ending. See 3.3.c.1 of the workbook and 3.3 of the textbook.) All verbs that end in ___ will follow this pattern.

11.4.a The _____ use of the direct middle refers to the result of the action directly to the agent.

11.4.a.1 The _____ use of the direct middle refers to a plural subject engaging in an interchange of action.

11.4.b The _____ middle has the subject acting with reference to itself or in behalf of itself.

11.4.c The _____ middle places stress on the agent producing the action rather than participating in it. The word "self" may be used in the translation into English to show the strong involvement of the subject.

11.4.d The _____ /deponent as middle appears middle in form; however, it is active in function. Sometimes these verbs use the passive voice, but these forms will be the same as the middle use in the present tense.

11.5.a When the _____ or _____ agent produces the action on the subject, the usual construction is the preposition ὑπό with the ablative case. ἀπό is occasionally used in this manner.

11.5.b When there is a(n) _____ agent through which the original agent acts, the usual construction is the preposition διά with the ablative case.

11.5.c When the agent is _____, the usual construction is the instrumental case either with or without the preposition ἐν.

11.5.d Sometimes the passive is used with no _____ expressed.

11.6 The student should be aware that some verbs take their objects in a case other than the _____. ἀκούω takes its object in either the _____ or _____ case. In the present active indicative, ἄρχω is translated "I rule"; however, in the middle voice, ἄρχομαι is translated "I begin" and is often followed by an _____.

11.7 EXERCISES:

1. καὶ γίνεται τὰ ἔσχατα τοῦ ἀνθρώπου ἐκείνου χείρονα (worse than) τῶν πρώτων (Matt. 12:45).

a. Is τοῦ ἀνθρώπου genitive or ablative in case? (4.1, 4.5.b, and 4.8.a) What is the significance of the case of this phrase in this sentence? (4.5.b)

b. What use are the adjectives ἔσχατα and πρώτων in? What is the significance of this use? (6.1, 6.3, and 6.4.c)

2. ἡ ἀλήθεια διδάσκεται ἐν τοῖς λόγοις τοῦ ἀποστόλου.

a. What two factors confirm that ἀλήθεια is the subject of this sentence? (5.1, 5.3, 5.4.a.1, 4.5.a, and 7.5)

b. Why does ἐν not have an accent? (See 8.1.1 of the workbook and 9.6.b of the textbook.)

c. Is ἀποστόλου masculine or neuter in gender? On what do you base your answer? (4.1, 4.3, 4.6, and 4.8.a)

3. ὁ πιστὸς ἀδελφὸς σῴζεται διὰ τοῦ μαθητοῦ τοῦ κυρίου.

a. How can you be sure that πιστὸς is in the attributive use rather than the predicative use? Demonstrate the difference between these two constructions. (6.1, 6.3, and 6.4.a and b)

b. Is διὰ used with the genitive or the accusative case in this sentence? (4.5.b, 8.1, and 11.5) How can you be sure? (5.1, 5.4.b, and 7.5) Explain the significance. (4.5.b and 11.5)

c. Locate κυρίου. (4.1, 4.5.b, and 4.8.a)

PART OF SPEECH: FUNCTION IN THE SENTENCE:

CASE: GENDER: DECLENSION:

NUMBER: LEXICAL FORM:

4. καρδίᾳ γὰρ πιστεύεται εἰς δικαιοσύνην (righteousness) (Rom. 10:10).

a. Is καρδίᾳ dative, locative, or instrumental? How can you be sure? (4.5.f, 5.1, 5.4.a.1, and 7.5)

b. Why is γὰρ the second word of the sentence and yet is translated as the first word? (See 9.5 and 10.1 of the textbook and 10.1.b of the workbook.)

c. What is the subject of πιστεύεται? On what do you base your answer? (3.3, 10.1, and 11.3)

5. ὁ υἱὸς τοῦ θεοῦ κηρύσσει ἀγάπην καὶ ἀλήθειαν.

a. Is the phrase ὁ υἱὸς τοῦ θεοῦ translated "the Son of God" or "the Son from God?" On what do you base your answer? (4.1, 4.5.b, 4.8.a, 7.1, and 7.5) What is the significance of the case in which τοῦ θεοῦ is translated in this sentence? (4.5.b)

b. Both ἀγάπην and ἀλήθειαν are first declension accusative singular feminine nouns that function as a compound direct object. Why do the endings of these nouns differ? (4.5.g, 5.1, 5.4.a.1, and 5.4.a.3)

6. ἄρχονιαι βάλλειν λίθους πρὸς ἁμαρτωλούς.

a. What is unusual about the result of the change in voice of ἄρχονται? (11.1, 11.3, and 11.6)

b. What part of speech is βάλλειν and the significance of this part of speech? (3.3.b and 11.1)

c. What is the function of λίθους in this sentence? (4.1, 4.5.g, and 4.8.a) What is the significance of this function? (4.5.g)

7. φωνὴ ἀκούεται ἐν τῇ ἐρήμῳ καὶ ὁδὸς βλέπεται εἰς οὐρανόν.

a. What is the significance of the function of the voice of ἀκούεται in this sentence? (2.1, 11.3, and 11.5)

b. Is οὐρανόν accusative singular masculine, nominative singular neuter, or accusative singular neuter? (4.5.g, 4.8.a, and 11.1) On what do you base your answer? (4.6, 7.5, 8.1, and 8.4)

8. ὅταν (when) ἀκούουσιν μετὰ χαρᾶς δέχονται τὸν λόγον (Luke 8:13).

a. Why does μετὰ have a grave rather than an acute accent? (2.7 and 8.1 See Appendix, page 159, section a)

b. How can you be sure of the case of χαρᾶς? (5.4.a.1, 8.1, 8.4, and 10.1)

c.. Identify the case and the case function of λόγον. (2.1, 4.5.5.g, and 4.8.a)

9. ὁ ἀγαθὸς προφήτης ἀπέρχεται ἀπὸ τοῦ ὄχλου.

a. In what other way might the attributive use of the adjective be written for the phrase ὁ ἀγαθὸς προφήτης? (6.1, 6.3, and 6.4.a)

b. Is ὄχλου genitive or ablative in case? (4.1, 4.5.c, and 4.8.a) How can you be sure? (7.5, 8.1, and 8.4) What is the significance of this case? (4.5.c)

10. γινώσκει ὁ θεὸς τὰς καρδίας τῶν ἀνθρώπων καὶ πέμπει λόγους ζωῆς.

a. What effect does the order of the subject and verb, γινώσκει ὁ θεὸς, have on the translation of this sentence? Explain. (4.7)

b. Is καρδίας genitive singular feminine, ablative singular feminine, or accusative plural feminine? How can you be sure? (4.5.b, 5.4.a.1, 7.5, and 11.1) What is the significance of the case function? (4.5.b)

c. Locate λόγους. (2.1, 4.5.g, and 4.8.a)

PART OF SPEECH: FUNCTION IN THE SENTENCE:

CASE: GENDER: DECLENSION:

NUMBER: LEXICAL FORM:

11. τί (why) καὶ βαπτίζονται ὑπὲρ αὐτῶν; (1 Cor. 15:29).

a. τί is a nominative singular neuter interrogative pronoun. (27.1 and 27.3.b)

b. Is it necessary for the verb βαπτίζονται to have the subject stated? Why or why not? (3.3, 7.1, 7.5, 9.3.b, and 11.3)

c. Though the antecedent of αὐτῶν is not stated in this sentence, what can be known about the antecedent? (9.1, 9.2, and 9.3.a)

12. ἀποκρίνεται 'Ιησοῦς (Jesus), Τὴν ψυχήν (life) σου ὑπὲρ ἐμοῦ θήσεις (will you lay down); (John 13:38).

a. What is the subject of ἀποκρίνεται in this sentence? (11.1, 11.3, and 12.1). What is the significance of this subject according to accidence? (7.2 and 12.1)

b. What is the significance of the construction of σου in this sentence? (9.1, 9.2, and 9.6.b)

c. Parse θήσεις. (See 11.1.a of the workbook and 14.2.d of the textbook.)

PART OF SPEECH: **VERB**	TENSE: **fut.**	STEM: Ζθη-
PERSON: **2nd**	VOICE: **act.**	SUBJECT: **(2nd sing.)**
NUMBER: **sing.**	MOOD: **indic.**	LEXICAL FORM: τίθημι

13. οἱ ὄχλοι ἀκούουσιν τὰ ἀγαθὰ τῆς βασιλείας τοῦ θεοῦ καὶ σῴζονται ἀπὸ τοῦ κόσμου.

a. Is οἱ ὄχλοι or τὰ ἀγαθὰ the subject of ἀκούουσιν? (4.1, 4.3, 4.8.a, 6.1, 6.2, and 6.3.a) On what do you base your answer? (7.5)

b. How can the translator be sure βασιλείας is not accusative plural feminine? (5.1, 5.3, and 5.4.a.1)

c. Dissect and parse σῴζονται. (7.5, 11.1, and 11.3)

PART OF SPEECH:	AUGMENT: NONE	STEM:
TENSE:	PERSON:	ENDING:

VOICE: NUMBER: CONNECTING VOWEL:

MOOD: LEXICAL FORM: SUBJECT:

14. ἐγήγερται (he was raised) τῇ ἡμέρᾳ τῇ τρίτῃ (third) κατὰ τὰς γραφάς (1 Cor. 15:4).

a. Dissect and parse ἐγήγερται. (3.1, 7.5, and 23.2)

PART OF SPEECH: **VERB**   AUGMENT: **n/a**   STEM: ηγερ-
TENSE: **perf.**   PERSON: **3rd**   ENDING: -ται
VOICE: **mid.**   NUMBER: **sing.**   CONNECTING VOWEL: **n/a**
MOOD: **indic.**   LEXICAL FORM: ἐγείρω   SUBJECT: **(3rd sing.)**

b. What use is the adjective τρίτῃ in the phrase τῇ ἡμέρᾳ τῇ τρίτῃ? What is the significance of this use? (5.1, 5.4.a.1. 6.1, 6.3, 6.4.a, and 31.1 of the textbook and 11.1.a of the workbook.)

c. How can one be sure that κατὰ is translated "along, according to" rather than "down" or "down from?" (5.1, 5.3, 5.4.a.1, 7.5, 8.1, and 8.4)

15. τὸν λόγον τῆς ἀληθείας οἱ μαθηταὶ διδάσκονται.

a. Locate μαθηταί. (4.3, 4.5.a, 5.1, and 5.4.b)

PART OF SPEECH: FUNCTION IN THE SENTENCE:

CASE: GENDER: DECLENSION:

NUMBER: LEXICAL FORM:

b. What is the significance of the function of the voice of διδάσκονται in this sentence? (3.1, 11.3, and 11.4.a)

16. κρίνεται ἐν τῇ παραβολῇ τοῦ προφήτου.

a. Dissect and parse κρίνεται. (7.1, 7.5, and 11.3)

PART OF SPEECH: AUGMENT: STEM:

TENSE: PERSON: ENDING:

VOICE: NUMBER: CONNECTING VOWEL:

MOOD: LEXICAL FORM: SUBJECT:

b. Is παραβολῇ dative, locative, or instrumental? How can you be sure? (4.5.e, 5.1, 5.4.a.3, and 7.5) How does the preposition ἐν help in the identification of the case of παραβολῇ? (8.1) What other factors must be considered in locating the case of παραβολῇ? (7.5, 8.4, and 11.5)

17. παραβολὴ τῆς βασιλείας τῶν οὐρανῶν διδάσκεται ὑπὸ τοῦ πιστοῦ ἀποστόλου.

a. Locate παραβολὴ. (4.5.a, 5.1 and 5.4.a.3)

PART OF SPEECH: FUNCTION IN THE SENTENCE:

CASE: GENDER: DECLENSION:

NUMBER: LEXICAL FORM:

b. What is the significance of the function of the voice of διδάσκεται in this sentence? (3.1, 11.3, and 11.5)

18. ὁ διδάσκαλος προσέρχεται τοὺς λαοὺς εἰς τὸν οἶκον.

a. What is the significance of the function of the voice of προσέρχεται in this sentence? (11.1, 11.2, and 11.4.d)

b. What is the relationship of οἶκον to the preposition εἰς? (See 4.1, 4.5.g, 4.8.a, 8.1, and 8.4 of the textbook and 8.2.c of the workbook.)

19. ἄνθρωποι τοῦ κόσμου δοξάζονται· τὸν θεὸν δίκαιοι ἄνθρωποι δοξάζουσιν.

a. Is this sentence a compound sentence or a complex sentence? Explain the significance of the choice that you made. (7.4.d)

b. Within the context of the sentence what is the significance of the function of the voice of δοξάζονται? (9.1, 11.3, and 11.4.a)

c. What use is the adjective δίκαιοι in? What is significant about this use? (6.4.a) What is the function in this sentence of the noun that δίκαιοι modifies? (4.1, 4.5.a, 4.8.a, 6.1, and 6.3)

20. τὸ εὐαγγέλιον . . . δι' οὗ (which) καὶ σῴζεσθε (1 Cor. 15:1-2).

a. Note that οὗ is a genitive singular masculine relative pronoun. (See 27.1 and 27.3.a) How can you be sure that οὗ is not a negative particle? (9.1 and 9.5)

b. Dissect and parse σῴζεσθε. (11.1, 11.3, and 11.5)

PART OF SPEECH: AUGMENT: STEM:

TENSE: PERSON: ENDING:

VOICE: NUMBER: CONNECTING VOWEL:

MOOD: LEXICAL FORM: SUBJECT:

LESSON 12: Imperfect Active Indicative

12.1.a Supplemental vocabulary.

ἔλεος, ὁ   - mercy (20.1)
Ναζαρέθ, ἡ - Nazareth
πλήρωμα, -ατος, τό - fullness,
  completeness

προσευχή, ἡ - prayer
σχίσμα, -ατος, τό - division
τίς, τί - who, what (27.1)
ὥρα, ἡ - hour (22.1)

12.1.b Adverbs are closely related to adjectives in that they qualify the meaning of words, namely, verbs, other adverbs, adjectives, and (only in rare instances) substantives. Adjectives are used primarily with substantives. Adverbs are used to express relationships of time, place, manner, and degree by answering questions such as how, when, or where. In a broad sense, prepositions, conjunctions, particles, and interjections are adverbial. The most common way to form an adverb is to take an adjective in its genitive plural form and replace the ν at the end with ς. The accent remains the same as the genitive plural adjective (Dana and Mantey, pp. 234-239). (See 28.4 and 28.5.)

12.1.c The conjunction ἀλλά strongly reverses the direction of thought or presents a strong contrast between two clauses. This conjunction is built on the root ἀλλ', i.e., ἀλλά.

12.1.d Explain the irregularity of the second declension noun Ἰησοῦς.

12.2.a The present stem of the verb does not distinguish between simple and continuous action. The present stem should be associated with progressive or continuous action regardless of the time indicated by the augment and/or ending.

12.2.a.1 The imperfect tense uses the stem of the _____ tense on which to build its forms; therefore, if one sought to conjugate the imperfect active indicative forms of λύω, one would build on the present stem _____.

12.2.a.2 The three component parts of the imperfect active indicative are:

1.   2.   3.

12.2.a.3 What process does one go through in order to form an imperfect active indicative verb?

12.2.b The ε at the beginning of the word is the _____, which indicates that the verb is a secondary tense, or one which expresses past time.

12.2.b.1 Verbs that begin with a consonant form a _____ _____ by adding ___ to the beginning of the verb stem.

12.2.b.2 Verbs that begin with a vowel form a _____ _____ by lengthening the vowel to the corresponding long vowel. This type of augment results from the _____ or _____ of two vowels.

12.2.c The augment of a compound verb comes _____ the preposition and _____ the verb stem.

12.2.d The verb of being εἰμί has no _____ or _____ function in the imperfect tense.

12.3 The imperfect tense may be translated in various ways; however, it always represents _____ action in the past.

12.3.a The _____ imperfect gives a vivid presentation of what was going on in past time. This imperfect is a picture of the movement of an event. (- - - - - - - - -)

12.3.b The _____ or _____ imperfect shows continual or repeated action in past time. (•————)

12.3.c The _____ imperfect depicts continuous action in past time, but the emphasis is on the beginning of the action rather than its progress. (————)

12.4 EXERCISES:

12.4.a Be sure to conjugate all the verbs that you have studied up to this point through the imperfect active indicative form.

12.4.b Translate the following sentences and answer the grammatical questions.

1. τότε ἠκούομεν τῆς φωνῆς αὐτοῦ, νῦν δὲ οὐκέτι ἀκούομεν αὐτῆς.

    a. Is ἠκούομεν translated "we were hearing" or "we heard?" On what do you base your answer? (12.3) Is the η a syllabic or a temporal augment? (12.2.b)

b. Why is νῦν δὲ translated "but now" when the Greek literally reads "now but?" (9.1, 9.5, and 12.1)

c. What is the difference between ἠκούομεν and ἀκούομεν? (2.1, 3.3, and 12.2.b.2)

2. ἐκεῖνοι μὲν οἱ ἁμαρτωλοὶ μένουσιν ἐν τῇ σκοτίᾳ, οὗτοι δὲ εἰσέρχονται εἰς τὴν βασιλείαν τοῦ θεοῦ.

a. Is τῇ σκοτίᾳ dative, locative, or instrumental? On what do you base your answer? (4.5.e, 7.5, 8.1, and 8.4)

b. Dana and Mantey classified μὲν . . . δὲ as a combination of the particle and conjunction which differentiates the clause in which it occurs from the clause which follows (p. 261). (See 9.1.)

c. Is τοῦ θεοῦ genitive or ablative? On what do you base your answer? (4.5.b, 4.8.a, 7.1, and 7.5)

3. καθ' ἡμέραν (daily) ἤμην πρὸς ὑμᾶς ἐν τῷ ἱερῷ (Mark 14:49).

a. καθ' ἡμέραν is often used to mean "every day" or "daily."

b. Explain why κατά spelled καθ' in this sentence? (2.5, 8.1, 8.4, and 8.5)

c. Locate ὑμᾶς. (8.1, 8.4, 9.1, and 9.2)

CASE: PART OF SPEECH:

NUMBER: FUNCTION IN THE SENTENCE:

GENDER: LEXICAL FORM:

4. ἐν ἐκείναις ταῖς ἡμέραις ὁ κύριος ἐθεράπευεν τοὺς ὄχλους καὶ ἔσῳζεν αὐτοὺς ἀπὸ τῶν ἁμαρτιῶν αὐτῶν.

a. How does the translation of the demonstrative pronoun ἐκείναις in the phrase ἐκείναις ταῖς ἡμέραις compare with an adjective in the same use? (6.4.b, 10.1, 10.2, 10.3.b) What use of the adjective best compares with the translation of this use of the demonstrative pronoun? (6.4.a)

b. Parse ἔσῳζεν. (9.1, 12.1, and 12.2.a)

PART OF SPEECH: TENSE: PERSON:

SUBJECT: VOICE: NUMBER:

STEM: MOOD: LEXICAL FORM:

c. Is τῶν ἁμαρτιῶν genitive or ablative? On what do you base your answer? (4.5.c, 5.1, 5.4.a.1, 7.5, 8.1, and 8.4)

5. ἡτοίμαζον τὰς καρδίας αὐτῶν πονηροὶ ἄνθρωποι ὅτι ἤκουον τὰς γραφὰς καὶ ἐπίστευον αὐταῖς.

a. Is ἡτοίμαζον a descriptive, repeated/iterate, or an inceptive imperfect? On what do you base your answer? (12.1, 12.2, and 12.3.c) Is the η a syllabic or a temporal augment? (12.2.b)

b. What is the antecedent of αὐτῶν? On what do you base your answer? (9.1, 9.2, and 9.3.a)

c. Are τάς καρδίας and τὰς γραφὰς genitive singular feminine, ablative singular feminine, or accusative, plural, feminine. On what do you base your answer? (5.1, 5.3, 5.4,a.1 and 3, and 7.5)

6. αὐτὸς γὰρ ἐγίνωσκεν τί (what) ἦν ἐν τῷ ἀνθρώπῳ (John 2:25).

a. What is the significance of the presence of αὐτὸς in this sentence? (9.1, 9.2, and 9.3.c)

b. Why is γὰρ the second word of the sentence and is translated as the first word of the sentence? (See 9.5 and 10.1 of the textbook and 10.1.b of the workbook)

c. How can you know for certain the gender of ἀνθρώπῳ? (4.1, 4.6, and 4.8.a)

7. διὰ μὲν τὴν ἀγάπην τοῦ θεοῦ ἐρχόμεθα εἰς τὴν βασιλείαν τοῦ θεοῦ, δεχόμεθα δὲ τὴν ζωὴν σὺν τῷ υἱῷ αὐτοῦ.

a. How is διὰ translated? On what do you base your answer? (7.5, 8.1, and 8.4)

b. Dissect and parse ἐρχόμεθα. (11.1, 11.3, and 11.4.d)

PART OF SPEECH: AUGMENT: STEM:

TENSE: PERSON: ENDING:

VOICE: NUMBER: CONNECTING VOWEL:

MOOD: LEXICAL FORM: SUBJECT:

c. Is δεχόμεθα translated as active, passive, or middle? How are you able to decide? (7.5, 11.1, and 11.3) Is δεχόμεθα deponent? Explain. (11.4.d)

8. Πέτρος δὲ καὶ Ἰωάννης ἀνέβαινον εἰς τὸ ἱερὸν ἐπὶ τὴν ὥραν (hour) τῆς προσευχῆς (of prayer) (Acts 3:1).

a. What is the significance of Πέτρος and Ἰωάννης beginning with capital letters? (1.2.e)

b. Is ἀνέβαινον a descriptive, repeated/iterate, or an inceptive imperfect? On what do you base your answer? (9.1, 12.2, and 12.3.a) Identify the augment in ἀνέβαινον. (12.2.c)

c. Is τῆς προσευχῆς genitive or ablative? On what do you base your answer? (See 4.5.b, 5.3, 5.4.a.3, and 7.5 of the textbook and 12.1.a of the workbook.)

9. ὡς πονηροὶ ἦτε, οὐκ ἐγινώσκετε τὸν Χριστόν.

a. In what use is the adjective πονηροὶ? What is the significance of this use? (6.1, 6.3, and 6.4.b)

b. What is the significance of the placement of οὐκ in this sentence? (9.1 and 9.5)

c. Why is the nominative substantive not necessary with ἐγινώσκετε? (3.3)

10. οἱ δὲ ὄχλοι ἔλεγον, Οὗτός ἐστιν ὁ προφήτης Ἰησοῦς, ὁ (the one) ἀπὸ Ναζαρὲθ (Nazareth) τῆς Γαλιλαίας (Matt. 21:11).

a. Why is the verb of being ἐστιν necessary in the phrase Οὗτός ἐστιν ὁ προφήτης ? (6.4.b and 10.3.b)

b. Why does προφήτης have a masculine article and an ending that resembles a feminine ending? (4.3, 5.1, and 5.4.b)

c. How can you be sure that Ναζαρὲθ is ablative in case? (8.1 and 8.4)

11. τότε ὁ κύριος ἐδίδασκεν ἡμᾶς, νῦν δὲ διδάσκομεν τὴν ἐκκλησίαν.

a. In this sentence τότε and νῦν are _____ with τότε being associated with a form of the _____ tense and νῦν being associated with the _____ tense. (7.5, 12.1, and 12.3)

b. Dissect and parse διδάσκομεν. (3.1 and 3.3)

PART OF SPEECH: AUGMENT: STEM:

TENSE: PERSON: ENDING:

VOICE: NUMBER: CONNECTING VOWEL:

MOOD: LEXICAL FORM: SUBJECT:

c. δὲ is translated into English as the first word of the second phrase of this sentence. Why is δὲ the second word in the Greek phrase νῦν δὲ διδάσκομεν? (9.1 and 9.5)

12. ἀκούω σχίσματα (divisions) ἐν ὑμῖν ὑπάρχειν (1 Cor. 11:18).

a. Locate σχίσματα. (See 12.1.a of the workbook and 19.3.b of the textbook.)

PART OF SPEECH: **NOUN**   FUNCTION IN THE SENTENCE: **do.** of ἀκούω
CASE: **acc.**   GENDER: **neut.**   DECLENSION: **3rd**
NUMBER: **pl.**   LEXICAL FORM: σχίσμα

b. What is the significance of the verb form ὑπάρχειν? (3.3 and 12.1)

13. οἱ ἄνθρωποι οἱ πονηροὶ ἀπέκτεινον τοὺς προφήτας καὶ μένουσιν ἐν σκοτίᾳ.

a. Is ἀπέκτεινον a first person singular or third person plural imperfect active indicative? On what do you base your answer? (7.5, 12.1, and 12.2.a)

b. What is the subject of μένουσιν? How can you be sure? (3.3, 4.1, 4.5.a, 4.8.a, 7.1, and 7.5)

c. Is ἐν σκοτίᾳ locative or instrumental? How do you be sure? (7.5, 8.1, and 8.4)

14. ἐν τῷ κόσμῳ ἦν, . . . καὶ ὁ κόσμος αὐτὸν οὐκ ἔγνω (knew) (John 1:10).

a. Parse ἦν. (9.1, 9.4, and 12.2.d)

PART OF SPEECH: TENSE: PERSON:

SUBJECT: VOICE: **N/A**   NUMBER:

STEM: MOOD: LEXICAL FORM:

b. What is the function of οὐκ in this sentence? (9.1 and 9.5)

c. ἔγνω is a third person singular second aorist active indicative of γινώσκω . This form will be discussed in lesson 16.

15. ἐγένετο (came) Ἰωάννης ὁ βαπτίζων (baptizing) ἐν τῇ ἐρήμῳ (Mark 1:4).

a. What does γίνομαι (ἐγένετο) have in common with εἰμί? (9.1, 9.4, and 11.1)

b. βαπτίζων is a nominative singular masculine present active participle that is in the attributive use. (7.1, 20.2, and 20.7.b.1)

c. Locate ἐρήμῳ . (4.8.a, 5.3, and 11.1)

PART OF SPEECH: FUNCTION IN THE SENTENCE:

CASE: GENDER: DECLENSION:

NUMBER: LEXICAL FORM:

16. ἐν ταῖς ἁμαρτίαις αὐτῶν ἔτι εἰσὶν ὅτι οὐκ ἔρχονται εἰς τὴν βασιλείαν τοῦ θεοῦ.

a. Is ἐν ταῖς ἁμαρτίαις locative or instrumental? Explain the significance of this case. (5.1, 5.4.a.1, 7.5, 8.1, and 8.4)

b. Dissect and parse ἔρχονται. (11.1, 11.3, and 11.4.d)

PART OF SPEECH: AUGMENT: STEM:

TENSE: PERSON: ENDING:

VOICE: NUMBER: CONNECTING VOWEL:

MOOD: LEXICAL FORM: SUBJECT:

c. Locate βασιλείαν. (5.1, 5.3, and 5.4.a.1)

PART OF SPEECH: FUNCTION IN THE SENTENCE:

CASE: GENDER: DECLENSION:

NUMBER: LEXICAL FORM:

17. Ἰησοῦς αὐτὸς οὐκ ἐβάπτιζεν ἀλλ' οἱ μαθηταὶ αὐτοῦ (John 4:2).

a. What is the function of αὐτὸς in this sentence? Why can αὐτὸς not be the subject of ἐβάπτιζεν? (9.1, 9.2, and 9.3.b)

b. Is the ε of ἐβάπτιζεν a syllabic or a temporal augment? What is the difference between these two types of augments? (12.2.b)

c. οἱ μαθηταὶ is the subject of the implied verb ἐβάπτιζεν based on context and its connection with the phrase Ἰησοῦς αὐτὸς οὐκ ἐβάπτιζεν. The purpose of this construction is to avoid redundancy.

18. ἡτοίμαζον οἱ ἀπόστολοι τὰς καρδίας αὐτῶν καὶ ἐκήρυσσον τὸ εὐαγγέλιον ἁμαρτωλοῖς.

a. Is this sentence a compound sentence or a complex sentence? Explain the significance of the choice that you made. (7.4.d)

b. Is τὰς καρδίας genitive singular feminine, ablative singular feminine, or accusative plural feminine? (4.5.b, 5.1, and 5.4.a.1) On what do you base your answer? (7.5)

c. Is ἁμαρτωλοῖς dative, locative, or instrumental in this sentence? Explain your answer. (4.5.d, 4.8.a, 7.1, and 7.5)

19. τοῦ κυρίου γὰρ ἡ γῆ καὶ τὸ πλήρωμα (fullness) αὐτῆς (1 Cor. 10:26).

a. Is κυρίου genitive singular masculine or ablative singular masculine? (4.1, 4.3, 4.5.c, and 4.8.a) On what do you base your answer? (7.5)

b. How can you be sure that πλήρωμα is neuter in gender? (See 4.3 and 4.6 of the textbook and 12.1.a of the workbook.) How can you be sure of the case of πλήρωμα? (7.5, 12.1.2, and 19.3.b)

c. What is the antecedent of αὐτῆς? On what do you base your answer? (5.4.a.3, 9.1, 9.2, 9.3.a, and 12.1)

20. εἰρήνη ἐπ᾽ αὐτοὺς καὶ ἔλεος (mercy) καὶ ἐπὶ τὸν Ἰσραὴλ τοῦ θεοῦ (Gal. 6:16).

a. What part of speech is καὶ? How is καὶ used in this sentence? (4.1 and 13.3.a)

b. Locate αὐτοὺς. (9.1 and 9.2)

PART OF SPEECH: FUNCTION IN THE SENTENCE:

CASE: GENDER: DECLENSION:

NUMBER: LEXICAL FORM:

c. Note that Ἰσραὴλ is an indeclinable noun. An indeclinable noun is a noun whose form is the same in all cases. (12.1)

LESSON 13: Imperfect Middle and Passive Indicative

13.1 Supplemental Vocabulary

ἀκάθαρτος, -ον, ὁ, ἡ - unclean, impure (adj)

ἀναχωρέω - I withdraw, go backward

βάπτισμα, τό - baptism

ἐάν - if (w/ subjunctive mood) (24.1)

ζάω - I live (26.1)

Ἰορδάνης, -ου, ὁ - Jordan

κατέρχομαι - I come/go down

οὔπω - not yet (adv.) (30.1)

πνεῦμα, πνεύματος, τό - spirit (19.1)

πόθεν - from where (adv.)

ποταμός, ὁ - river (30.1)

13.2.a The middle and passive forms of the imperfect are identical as they are in the present tense. How can you differentiate between the two voices? (13.2)

13.2.b The imperfect tense uses the stem of the _____ tense on which it builds its forms; therefore, if you sought to conjugate the imperfect middle/passive indicative forms of λύω, you would build on the present stem _____.

13.2.c The four component parts of the imperfect middle/passive indicative are:

1.   3.

2.   4.

13.2.d Verbs which are defective or _____ in the present tense are also defective in the imperfect tense. There is no active form of the deponent verb; therefore, the middle/passive form will also have the active function.

13.3 _____ in both Greek and English are used to connect sentences, clauses, phrases, and words.

13.3.a The two main types of conjunctions that appear in the New Testament are coordinating and subordinating conjunctions. _____ conjunctions usually connect two equal grammatical elements; whereas _____ conjunctions introduce dependent clauses.

13.3.b Conjunctions often express a change in the progression of _____ of a sentence.

13.3.c καί has uses other than as a simple connective "and" since it is often used to mean "also" or "even," and demonstrate emphasis. When καί is used to mean "also" or "even," where is it placed in this sentence? What determines the meaning of καί in a sentence? (7.5)

13.3.d The conjunction _____ is used much like καί as a connecting particle and also as a correlative meaning "both . . . and." What does a correlative conjunction imply?

13.3.e οὐδέ can be a simple negative _____ and as such is translated how? At other times οὐδέ is used _____ and should be translated "not even." A third use of οὐδέ is as a _____ in which οὐδέ . . . οὐδέ is translated how?

13.4 EXERCISES:

1. ὁ Ἰησοῦς ἀπὸ τοῦ ἱεροῦ ἐπορεύετο (Matt. 24:1).

  a. Why is the definite article ὁ not translated in the phrase ὁ Ἰησοῦς? (7.4.a) What is the significance of the presence of the definite article in this phrase? (7.4.b, 7.5, and 9.4)

  b. Is ἀπὸ τοῦ ἱεροῦ genitive or ablative? (8.1) How are you able to determine the case? (7.5 and 8.4)

  c. What time element is expressed by the augment in ἐπορεύετο? (12.2.b) What type of action is expressed by the imperfect tense? (12.3)

2. καὶ οἱ λόγοι καὶ αἱ διδαχαὶ τῶν προφητῶν ἠκούοντο ὑπὸ τῶν ἁμαρτωλῶν.

  a. What is the subject of ἠκούοντο? On what do you base your answer? What is the significance of the article(s) preceding the subject(s)? (2.1, 4.5.a, 4.8.a, 5.1, 5.4.a.3, and 7.5)

b. Locate διδαχαί. (5.1 and 5.4.a.3)

PART OF SPEECH: FUNCTION IN THE SENTENCE:

CASE: GENDER: DECLENSION:

NUMBER: LEXICAL FORM:

c. Is τῶν προφητῶν genitive or ablative? (4.5.b, 5.1, 5.4.b, and 7.5) Is προφητῶν masculine, feminine, or neuter? How can you be sure? (See 4.6 of the workbook and the textbook.)

3. ἐν ἐκείναις ταῖς ἡμέραις οὐδὲ ἐδιδασκόμεθα ὑπ' αὐτοῦ οὐδὲ ἐδιδάσκομεν τοὺς ἄλλους.

a. In what use is ἐκείναις? (10.1, 10.2, and 10.3.b) Is ἡμέραις dative, locative, or instrumental? (5.1, 5.4.a.1, and 7.5) What is the significance of this case? (4.5.e)

b. Is the use of οὐδὲ in this sentence connective, emphatic, or correlative? Explain your answer. (13.3.e)

c. Is ἄλλους in the attributive, predicate, or substantive use? How did you translate this adjective? What is the significance of this use? (6.1, 6.3, and 6.4.c)

4. ἐβαπτίζοντο ὑπ' αὐτοῦ (Mark 1:5).

a. Dissect and parse ἐβαπτίζοντο. (7.1 and 13.2)

PART OF SPEECH: AUGMENT: STEM:

TENSE: PERSON: ENDING:

VOICE: NUMBER: CONNECTING VOWEL:

MOOD: LEXICAL FORM: SUBJECT:

b. Why is ὑπό spelled ὑπ' in this sentence. (2.5) Is ὑπ' translated as genitive or ablative? (8.1 and 8.4)

5. ἀγαθὰ δῶρα ἐφέρετο πρὸς τοὺς ἀγαθοὺς ἀδελφούς.

a. Is ἀγαθὰ attributive, predicate, or substantive? What about ἀγαθούς? What is the significance of this use? (6.1, 6.3, and 6.4.a)

b. Dissect and parse ἐφέρετο. (3.1 and 13.2)

PART OF SPEECH: AUGMENT: STEM:

TENSE: PERSON: ENDING:

VOICE: NUMBER: CONNECTING VOWEL:

MOOD: LEXICAL FORM: SUBJECT:

6. βλέπουσιν τὸν κύριον ἐν τῇ δόξῃ αὐτοῦ, καὶ ἐδιδάσκοντο ὑπ' αὐτοῦ καὶ ἐν ταῖς ἡμέραις ταῖς κακαῖς.

a. Dissect and parse βλέπουσιν. (3.1 and 3.3)

PART OF SPEECH: AUGMENT: STEM:

TENSE: PERSON: ENDING:

VOICE: NUMBER: CONNECTING VOWEL:

MOOD: LEXICAL FORM: SUBJECT:

b. Is δόξῃ dative, locative, or instrumental? What does this case describe? On what do you base your answer? (4.5, 5.1, 5.4.a.1, and 7.5)

c. Is ἐδιδάσκοντο descriptive, iterate, or inceptive? (12.3) Is ἐδιδάσκοντο active, middle, or passive in voice? What type of action is described by this verb? (13.2 and 12.3.b)

7. ὁ ὄχλος ἤρχετο πρὸς αὐτόν, καὶ ἐδίδασκεν αὐτούς (Mark 2:13).

a. Is πρὸς αὐτόν translated "for him," "at him," or "to/toward him" in this sentence? (8.1, 9.1, and 9.2) On what do you base your answer? (7.5 and 8.4)

b. Is καὶ connective or correlative? What is the significance of its use? Contrast the use of καὶ in this sentence with its use in the previous sentence. (13.3.a)

c. What is the subject of ἐδίδασκεν? How can you be sure? (3.1, 3.3, and 12.2.a)

8. οἱ μαθηταὶ κατήρχοντο πρὸς τὴν θάλασσαν καὶ εἰσηρχόμεθα εἰς τὸ πλοῖον σὺν τῷ κυρίῳ.

a. Why does the first declension noun μαθηταὶ have a masculine definite article? (4.3, 5.1, and 5.4.b)

b. Is εἰσηρχόμεθα descriptive, iterate, or inceptive? (12.3.c) Is the augment syllabic or temporal? How can you tell? (12.2.b)

c. What redundant feature occurs in the phrase εἰσηρχόμεθα εἰς τὸ πλοῖον? How does this affect the translation? (See 8.6 of the textbook and 8.6.a and 8.6.b of the workbook.)

9. διὰ τοῦτο οὐκ ἠδύναντο πιστεύειν (John 12:39).

a. In what use is the word τοῦτο? What is the significance of this use? (10.1, 10.2, and 10.3.a)

b. What is the function of οὐκ in this sentence? (9.1 and 9.5)

c. What is the function of the verb form πιστεύειν? (3.3 and 10.1)

10. ἐξέβαλλεν ὁ Ἰησοῦς τὰ δαιμόνια ἐκ τῶν ἀνθρώπων καὶ ἐκαθάριζεν αὐτοὺς ἀπὸ τῶν ἁμαρτιῶν αὐτῶν.

a. Dissect and parse ἐξέβαλλεν. (12.2 and 13.1)

PART OF SPEECH: AUGMENT: STEM:

TENSE: PERSON: ENDING:

VOICE: NUMBER: CONNECTING VOWEL:

MOOD: LEXICAL FORM: SUBJECT:

b. Why is the verb spelled ἐξέβαλλεν rather than ἐκέβαλλεν? (8.1)

c. Is ἁμαρτιῶν genitive or ablative? What does this case express? How can you be sure? (4.5.c, 4.8.a, 7.1, and 7.5)

11. καὶ ὁ Ἰησοῦς μετὰ τῶν μαθητῶν αὐτοῦ ἀνεχώρησεν (withdrew) πρὸς τὴν θάλασσαν (Mark 3:7).

a. What kind of conjunction is καί? What is the significance of this kind of conjunction? (4.1 and 12.3.a)

b. Locate μαθητῶν. (5.1 and 5.4.b)

PART OF SPEECH: FUNCTION IN THE SENTENCE:

CASE: GENDER: DECLENSION:

NUMBER: LEXICAL FORM:

c. Why is the ending of θάλασσαν and the definite article is τὴν? (5.1, 5.3, and 5.4.a.1)

12. διὰ τὸν λόγον τοῦ κυρίου τὰ δαιμόνια ἐξήρχετο ἐκ τῶν ἀνθρώπων.

a. How is διὰ best translated in this sentence? How can you be sure? (7.5, 8.1, and 8.4)

b. δαιμόνια is the plural subject of ἐξήρχετο (a singular ending verb). Explain this phenomenon. (See 10.4 of the textbook and 10.4 of the workbook.)

c. Is ἐξήρχετο active, middle, or passive? (11.1 and 13.2) Is the augment syllabic or temporal? On what do you base your answer? (12.2.b)

13. οὐδὲ ἐδεχόμεθα τὴν ἀλήθειαν ἀπὸ ὑμῶν οὐδὲ ἐλέγετε αὐτὴν πρὸς ἄλλους.

a. How is οὐδὲ . . . οὐδὲ used in this sentence? (13.3.e)

b. What is the antecedent of αὐτὴν? How can you be sure? (9.1, 9.2, and 9.3.a)

c. Is ἄλλους in the attributive, predicate, or substantive use in this sentence? How can you be sure? (6.1, 6.3, and 6.4.c)

14. καὶ εὐθὺς τὸ πνεῦμα (Spirit) αὐτὸν ἐκβάλλει (drove out) εἰς τὴν ἔρημον (Mark 1:12).

   a. What part of speech is εὐθὺς? (13.1) What is the significance of this part of speech? (See 12.1.b of the workbook.)

   b. πνεῦμα is a third declension nominative singular neuter noun. (19.1 and 19.3.b)

   c. Why does second declension noun ἔρημον have a feminine definite article? (5.3 and 11.1)

15. τὰ βιβλία γινώσκουσιν τῶν ἀνθρώπων, ἀλλὰ τὰς γραφὰς γινώσκουσιν καὶ τοῦ θεοῦ.

   a. ἀλλὰ is a strong adversative conjunction (Dana and Mantey, p.. 240). Is ἀλλὰ a coordinating or a subordinating conjunction? What is the significance of this type conjunction? (13.3.a and b)

   b. Is τὰς γραφὰς genitive singular feminine, ablative singular feminine, or accusative plural masculine? How can you be sure? (5.1, 5.4.a.2, and 7.5)

   c. How is καὶ used in this sentence? Can it be a simple connective translated "and?" What would be the proper translation, and how can you determine the translation here? (13.3.c)

16. ἐὰν (if) τε γὰρ ζῶμεν (we live, **subjunctive mood**), τῷ κυρίῳ ζῶμεν, ἐάν τε ἀποθνήσκωμεν (we die, **subjunctive mood**), τῷ κυρίῳ ἀποθνήσκομεν. ἐάν τε οὖν ζῶμεν ἐάν τε ἀποθνήσκωμεν, τοῦ κυρίου ἐσμέν (Rom. 14:8).

   a. ἐὰν is a particle that is used with a subjunctive mood verb. (See 24.1 and 24.5.c) The purpose of this particle is to introduce a conditional sentence or clause. In this sentence, ζῶμεν and ἀποθνήσκωμεν are subjunctive mood verbs.

b. What is the function of the reccurring use of τε in this sentence? (13.1 and 13.3.d)

c. What is paranomasia? List the occurrences of paranomasia in this sentence? (See lesson 6 sentence 17.b) Is this a point of accidence or syntax? Explain. (7.2)

17. καὶ ἐβαπτίζοντο ἐν τῷ Ἰορδάνῃ, (Jordan) ποταμῷ (river) ὑπ' αὐτοῦ (Matt. 3:6).

a. Is ἐβαπτίζοντο middle or passive in voice? (7.1 and 13.2) What is the significance of the voice of ἐβαπτίζοντο? (11.5)

b. Is ἐν τῷ Ἰορδάνῃ best translated "in the Jordan" or "by the Jordan?" (See 4.3 and 8.1 of the textbook and 13.1 of the workbook.) On what do you base your answer? (7.5 and 8.4)

c. Why does elision occur with the form ὑπ'? (2.5)

18. τὸ βάπτισμα (baptism) τὸ Ἰωάννου πόθεν (from whence) ἦν; ἐξ οὐρανοῦ ἢ ἐξ ἀνθρώπων; (Matt. 21:25).

a. The repetition of the definite article in τὸ βάπτισμα τὸ "is a device employed for emphasis, in which the article functions with more than its ordinary force, and appears as a mild relative pronoun" (Dana and Mantey, p. 148).

b. Locate βάπτισμα. (See 13.1 of the workbook and 19.3.b of the textbook.)

PART OF SPEECH: **NOUN**   FUNCTION IN THE SENTENCE: **subj.** of ἦν
CASE: **nom.**   GENDER: **neut.**   DECLENSION: **3rd**
NUMBER: **sing.**   LEXICAL FORM: βάπτισμα

c. What part of speech is ἤ? (13.1) What is the significance of this word in this sentence? (13.3.a)

19. οὔπω (not yet) γὰρ ἐδύνασθε δέχευθαι τὴν διδαχήν μου, ἀλλ' οὐδὲ ἔτι νῦν δύνασθε (1 Cor. 3:2).

a. Is this a compound or a complex sentence? What is the significance of this kind of sentence? (7.4.d)

b. Why does μου not have an accent? What is the significance of this phenomenon? (9.1, 9.2, and 9.6.b)

c. What part of speech is νῦν? (12.1) What is the significance of this part of speech? (See 12.1.b of the workbook.)

20. καὶ εὐθὺς ἦν ἐν τῇ συναγωγῇ αὐτῶν ἄνθρωπος ἐν πνεύματι (spirit) ἀκαθάρτῳ (unclean) (Mark 1:23).

a. Parse ἦν. (9.1 and 12.2)

PART OF SPEECH:	TENSE:	PERSON:
SUBJECT:	VOICE: **N/A**	NUMBER:
STEM:	MOOD:LEXICAL FORM:	

b. Locate πνεύματι. (See 4.5.f and 19.3.b of the textbook and 13.1 of the workbook.)

PART OF SPEECH: **NOUN**	FUNCTION IN THE SENTENCE: **obj.** of ἐν
CASE: **inst.**	GENDER: **neut.** DECLENSION: **3rd**
NUMBER: **sing.**	LEXICAL FORM: πνεῦμα

LESSON 14: Future Active and Middle Indicative

14.1 Supplemental vocabulary.

ἀναγγέλλω - I proclaim, announce   ὅτε - when (adv.) (18.1)
εἰ - if (24.1)   σάρξ, σαρκός, ἡ - flesh (18.1)
ἐντός - within (adv.)

14.2 The future stem is usually formed by adding ___ to the _____ stem. If one wanted to conjugate the future active or middle indicative forms of λύω, one would build on the present stem _____.

14.2.a The three component parts of the future middle indicative are:

1.   2.   3.

14.2.a.1 The active and middle voice endings of the future are identical to the present active and middle respectively. How do you differentiate between these two tenses?

14.2.b List the liquid, mute, and sibilant consonants.

14.2.b.1 Verbs ending in a liquid consonant (λ, μ, ν, ρ), usually drop the ____ and accent the ____ with a circumflex. Demonstrate this rule with the verb μένω, by listing the three component parts and the final form of the future form.

14.2.b.2 Verb stems ending in a mute consonant experience significant changes.

A _____ (π, β, φ) before σ changes to ψ.

A _____ (τ, δ, θ) before σ drops out.

A _____ (κ, γ, χ) before σ changes to ξ.

14.2.b.3 Verb stems ending in a _____ _____ drop the sibilant before the σ of the future.

14.2.c Why are some future stems different from their present stems? What is the only possible way to determine the form of the future tense?

14.2.d Some verbs are regular in the present tense; however, defective or _____ in the future tense.

14.2.d.1 Memorize the future active and middle indicative paradigm for λύω.

14.3 The time of the future tense is obvious; however, the kind of action may be either _____ or _____. The context will indicate its use.

14.3.a _____ This use of the future announces a future event.

14.3.b _____ This is the use of the future to express a command.

14.3.c _____ This future is occasionally found when a rhetorical question is asked.

14.4.a As in the present tense, εἰμί has no _____ or _____ function or voice in the future.

14.4.b The future indicative of εἰμί is formed on the stem ____, to which ____ is added for the future, then the thematic vowel _____, and then finally, the middle endings.

14.4.c The only exception to the above rule is the _____ _____ where the thematic vowel is omitted.

14.5 EXERCISES:

14.5.a Be sure to conjugate all verbs studied up to this point through their future active and middle forms.

14.5.b Translate each sentence and answer the following grammatical questions.

1. ὁ Χριστὸς ἄξει τοὺς μαθητὰς αὐτοῦ εἰς τὴν ὁδὸν τῆς ἀγάπης.

a. Why does the second declension noun ὁδὸν have a feminine article? (5.3 and 7.1)

b. Is τῆς ἀγάπης genitive or ablative? How can you be sure? (5.1, 5.4.a.3, and 7.5)

2. ἐν ἐκείνῃ τῇ ἡμέρᾳ ἐλεύσεται ὁ κύριος σὺν τοῖς ἀγγέλοις αὐτοῦ.

a. The prepositional phrase ἐν ἐκείνῃ τῇ ἡμέρᾳ is adverbial in that it answers the question "when?" What use is the demonstrative pronoun ἐκείνῃ in? How is this phrase translated based on the use of the demonstrative pronoun? (10.1, 10.2, and 10.3.b)

b. Is ἡμέρᾳ dative, locative, or instrumental? (4.5.e, 5.1, 5.4.a.2, and 8.1) How are you able to determine the case? (7.5 and 8.4)

c. Why does the verb ἐλεύσεται appear to be inconsistent with its present tense form? (2.1, 14.1, and 14.2.b and d)

3. καὶ ὁ θεὸς τῆς ἀγάπης καὶ εἰρήνης ἔσται μεθ' ὑμῶν (2 Cor. 13:11).

a. Is the definite article ὁ translated in the phrase ὁ θεός? Why or why not? The point of syntax in 7.4.a is flexible. (4.3, 7.1, 7.4.a, and 7.5)

b. The definite article τῆς is not repeated with εἰρήνης in the phrase τῆς ἀγάπης καὶ εἰρήνης. The Granville Sharp rule explains this phenomenon: "'When the copulative καὶ connects two nouns of the same case, if the article ὁ or any of its cases precedes the first of the said nouns and participles, and is not repeated before the second noun or participle, the latter always relates to the to the same person that is expressed or described by the first noun or participle. . . .'" (Dana and Mantey, p. 147).

c. Why does elision occur with the preposition μεθ'? (2.5 and 8.1)

4. νεκροὶ μὲν ἐν ταῖς ἁμαρτίαις ὑμῶν ἐστέ, γενήσεσθε δὲ υἱοὶ τοῦ θεοῦ.

a. μὲν . . . δὲ is a combination of the particle and conjunction which differentiates the clause with which it occurs from the clause which follows (Dana and Mantey, p. 261).

b. Dissect and parse γενήσεσθε. (11.1, 14.1, and 14.2.d)

PART OF SPEECH: STEM: ENDING:

TENSE: PERSON: CONNECTING VOWEL:

VOICE: NUMBER: SUBJECT:

MOOD: LEXICAL FORM: TENSE SIGN:

5. τότε γνώσονται ὅτι αὐτός ἐστιν ὁ κύριος.

a. τότε is a(n) _____ with τότε being associated in this sentence with a form of the _____ tense. (12.1)

b. What kind of conjunction is ὅτι? What type of clause does this conjunction introduce? (10.1 and 13.3.a)

c. What is the predicate nominative of ἐστιν? On what do you base your answer? (9.4)

6. λήμψεσθε καὶ τὰ δῶρα καὶ τοὺς οἴκους.

a. How is καὶ . . . καὶ used in this sentence? Explain the significance of this use. (13.3.c)

b. Locate οἴκους. (4.1 and 4.8.a)

PART OF SPEECH: FUNCTION IN THE SENTENCE:

CASE: GENDER: DECLENSION:

NUMBER: LEXICAL FORM:

7. ἀμὴν ἀμὴν λέγω ὑμῖν ὅτι ἔρχεται ὥρα (hour) καὶ νῦν ἐστιν ὅτε (when) οἱ νεκροὶ ἀκούσουσιν τῆς φωνῆς τοῦ υἱοῦ τοῦ θεοῦ (John 5:25).

a. What is the significance of the function of the voice of ἔρχεται? (11.1, 11.3, and 11.4.d)

b. ὥρα is so definite that the article is not included in Greek; however, it is included in the translation into English. (30.5)

c. Is ἀκούσουσιν predictive, imperative, or deliberate? What is the significance of this type of future tense verb? (2.1,, 14.1, 14.2.d, and 14.3.a)

8. ἀποστελεῖ ὁ υἱὸς τοῦ ἀνθρώπου τοὺς ἀγγέλους αὐτοῦ (Matt. 13:41).

a. What tense is ἀποστελεῖ? On what do you base your answer? (3.3, 7.1, 14.1, and 14.2.c and d)

b. What case is ἀγγέλους in? What is the significance of this case? (4.5.g and 4.8.a)

9. οὐδὲ ἐγὼ ταῦτα γνώσομαι ἀλλὰ ὁ θεός.

a. Is οὐδὲ a coordinating or subordinating conjunction? (13.1 and 13.3.a) Is the use of οὐδὲ in this sentence connective, emphatic, or correlative? Explain your choice. (13.3.e)

b. Dissect and parse γνώσομαι. (3.1, 14.1, and 14.2)

PART OF SPEECH: STEM: ENDING:

TENSE: PERSON: CONNECTING VOWEL:

VOICE: NUMBER: SUBJECT:

MOOD: LEXICAL FORM: TENSE SIGN:

c. What verb is θεός the subject of? Where does this verb come from? Why does this phenomenon occur? (This verb is a present tense verb. See lesson 12, section 12.4.b, sentence 17.d.)

10. αἱ ἡμέραι αἱ κακαὶ ἐλεύσονται.

a. Is the article essential in determining attributive or predicate use of the adjective κακαὶ? (6.4.a) If not, how can you know whether an adjective is in attributive or predicate use? (7.5)

b. Dissect and parse ἐλεύσονται. (2.1, 14.1, and 14.2.b and d)

PART OF SPEECH: STEM: ENDING:

TENSE: PERSON: CONNECTING VOWEL:

VOICE: NUMBER: SUBJECT:

MOOD: LEXICAL FORM: TENSE SIGN:

11. αὐτὸς γὰρ σώσει τὸν λαὸν αὐτοῦ ἀπὸ τῶν ἁμαρτιῶν αὐτῶν (Matt. 1:21).

a. Is σώσει present or future tense? On what do you base your answer? (3.3, 11.1, and 14.c and d)

b. What is the antecedent of αὐτοῦ? How about αὐτῶν? What rule does αὐτῶν violate with respect to its antecedent? (9.1, 9.2, and 9.3.a)

12. οἱ μαθηταὶ ἀκούσουσιν τῆς τοῦ κυρίου αὐτῶν φωνῆς καὶ ἄξουσιν τὰ τέκνα πρὸς αὐτόν.

a. What is the object of ἀκούσουσιν? Why is the object in the genitive case? What other case may ἀκούσουσιν take as its object? (11.6)

b. φωνῆς is so definite that the article is not included in Greek; however, it is included in the translation into English. (30.5)

c. Explain the origin and significance of ξ in ἄξουσιν. (14.1 and 14.2.b)

13. ἐκεῖνος ἐμὲ δοξάσει, ὅτι ἐκ τοῦ ἐμοῦ λήμψεται καὶ ἀναγγελεῖ (he will proclaim) ὑμῖν (John 16:14).

a. In what use is ἐκεῖνος in conjunction with the phrase ἐκεῖνος ἐμὲ δοξάσει? What is the significance of this use? (10.1, 10.2.b, and 10.3.a)

b. The definite article τοῦ is used as a relative pronoun in this sentence and is translated "that." (30.4) How can you be sure of the case of τοῦ. (8.1)

c. What is the subject of λήμψεται and ἀναγγελεῖ ? (10.1, 10.2.b, 14.1, and 14.2.d) How can you be sure? (3.3 and 7.5)

14. ἐσόμεθα σὺν αὐτῷ ἐν τῇ βασιλείᾳ αὐτοῦ.

a. Dissect and parse ἐσόμεθα. (9.1, 14.1, and 14.2.d)

PART OF SPEECH: STEM: ENDING:

TENSE: PERSON: CONNECTING VOWEL:

VOICE: NUMBER: SUBJECT:

MOOD: LEXICAL FORM: TENSE SIGN:

b. Is σὺν followed by a dative, locative, or instrumental? (4.5.e, 5.1, and 8.1) Could this preposition be properly translated any other way than the previously stated case? Explain. (7.5 and 8.4)

c. Locate βασιλείᾳ. (5.1 and 5.4.a.1)

PART OF SPEECH: FUNCTION IN THE SENTENCE:

CASE: GENDER: DECLENSION:

NUMBER: LEXICAL FORM:

15. εἰ πονηρός, ἀλλ' ἔσῃ ἀγαθός.

a. In what use is πονηρός in reference to εἰ? What about ἀγαθός in reference to ἔσῃ? Explain the significance of these uses. (6.1, 6.3, and 6.4.b)

b. What type of conjunction ἀλλ'? What is the significance of this type conjunction? (12.1 and 13.3.a) Why does elision occur with the form ἀλλ'? (2.5)

c. Compare and contrast εἰ and ἔσῃ as much as possible. (9.1, 9.4, 14.1, and 14.2.d)

16. Ἰδοὺ (behold) γὰρ ἡ βασιλεία τοῦ θεοῦ ἐντὸς (within) ὑμῶν ἐστιν (Luke 17:21).

a. What is unusual about the position of γὰρ in this sentence? (See 9.5 and 10.1 of the textbook and 10.1.b of this workbook.)

b. Harold Moulton classified ἐντὸς as an adverb (Moulton, p. 142). Though Walter Bauer confirmed the adverbial form, he also listed ἐντὸς as a preposition followed by a genitive, as we have here (Bauer, pp. 268-9).   According to William Chamberlain, adverbs may stand in the predicate use with εἰμί (Chamberlain, p. 111). Since prepositions are adverbial in nature, it would be appropriate for ἐντὸς to take on characteristics of both an adverb and a preposition. If the predicate nominative precedes the "to be" verb, it is stressed "the kingdom of God is AMONG YOU." (See 12.1.b and 14.1 of the workbook.)

c. Parse ἐστιν. (9.1 and 9.4)

PART OF SPEECH: TENSE: PERSON:

SUBJECT: VOICE: NUMBER:

STEM: MOOD: LEXICAL FORM:

17. ἄξουσιν τοὺς ἁμαρτωλοὺς καὶ τὰ τέκνα εἰς τὴν αὐτὴν ἐκκλησίαν.

a. Explain the form of ἄξουσιν. Is ἄξουσιν predictive, imperative, or deliberate? What is the significance of this type of future tense verb? (2.1, 14.1, 14.2.d, and 14.3.a)

b. Is τὰ τέκνα nominative or accusative plural neuter? How can you be sure? (4.5.g, 4.8.b, 7.5, and 9.1)

c. What use is αὐτὴν used in this sentence? How is this word translated according to this use? (9.1, 9.2, and 9.3.c)

18. ἡ φωνὴ τοῦ προφήτου ἑτοίμασει ὁδὸν ἐν ταῖς καρδίαις ἀνθρώπων.

a. Locate προφήτου. (5.1 and 5.4.b.2)

PART OF SPEECH: FUNCTION IN THE SENTENCE:

CASE: GENDER: DECLENSION:

NUMBER: LEXICAL FORM:

b. What gender and declension is the noun ὁδόν? On what do you base your decision? (4.6, 4.8.a, and 7.1)

c. Is καρδίαις dative, locative, or instrumental plural feminine? (4.5.e, 5.1, and 5.4.a.1) How can you be sure? (7.5, 8.1 and 8.4)

19. εἰ (if) γὰρ κατὰ σάρκα (flesh) ζῆτε (you live), μέλλετε ἀποθνήσκειν (Rom. 8:13).

a. εἰ is a conditional particle that introduces an indicative mood verb. (24.1)

b. Locate σάρκα. (See 14.1 of the workbook and 18.1 and 18.2 of the textbook.)

PART OF SPEECH: **NOUN**   **FUNCTION** IN THE SENTENCE: **obj.** of κατὰ
CASE: **acc.**   GENDER: **fem.**   DECLENSION: **3rd**
NUMBER: **sing.**   LEXICAL FORM: σάρξ

c. μέλλετε is used in this sentence with the infinitive "denoting action that necessarily follows a divine decree is destined, must, will certainly . . ." (Bauer, p. 502).

20. καταβήσεται εἰς τοὺς τόπους ἁμαρτίας καὶ πείσει ἀνθρώπους καταβαίνειν σύν αὐτῷ.

a. Is this a compound or a complex sentence? On what do you base your answer? (7.4.d)

b. Is ἁμαρτίας genitive singular feminine, ablative singular feminine, or accusative plural feminine? (4.5.b, 5.1, and 5.4.a) On what do you base your answer? (7.5)

LESSON 15: First Aorist Active and Middle Indicative

15.1 Supplemental vocabulary.

ἀρχιερεύς, ἀρχιερέως, ὁ - high priest, chief priest (19.1)

ἐάν - if (24.1)

ἐγγίζω - I come near, approach (23.1)

ἔθνος, -εος, τό - nation (pl. Gentiles) (21.1)

ἐμαυτοῦ, -ῆς, -οῦ - myself (rfx. prn.) (27.1)

εὐαγγελίζω - I preach the good news (25.1)

μετανοέω - I repent

πάντοτε - always (adv.)

συναγωγή, ἡ - synagogue (21.1)

15.2.a Like the past tense in English, the aorist tense does not always have the same form. Two English examples of this phenomenon are the similar forms of the present tense "preach" and the past form "preached;" however, the present tense "teach" differs somewhat to its past form "taught."

15.2.b Some verbs form the aorist by adding σ to the present stem and are called _____ _____. Other verbs do not add σ, and the stem is different from the present. These latter verbs are called _____ _____.

15.2.c Are there any differences in the translation of tense between first aorist and second aorist verbs? Do some verbs appear in both first and second aorist forms? Explain.

15.2.d When verbs are used in the _____ mood of the aorist tense, they will have a(n) _____.

15.2.e In the aorist tense, the predominant connecting vowel is ____ instead of _____.

15.2.f Like the future, the aorist middle and passive forms are different.

15.2.g To form the first aorist active indicative, locate the _____ stem and add the augment on the front of the stem. Then add the tense suffix ____ (a few verbs take κ as their tense suffix), after which comes the connecting vowel (usually ____), and finally the ending. The first aorist active indicative third singular usually has ____ for the connecting vowel and sometimes has a movable ν.

15.2.h The process for forming the first aorist middle is the same as the active with the exception that the _____ endings are added. These are identical to the _____

_____ endings with the exception of the second singular, which is the result of the contraction of vowels.

15.2.i Changes occur when the first aorist verb stem ends in a consonant followed by the ____ suffix. These changes are generally the same as the ones described in the previous lesson concerning the future tense. See 14.2.b of the textbook.

15.2.j Learn the first aorist active and middle indicative paradigms for λύω.

15.3.a Describe the significance of the aorist tense.

15.3.b The indicative mood of the imperfect and the aorist tenses are alike in the _____ of action; they are both past tense. They are different in the _____ of action.

15.3.c Describe the difference in the kind of action between the imperfect and the aorist tenses.

15.3.d The usual way to translate the aorist is with the simple _____ tense in English.

15.3.e Identify the following uses of the aorist tense:

_____ This aorist looks upon the action in its entirety. (- - - - - - - -) or (·)

_____ This aorist views the act as already having occurred but places emphasis on the initiation of the act. (· - - - - - - -)

_____ This aorist also views the action as having occurred, but the emphasis is on the end of the action. (- - - - - - - ·)

15.4 The first aorist infinitive has no _____. The reason is that the infinitive does not indicate past time as does the indicative mood. What is the primary difference between the present infinitive and the aorist infinitive?

15.5 EXERCISES:

15.5.a Be sure to conjugate all verbs studied up to this point through their first aorist active and middle forms. Remember that some verbs do not have first aorist forms.

15.5.b Translate each sentence and answer the following grammatical questions.

1. ἔλυσεν ὁ μαθητὴς τὸ πλοῖον αὐτοῦ.

a. Parse ἔλυσεν. (2.1, 15.1, and 15.2)

PART OF SPEECH: TENSE: PERSON:

SUBJECT: VOICE: NUMBER:

STEM: MOOD: LEXICAL FORM:

b. Why does the second declension noun μαθητὴς have a masculine definite article? (4.3, 5.1, and 5.4.b)

c. Is πλοῖον nominative singular masculine, nominative singular neuter, or accusative singular neuter? How can you be sure? (4.5.g, 4.8.b, 7.5, and 13.1)

2. τὰ τέκνα ἐπέμψαμεν ἐκ τοῦ οἴκου.

a. Dissect and parse ἐπέμψαμεν. (3.1, 14.2.b, 15.1, and 15.2)

PART OF SPEECH: AUGMENT: STEM:

TENSE: PERSON: ENDING:

VOICE: NUMBER: CONNECTING VOWEL:

MOOD: LEXICAL FORM: SUBJECT:

b. Why is τὰ τέκνα not the subject of ἐπέμψαμεν? (4.5.g, 4.8.b, 7.5, and 9.1)

c. Is οἴκου in the genitive or ablative case? On what do you base your answer? What is the significance of this case? (4.1, 4.5.c, 4.8.a, 7.5, 8.1, and 8.4)

3. ἐγὼ πάντοτε (always) ἐδίδαξα ἐν συναγωγῇ καὶ ἐν τῷ ἱερῷ (John 18:20).

a. Is ἐγὼ necessary in this sentence? What is the significance of the presence of ἐγὼ in this sentence? (9.1, 9.2, and 9.3.b)

b. Is συναγωγῇ dative, locative, or instrumental? (See 5.4.a.3 of the textbook and 15.1 of the workbook) On what do you base your answer? (7.5, 8.1, and 8.4)

c. Is ἱερῷ masculine or neuter in gender? (4.1 and 4.8.b and b) How can you be sure? (4.6)

4. οἱ μαθηταὶ ἐδόξασαν τὸν θεὸν καὶ τὸν υἱὸν αὐτοῦ.

a. How do you distinguish whether ἐδόξασαν is first singular or third plural aorist active indicative? (9.1, 15.1, and 15.2.c) Is ἐδόξασαν constative, ingressive, or culminative? What is the significance of this type of aorist? (9.1, 15.1, 15.2, and 15.3.a)

b. What is the antecedent of αὐτοῦ? On what do you base your answer? (9.1, 9.2, and 9.3.a)

5. οἱ δὲ ἀρχιερεῖς (chief priests) καὶ οἱ πρεσβύτεροι ἔπεισαν τοὺς ὄχλους (Matt. 27:20).

a. Why does δὲ appear as the second word of this sentence and is translated as the first word? What is the significance of this phenomenon? (9.1 and 9.5)

b. Dissect and parse ἔπεισαν. (14.1, 15.1, and 15.2)

PART OF SPEECH: AUGMENT: STEM:

TENSE: PERSON: ENDING:

VOICE: NUMBER: CONNECTING VOWEL:

MOOD: LEXICAL FORM: SUBJECT:

c. How can you be sure that ὄχλους is masculine? (4.1, 4.3, and 4.6)

6. διὰ τοὺς λόγους ὑμῶν ἐβλέψαμεν τὴν πονηρὰν ὁδὸν τοῦ κόσμου.

a. Why is διὰ translated "because of" in this sentence? (2.1, 4.8.a, 7.5, 8.1, and 8.4)

b. What use is πονηρὰν in this sentence? What is the significance of this use? (6.1, 6.2, and 6.3.a)

c. Does τοῦ κόσμου express description or separation? (4.5.b, 4.8.a, and 7.1)

7. ἐκήρυξας τὸ εὐαγγέλιον καὶ οἱ ἀδελφοί σου ἤκουσαν αὐτὸ καὶ ἐπίστευσαν.

a. Why is τὸ εὐαγγέλιον not the subject of ἐκήρυξας? What is the subject of ἐκήρυξας? (3.3, 4.8.b, 7.5, 10.1, 15.1, and 15.2)

b. How is the antecedent of σου expressed in this sentence? (7.5, 9.1, 9.2, and 9.3.d) What is the antecedent of αὐτὸ? (9.3.a)

8. καὶ ἐδόξασαν τὸν θεὸν Ἰσραήλ (Matt. 15:31).

a. What kind of conjunction is καί? What is the significance of this type of conjunction? (4.1 and 13.3.a)

b. List the points of grammar that identify θεὸν as accusative singular masculine. How can you be sure that θεὸν is not nominative or accusative singular neuter? (4.3, 4.6, 4.8.g, and 7.1)

c. Ἰσραήλ is an indeclinable noun. The case function of this noun (genitive) is determined by the context of this sentence.

9. ἔγραψεν παραβολὴν καὶ ἔπεμψεν αὐτὴν πρὸς τὴν ἐκκλησίαν.

a. Are ἔγραψεν and ἔπεμψεν constative, ingressive, or culminative respectfully? What is the significance of this type of aorist? (3.1, 15.1, 15.2 and 15.3.c)

b. Is πρὸς translated "for the sake of," "at, on," "to, toward." How can you be sure? (5.1, 5.4.a.1, 7.5, 8.1, and 8.4)

10. ἀπὸ τότε ἤρξατο ὁ Ἰησοῦς κηρύσσειν καὶ λέγειν, Μετανοῖτε (repent)· ἤγγικεν (is at hand or present) γὰρ ἡ βασιλεία τῶν οὐρανῶν (Matt. 4:17).

a. Is this a compound or a complex sentence? Explain the difference between compound and complex sentences. (7.4.d)

b. Parse Μετανοῖτε. (See 15.1 of the workbook and 25.2, 26.4.a.2, and 26.5 of the textbook.)

PART OF SPEECH: **VERB**	TENSE: **pres.**	PERSON: **2nd**
SUBJECT: **(2nd pl.)**	VOICE: **act.**	NUMBER: **pl.**
STEM: μετανοε-	MOOD: **imper.**	LEXICAL FORM: μετανοέω

c. What effect does the irregular order of the subject and verb have on the translation of the phrase ἤγγικεν γὰρ ἡ βασιλεία τῶν οὐρανῶν? Explain. (4.7)

11. καὶ ἐὰν (if) . . . ἑτοιμάσω τόπον ὑμῖν, πάλιν ἔρχομαι καὶ παραλήμψομαι ὑμᾶς πρὸς ἐμαυτόν (myself) (John 14:3).

a. Is the use of ἑτοιμάσω a syllabic or a temporal augment? On what do you base your answer? (12.1, 13.2.b, 14.1, and 14.2.d)

b. ἐὰν is a particle, and ἐμαυτόν is a reflexive pronoun. These two words will be studies in subsequent lessons.

c. Why is παραλήμψομαι translated as if it were a future active when it appears as future middle in form? (14.1 and 14.2.d)

12. ἐδίδαξα ὑμᾶς ἐγώ, ὑμεῖς δὲ οὐκ ἐδέξασθε ἐμὲ εἰς τοὺς οἴκους ὑμῶν.

a. Transliterate this sentence. (1.1 and 1.4)

b. What is the significance of the presence of ἐγώ in this sentence? (9.1, 9.2, and 9.3.b)

c. Locate ὑμῶν. (9.1 and 9.2)

CASE: PART OF SPEECH:

NUMBER: FUNCTION IN THE SENTENCE:

GENDER: LEXICAL FORM:

13. Διδάσκαλε, ἤνεγκα τὸν υἱόν μου πρὸς σέ (Mark 9:17).

a. What case is Διδάσκαλε? (4.8.a and 10.1) What is the significance of this case? (4.5.h)

b. What special classification does the unaccented form of μου fall under? How can you be sure? (9.1, 9.2, and 9.6.b)

14. ἠκούσατε ἐκείνας τὰς ἐντολὰς ἐν τῷ ἱερῷ, ἄλλας δὲ ἐν τῇ ἐκκλησίᾳ ἀκούετε.

a. Is ἠκούσατε constative, ingressive, or culminative? What is the significance of this type of aorist? (3.1, 15.1, 15.2 and 15.3.b)

b. What use is the demonstrative pronoun ἐκείνας in relation to ἐντολὰς? What is the significance of this use? (10.1, 10.2.b, and 10.3.b)

c. How does the preposition ἐν help in the identification of the case of ἱερῷ? What other factors must be considered in locating the case of ἱερῷ? (4.1, 4.8.b, 7.5, 8.1, and 8.4)

15. Ἄλλους ἔσωσεν, ἑαυτὸν (himself) οὐ δύναται σῶσαι (Matt. 27:42).

a. Explain the changes from the present tense form of σῴζω to the first aorist tense form ἔσωσεν. (11.1, 15.1, and 15.2)

b. Locate ἑαυτὸν. (27.1 and 27.3.e)

CASE: **acc.**   PART OF SPEECH: **rfx. prn.**
NUMBER: **sing.**   FUNCTION IN THE SENTENCE: **do.** of οὐ δύναται σῶσαι
GENDER: **masc.**   LEXICAL FORM: ἑαυτοῦ

c. What is the significance of οὐ in this sentence? Why is the οὐ form used? (9.1 and 9.5)

16. ἐκηρύξαμεν τὸ εὐαγγέλιον αὐτοῖς καὶ ἐβαπτίσαμεν τοὺς υἱοὺς αὐτῶν.

a. Parse ἐκηρύξαμεν. (11.1, 14.2.b, 15.1, and 15.2)

PART OF SPEECH: TENSE: PERSON:

SUBJECT: VOICE: NUMBER:

STEM: MOOD: LEXICAL FORM:

b. Locate εὐαγγέλιον. (4.8.b and 10.1)

PART OF SPEECH: FUNCTION IN THE SENTENCE:

CASE: NUMBER: GENDER:

LEXICAL FORM: DECLENSION:

17. ἠκούσατε τὰς αὐτὰς παραβολὰς καὶ ἐπιστεύσατε εἰς τὸν Χριστὸν.

a. What use is the third personal pronoun αὐτὰς in? What is the significance of this use? (9.1, 9.2, and 9.3.c)

b. Locate παραβολὰς. (5.1 and 5.4.a.3)

PART OF SPEECH: FUNCTION IN THE SENTENCE:

CASE: NUMBER: GENDER:

LEXICAL FORM: DECLENSION:

c. Do the verbs ἠκούσατε and ἐπιστεύσατε have a syllabic or a temporal augment respectively? Explain. (12.2.b, 15.1, and 15.2)

18. ἤκουσαν δὲ οἱ ἀπόστολοι καὶ οἱ ἀδελφοὶ . . . ὅτι καὶ τὰ ἔθνη (Gentiles) ἐδέξαντο τὸν λόγον τοῦ θεοῦ (Acts 11:1).

a. How can you be sure that ἀπόστολοι and ἀδελφοί are masculine? (2.1, 4.1, 4.3, and 4.6)

b. What kind of conjunction is καί? What is the significance of this type of conjunction? (4.1 and 13.3.a) What is the significance of the second use of καί in this sentence? (13.3.c)

c. What case is τὰ ἔθνη in this sentence? (See 4.8.b of the textbook and 15.1 of the workbook.) On what do you base your answer? (7.5) What is the significance of this case? (4.5.g)

19. αὗται αἱ ἀγαθαὶ ἐδόξασαν τὸν θεὸν ὅτι ἐθεράπευσεν τοὺς ἀδελφοὺς αὐτῶν καὶ ἔσωσεν τοὺς υἱοὺς αὐτῶν.

a. What use is the demonstrative pronoun αὗται in? What is the significance of this use? (10.1, 10.2.a, and 10.3.b)

b. Is ὅτι a coordinating or a subordinating conjunction? What is the significance of the type of conjunction? (13.3.a)

20. ἀπὸ τῆς γραφῆς ταύτης εὐηγγελίσατο (he preached) αὐτῷ τὸν Ἰησοῦν (Acts 8:35).

a. Is γραφῆς genitive or ablative singular feminine? (5.1, 5.3, and 5.4.a.3) On what do you base your answer? (7.5, 8.1, and 8.4) What is the significance of the case of γραφῆς? (4.5.c)

b. What use is the demonstrative pronoun ταύτης in this sentence? What is the significance of this use? (10.1, 10.2.a, and 10.3.b)

LESSON 16: Second Aorist Active and Middle Indicative

16.1 Supplemental vocabulary.

καλέω - I call (26.1)   πούς, ποδός, ὁ - foot (18.1)
κατέρχομαι - I go down, I come down   σῶμα, σώματος, τό - body (19.1)
πατήρ, πατρός, ὁ - father (18.1)

16.2.a The second aorist does not add a _____ to the stem and uses an entirely different stem from the first aorist.

16.2.b How can you determine whether a verb is first or second aorist?

16.2.c How does one locate the stem of the second aorist active indicative verb?

16.2.d The second aorist indicative is formed by adding a(n) _____ to the stem, then the connecting vowel _____, and finally the active or middle _____.

16.2.e The second aorist middle is formed like the active except the _____ endings are added.

16.3.a The function and translation of the second aorist are the same as that of the first aorist; therefore, the student should review the use of the aorist as described in the previous lesson. (15.3.5) Identify the following uses of the aorist tense:

_____ This aorist views the action as having occurred, but places emphasis on the end of the action. (- - - - - - - •)

_____ This aorist looks upon the action in its entirety. (- - - - - - -) or (•)

_____ This aorist views the act as already having occurred, but places emphasis on the initiation of the act. (• - - - - - - -)

16.3.b The second aorist is not a different tense from the first aorist. It only uses a different _____.

16.4.a Several second aorist forms are entirely different from the present stems. How can you know with certainty the aorist form if it differs from the present stem?

16.4.b ἔγνω, the second aorist of γινώσκω, uses _____ as the connecting vowel.

16.5 EXERCISES:

16.5.a Be sure to conjugate all verbs studied up to this point through their second aorist active and middle forms. Some verbs have both first and second aorist forms, but not all verbs do.

16.5.b Translate each section and answer the following grammatical questions.

1. παρέλαβεν τὴν ἐπαγγελίαν παρὰ τοῦ Χριστοῦ, καὶ κηρύσσει αὐτὴν ἐν τῷ κόσμῳ.

a. Is τοῦ Χριστοῦ genitive or ablative? What part does the preposition παρὰ play in identifying whether τοῦ Χριστοῦ is genitive or ablative? (4.5.b, 4.8.a, 7.1, 8.1, and 8.4)

b. Parse κηρύσσει. (3.3 and 11.1)

PART OF SPEECH: TENSE: PERSON:

SUBJECT: VOICE: NUMBER:

STEM: MOOD: LEXICAL FORM:

c. What is the antecedent of αὐτὴν? How can you be sure? (9.1, 9.2, and 9.3.a)

2. ὁ λόγος σὰρξ (flesh) ἐγένετο (John 1:14).

a. Is σὰρξ the subject or predicate nominative of ἐγένετο? Explain. (See 14.1 of the workbook and 18.1 and 18.4 of the textbook.)

b. Parse ἐγένετο. (11.1, 16.1, and 16.2)

PART OF SPEECH: TENSE: PERSON:

SUBJECT: VOICE: NUMBER:

STEM: MOOD: LEXICAL FORM:

3. ὁ Χριστὸς ἐξέβαλεν τὰ δαιμόνια ἐκ τοῦ λαοῦ καὶ ἐθεράπευσεν αὐτούς.

   a. Compare and contrast the two verbs ἐξέβαλεν and ἐθεράπευσεν. (See 2.1, 8.4, 12.1, 15.1, 15.2, 16.1, and 16.2 of the textbook and 16.1 of the workbook.)

   b. What is the subject of ἐξέβαλεν and ἐθεράπευσεν? (4.5.a, 4.8.a, 7.1, and 7.5) Why may one be confused and choose δαιμόνια as the subject of the two verbs? (4.8.b, 13.1, and 13.3)

4. καὶ εἴδομεν τὸν κύριον καὶ ἠκούσαμεν τῶν λόγων αὐτοῦ.

   a. What meaning does the double use of the coordinating conjunction καὶ have? Explain the significance of this use. (13.3.d)

   b. Is the augment of ἠκούσαμεν syllabic or temporal? (2.1, 12.2.b, 16.1, and 16.2) Is ἠκούσαμεν constative, ingressive, or culminative? What is the significance of this type of aorist? (15.3.a)

   c. What is the direct object of ἠκούσαμεν? What is unusual about this object? (11.6)

5. καὶ αὐτός ἐστιν ἡ κεφαλὴ τοῦ σώματος (of the body) τῆς ἐκκλησίας (Col. 1:18).

   a. Is the presence of αὐτός necessary as the subject of ἐστιν? Why or why not? What is the significance of the presence of αὐτός in this sentence? (3.3, 9.1, 9.2, 9.3.b, and 9.4)

b. Explain why ἐστιν is not accented in this sentence? (9.1, 9.4, and 9.6.b)

c. Locate σώματος. (See 16.1 of the workbook and 4.5.b, 19.1, and 19.3.b of the textbook.)

PART OF SPEECH: **NOUN**   FUNCTION IN THE SENTENCE: **descrip.** of κεφαλὴ
CASE: **gen.**   GENDER: **neut.**   DECLENSION: **3rd**
NUMBER: **sing.**   LEXICAL FORM: σῶμα

6. οἱ ἀπόστολοι εἶδον τὸν υἱὸν τοῦ θεοῦ, ἐγένετο γὰρ αὐτὸς ἄνθρωπος καὶ ἔμενεν ἐν τῷ κόσμῳ.

a. Is εἶδον a first person singular or third person plural second aorist active indicative? On what do you base your answer? (2.1, 4.1, 4.5.a, 4.8.a, 7.5, 16.1, and 16.2)

b. Why is ἄνθρωπος the predicate nominative of ἐγένετο? (4.1, 4.8.a, and 9.4) Why not ἄνθρωπον? (11.1)

c. What use is αὐτὸς in and what is the significance of this use in this sentence? (9.1, 9.2, and 9.3.c)

7. πάλιν εἶπεν ἐν παραβολαῖς αὐτοῖς (Matt. 22:1).

a. What is the significance of πάλιν in this sentence? (See 7.1 of the textbook and 12.1.b of the workbook.)

b. Is παραβολαῖς dative, locative, or instrumental? How can you be sure? (5.1, 5.4.a.3, 7.5, 8.1, and 8.4) What is the significance of this use? (4.5.f)

c. Is the antecedent of αὐτοῖς stated in this sentence? What can be known for sure about the antecedent of αὐτοῖς no matter whether the antecedent is stated or not? (9.1, 9.2, and 9.3.a)

8. ταῦτα εἴπατε ἡμῖν ἐν τῷ ἱερῷ, ἐκεῖνα δὲ ἐν τῷ οἴκῳ.

a. The verb, in the phrase ἐκεῖνα δὲ τῷ οἴκῳ, is an implied εἴπατε. The reason why the verb is not repeated is to prevent redundancy.

b. Locate ἡμῖν. (9.1 and 9.2)

CASE: PART OF SPEECH:

NUMBER: FUNCTION IN THE SENTENCE:

GENDER: LEXICAL FORM:

c. Are the objects of the two uses of the preposition ἐν dative, locative, or instrumental respectively? What is the significance of this use? (7.5, 8.1, and 8.4)

9. καὶ ἔπεσεν ἐπὶ πρόσωπον (face) παρὰ τοὺς πόδας (feet) αὐτοῦ (Luke 17:16).

a. Why does ἔπεσεν end with ν? (3.3.f, 16.1, and 16.2)

b. There is an implied form of αὐτοῦ used with πρόσωπον in the translation of this sentence. (7.5, 9.1, 9.2, and 9.3)

c. How can you be sure of the translation of ἐπὶ and παρὰ? (7.5, 8.1, and 8.4)

10. οὐδὲ εἰσῆλθες εἰς τὴν ἐκκλησίαν, οὐδὲ εἶπες λόγους ἀγάπης τοῖς τέκνοις.

a. Is the use of οὐδὲ in this sentence connective, emphatic, or correlative? Explain your answer. (13.3.e)

b. Is the augment of εἰσῆλθες syllabic or temporal? (12.2.b) Is εἰσῆλθες constative, ingressive, or culminative? What is the significance of this type of aorist? (15.3.b)

c. Parse εἶπες. (3.1, 16.1, 16.2, and 16.4)

PART OF SPEECH: TENSE: PERSON:

SUBJECT: VOICE: NUMBER:

STEM: MOOD: LEXICAL FORM:

11. τοῦ ἱεροῦ αἱ πισταὶ ἐξῆλθον, καὶ κατῆλθον (they went down) εἰς τοὺς οἴκους αὐτῶν.

a. Is πισταὶ attributive, predicative, or substantive? Explain the significance of the use of this adjective. (6.1, 6.3, and 6.4.c)

b. Compare and contrast ἐξῆλθον and κατῆλθον. (11.1, 16.1, and 16.2)

c. What is the antecedent of αὐτῶν? How can you be sure? (7.5, 9.1, 9.2, and 9.3.a)

12. εἰς τοῦτο γὰρ ἐκλήθητε (you were called), ὅτι καὶ Χριστὸς ἔπαθεν ὑπὲρ ὑμῶν (1 Pet. 2:21)

a. Is this a compound or a complex sentence? What is the significance of this type of sentence? (7.4.d)

b. How is τοῦτο used in this sentence? What is the significance of this use? (10.1, 10.2, and 10.3.a)

c. Is ὑμῶν genitive or ablative in case in this sentence? (4.5.b, 9.1, and 9.2) On what do you base your answer? (7.5, 8.1, and 8.4)

13. ἐκεῖνος ἤγαγεν τὰ τέκνα πρὸς τὸν κύριον ὅτι ἔσχεν τὴν ἀγάπην τοῦ θεοῦ ἐν τῇ καρδίᾳ αὐτοῦ.

a. Locate κύριον. (4.1, 4.8.a, 8.1, and 8.4)

PART OF SPEECH: FUNCTION IN THE SENTENCE:

CASE: GENDER: DECLENSION:

NUMBER: LEXICAL FORM:

b. Is ὅτι a coordinating or a subordinating conjunction? What is the significance of the type of conjunction? (13.3.a)

c. Is τοῦ θεοῦ genitive or ablative? How can you be sure? (4.5.b, 4.8.a, 7.1, and 7.5)

14. εἰς τὰ ἴδια (his own things) ἦλθεν, καὶ οἱ ἴδιοι (his own people) αὐτὸν οὐ παρέλαβον (John 1:11).

a. Parse ἦλθεν. (12.1, 16.1, and 16.2)

PART OF SPEECH: TENSE: PERSON:

SUBJECT: VOICE: NUMBER:

STEM: MOOD: LEXICAL FORM:

b. Are ἦλθεν and παρέλαβον constative, ingressive, or culminative? What is the significance of this type of aorist? (11.1, 14.1, 15.3.a, 16.2, and 16.1)

c. What is the significance of οὐ in this sentence? Why use this spelling rather than οὐκ or οὐχ? (9.1 and 9.5)

15. οἱ δίκαιοι ἔφαγον ἄρτον ἐν τῇ ἐρήμῳ καὶ ἐδόξασαν τὸν θεόν.

a. Compare and contrast ἔφαγον and ἐδόξασαν as much as possible. (9.1, 15.1, 15.2, 16.1, and 16.2)

b. καὶ a coordinating or a subordinating conjunction? What is the significance of the use of this conjunction? (13.3.a)

c. Why is the article present but not translated with θεόν in this sentence? (4.3, 7.1, and 7.4.a)

16. Χριστὸς ὑπὲρ ἡμῶν ἀπέθανεν (Rom. 5:8).

a. Is ὑπὲρ translated "in behalf of" or "over, above." (4.5.b and 8.1) What determines the translation of the preposition? (7.5 and 8.4)

b. Is the augment of ἀπέθανεν a temporal or a syllabic augment? Explain the significance of this type of augment. (12.2.b, 13.1, 16.1, and 16.2)

c. Parse ἀπέθανεν. (13.1, 16.1, and 16.2)

PART OF SPEECH: TENSE: PERSON:

SUBJECT: VOICE: NUMBER:

STEM: MOOD: LEXICAL FORM:

17. πάτερ (Father) δίκαιε, καὶ ὁ κόσμος σε οὐκ ἔγνω, ἐγὼ δὲ σε ἔγνων, καὶ οὗτοι ἔγνωσαν ὅτι σύ με ἀπέστειλας (John 17:25).

a. Locate πάτερ. (18.1 and 18.3)

PART OF SPEECH: **NOUN**   FUNCTION IN THE SENTENCE: **direct address**
CASE: **voc.**   GENDER: **masc.**   DECLENSION: **3rd**
NUMBER: **sing.**   LEXICAL FORM: πατήρ

b. Explain the radical stem change with the aorist forms of γινώσκω in this sentence? (3.1, 16.1, 16.2, and 16.4)

c. What is *paranomasia*? List the occurrences of *paranomasia* in this sentence. (See lesson six, sentence 17.b of the workbook.)

18. οἴκους οἱ ἁμαρτωλοὶ ἔσχον, ἀλλ' ἔλιπον αὐτοὺς ὅτι ἡ φωνὴ τοῦ κυρίου ἠκούετο ἐν τῇ ἐκκλησίᾳ.

a. Contrast ἀλλ' and ὅτι as much as possible. (10.1, 12.1, 13.3.a)

b. Dissect and parse ἠκούετο. (2.1 and 13.2)

PART OF SPEECH: TENSE: CASE:

STEM: VOICE: NUMBER:

LEXICAL FORM: VERBAL FORM: GENDER:

CONNECTING VOWEL: PART. SIGN: ENDING:

c. Is the augment of ἠκούετο syllabic or temporal? Explain the significance of this augment. (2.1, 12.2.b, and 13.2)

19. ταῦτα δὲ ὑμῖν ἐξ ἀρχῆς οὐκ εἶπον, ὅτι μεθ᾽ ὑμῶν ἤμην (John 16:4).

a. What is the function of ταῦτα in this sentence? On what do you base your answer? (4.5.a, 7.5, 10.1, 10.2, and 10.3.a)

b. Explain the spelling of μεθ᾽ in this sentence. (2.5 and 8.1)

c. What part of speech is ἤμην? What is the significance of this part of speech? (9.1, 9.4, and 12.2.d)

20. τὰ τέκνα εἶπεν κακοὺς λόγους ὅτι ἤκουσεν αὐτοὺς ἀπὸ τῶν πονηρῶν ἀνθρώπων.

a. Why is the subject plural and the verb ending singular? (10.4)

b. Is κακοὺς attributive, predicative, or substantive? Explain the significance of the use of this adjective. (6.1, 6.3, and 6.4.a)

c. Is ἤκουσεν first or second aorist? How can you be sure? (2.1, 15.1, and 15.2)

LESSON 17: Aorist and Future Passive Indicative

17.1 Supplemental vocabulary.

διάβολος, ὁ - devil (20.1)
λίμνη, ἡ - lake
μακάριος, -ια, -ιον - blessed (22.1)
ὅς, ἥ, ὅ - who, which, what (27.1)

ὅτε - when (18.1) (adv.)
πιστεύω - I believe, I have faith in (23.1)
πῦρ, πυρός, τό - fire (18.1)
ὧδε - here (22.1) (adv.)

17.2.a In contrast to the _____ and _____ tenses, the aorist has different forms for the middle and passive. The aorist will have a(n) _____ since it is past tense.

17.2.b The aorist passive will not always be formed on the _____ stem; therefore, the aorist passive must be learned as a separate form. Once the stem is located, then the ending is added.

17.2.c The first aorist passive verb is formed by attaching the augment ___ to the present stem, followed by ___ (the sign of the first aorist passive), then the thematic vowel ___, and finally the personal ending.

17.2.d The infinitive does not have a(n) _____ .

17.2.e When the stem ends with a _____, various changes occur before the θη of the first aorist passive.

17.2.e.1 Liquid consonants:

ν drops out before ____ .

___ and ___ are retained before θ.

μ inserts ___ before θ.

17.2.5.e.2 Mute consonants:

_____ π and β change to φ before θ. (φ causes the θ to drop out and the form becomes second aorist.)

_____ τ, δ, and θ change to σ before θ.

_____ κ and γ change to χ before θ. (χ is retained before θ.)

17.2.e.3 Sibilant consonants:

ζ, ξ, and ψ change to ___ before θ.

17.3 The second aorist passive is like the first aorist passive except for the absence of the _____. The _____ and _____ of the first and second aorist passive are identical.

17.4.a The future passive indicative is based on the _____ _____ stem. The future does not have an augment, and this form uses the same endings as does the _____ _____. The future tense suffix ___ appears here as in the other future tense forms.

17.4.b What is the function of the future passive? What kind of action is expressed by the future passive? What dictates the way the future active verb is translated?

17.5 How do deponent verbs vary in the future and aorist forms? How are deponent middle or passive verbs translated? (8.4.d)

17.6 EXERCISES:

1. ἀπεκρίθη Ἰησοῦς καὶ εἶπεν, Οὐ δι᾽ ἐμὲ ἡ φωνὴ αὕτη γέγονεν (has come) ἀλλὰ δι᾽ ὑμᾶς (John 12:30).

   a. List the factors that identify the tense and voice of ἀπεκρίθη. (11.1, 17.1, and 17.2)

   b. Explain the spelling of the preposition δι᾽ in this sentence. (2.5 and 8.1)

   c. Parse γέγονεν. (11.1, 23.1, and 23.2)

PART OF SPEECH: **VERB**	TENSE: **2 perf.**	PERSON: **3rd**
SUBJECT: **(3rd sing.)**	VOICE: **act.**	NUMBER: **sing.**
STEM: γον-	MOOD: **indic.**	LEXICAL FORM: γίνομαι

2. ἐν ἐκείνῃ τῇ ἡμέρᾳ οἱ νεκροὶ ἐγερθήσονται ἐν τῷ λόγῳ τοῦ θεοῦ.

a. Is ἡμέρᾳ dative, locative, or instrumental? (4.5.e, 5.1, and 5.4.a.1) Is λόγῳ dative, locative, or instrumental? (2.1, 4.8.a) How can you to determine the case? (7.5, 8.1, and 8.4)

b. Why does νεκροὶ have a grave accent in this sentence? (See 2.7 of the textbook and 2.7.c of the workbook.)

c. Why is the definite article τοῦ not translated in the phrase τοῦ θεοῦ? (4.3, 7.1, and 7.4.a)

3. ταῦτα ἐγράφη ἐν ταῖς γραφαῖς.

a. Why is the plural ταῦτα the subject of ἐγράφη with the third singular ending? (10.1, 10.2.b, and 13.3)

b. Is γραφαῖς dative, locative, or instrumental? (4.5.e, 5.1, and 5.4.a.3) How are you able to determine the case? (7.5, 8.1, and 8.4)

4. οὗτοι οἱ ἄνθρωποι συνήχθησαν εἰς τὸν τοῦ προφήτου οἶκον.

a. What use is οὗτοι in the phrase οὗτοι οἱ ἄνθρωποι? How is this phrase translated? (10.1, 10.2.a, and 10.3.b)

b. Parse συνήχθησαν. (7.1, 17.1, and 17.2)

PART OF SPEECH: TENSE: PERSON:

SUBJECT: VOICE: NUMBER:

STEM: MOOD: LEXICAL FORM:

c. Locate προφήτου. (4.5.b, 5.1, 5.4.b, and 7.5)

PART OF SPEECH: FUNCTION IN THE SENTENCE:

CASE: GENDER: DECLENSION:

NUMBER: LEXICAL FORM:

5. ἠγέρθη οὐκ ἔστιν ὧδε (here) (Mark 16:6).

   a. What is the subject of ἠγέρθη? How can you be sure? (3.3, 7.5, 17.1, and 17.2)

   b. What is the significance of οὐκ in this sentence? Why not use the form of οὐ? (9.1 and 9.5)

   c. What part of speech is ὧδε? (See 17.1 of the workbook and 18.1 of the textbook.) What is the significance of this part of speech? (See 12.1.b of the workbook.)

6. νῦν μὲν πέμπονται οἱ διδάσκαλοι, τότε δὲ ἐπέμφθησαν καὶ οἱ ἀπόστολοι καὶ οἱ μαθηταί.

   a. What tense is the adverb νῦν generally used with? (3.3, 11.3, and 12.1) Would it be proper to use this adverb with any other tenses? (7.5, 12.1, and 12.3)

   b. Is it necessary to translate μὲν? On what do you base your answer? (See 12.1 of the textbook and 12.1.c of the workbook.)

7. διὰ τῆς ἀγάπης τοῦ Χριστοῦ οἱ ἁμαρτωλοὶ ἐσώθησαν καὶ ἐγενήθησαν μαθηταὶ τοῦ κυρίου.

a. Is διὰ translated as "through" or "because of" in this sentence? (8.1) On what do you base your answer? (7.5 and 8.4)

b. Other than having augments, how can you be sure that both ἐσώθησαν and ἐγενήθησαν are first aorist passive indicative verbs? (11.1, 17.1, and 17.2)

c. Why is the iota of μαθηταὶ accented with a grave accent in this sentence? (See 2.7 of the textbook and 2.7.c of the workbook.)

8. ἀπεκρίθη Ἰησοῦς καὶ εἶπεν αὐτῷ, Σὺ εἶ ὁ διδάσκαλος τοῦ Ἰσραὴλ καὶ ταῦτα οὐ γινώσκεις; (John 3:10).

a. Is the antecedent of αὐτῷ stated in this sentence? What can be determined about the antecedent on the basis of αὐτῷ? (9.1, 9.2, and 9.3.b)

b. What is the case of Ἰσραὴλ? On what do you base your answer? (4.3 and 7.5) Why is the location of Ἰσραὴλ problematic? (12.1)

c. What part of speech is ταῦτα? (10.1 and 10.2) In what use is ταῦτα in this sentence? What is the significance of this use? (10.3.a)

9. ἐπορεύθημεν εἰς ἕτερον τόπον, ἐκεῖνοι γὰρ οὐκ ἐδέξαντο ἡμᾶς.

a. Parse ἐπορεύθημεν. (9.1, 17.1, and 17.2)

PART OF SPEECH: TENSE: CASE:

STEM: VOICE: NUMBER:

LEXICAL FORM: MOOD: LEXICAL FORM:

b. What use is the adjective ἕτερον in this sentence? What is the significance of this use? (6.1, 6.3, and 6.4.a)

c. What is the antecedent of ἡμᾶς? Explain. (7.5, 9.1, 9.2, and 9.3.a)

10. τὸ εὐαγγέλιον ἐκηρύχθη ἐν ἐκείναις ταῖς ἡμέραις, καὶ κηρυχθήσεται καὶ νῦν.

     a. Locate ἐκείναις. (4.5.d, 10.1, and 10.2.b)

PART OF SPEECH: FUNCTION IN THE SENTENCE:

CASE: GENDER: DECLENSION:

NUMBER: LEXICAL FORM:

     b. Parse κηρυχθήσεται. (9.1, 17.1, and 17.2)

PART OF SPEECH: TENSE: PERSON:

SUBJECT: VOICE: NUMBER:

STEM: MOOD: LEXICAL FORM:

     c. The adverb νῦν generally relates to the present tense. What tense is νῦν used with in this sentence? (7.5, 12.1, and 12.3)

11. ὅτε (when) οὖν ἐξῆλθεν, λέγει Ἰησοῦς, Νῦν ἐδοξάσθη ὁ υἱὸς τοῦ ἀνθρώπου, καὶ ὁ θεὸς ἐδοξάσθη ἐν αὐτῷ (John 13:31).

     a. λέγει is a present active indicative verb that is translated as past tense. This is classified as the historical present tense verb, in which "the present tense is thus employed when a past event is viewed with the vividness of a present occurrence" (Dana and Mantey, p. 185).

b. ἐξῆλθεν and ἐδοξάσθη are aorist tense verbs. They are translated as present tense. These two verbs fall under the classification of dramatic aorist. The dramatic aorist, "may be used for stating a present reality with the certitude of a past event. This idiom is a device for emphasis" (Dana and Mantey, p. 198).

c. Is ἐξῆλθεν constative, ingressive, or culminative? What about ἐδοξάσθη? What is the significance of this type of aorist? (9.1, 11.1, 15.1, 15.2, 15.3.b, 16.1, and 16.2)

12. ἡ φωνὴ ἠκούσθη καὶ ὁ ἀπόστολος ἀπεστάλη εἰς τὸν κόσμον.

a. Compare and contrast the verbs ἠκούσθη and ἀπεστάλη as much as possible. (2.1, 7.1, 17.1, 17.2, and 17.3) Are the augments of each of these words syllabic or temporal? (12.2.b)

b. Is καὶ a coordinating or subordinating conjunction? What is the significance of this type of conjunction? (13.3.a)

c. What is *paranomasia*? Identify the occurrence of *paranomasia* in this sentence. (See the workbook, lesson 6, question 17.b)

13. Χριστὸς Ἰησοῦς ἦλθεν εἰς τὸν κόσμον ἁμαρτωλοὺς σῶσαι, ὧν (of whom) πρῶτός εἰμι ἐγώ (1 Tim. 1:15).

a. Why is Χριστὸς in the nominative case and Ἰησοῦς appears to be in the accusative plural case when both are the subject of ἦλθεν? (4.8.a, 7.1 and 12.1)

b. Parse σῶσαι. (9.1, 15.1, and 15.2)

PART OF SPEECH: TENSE: PERSON:

SUBJECT: VOICE: NUMBER:

STEM: MOOD: LEXICAL FORM:

   c. Why does the adjective πρῶτός have two accents? (9.6.b)

14. εἰσῆλθες εἰς τὴν ἐκκλησίαν τοῦ κυρίου καὶ ἐβαπτίσθης.

   a. Parse εἰσῆλθες. (11.1, 16.1, and 16.2)

PART OF SPEECH: TENSE: PERSON:

SUBJECT: VOICE: NUMBER:

STEM: MOOD: LEXICAL FORM:

   b. Locate ἐκκλησίαν. (4.5.g, 5.1, 5.4.a.1, and 7.5)

PART OF SPEECH: FUNCTION IN THE SENTENCE:

CASE: GENDER: DECLENSION:

NUMBER: LEXICAL FORM:

   c. What case is κυρίου in? On what do you base your answer? (4.1, 4.5.b, 4.8.a, 7.1, and 7.5)

15. ἐν ἐκείναις ταῖς ἡμέραις ἀκουσθήσεται ὁ λόγος τῆς εἰρήνης.

   a. The demonstrative pronoun ἐκείναις is the classical predicate use. Why is ἐκείναις translated as attributive? (10.1, 10.2.b, and 10.3.b).

   b. Is ἀκουσθήσεται future or aorist passive indicative? (17.4) What confirms your answer? (2.1 and 12.2.b)

16. κατὰ τὸ εὐαγγέλιον τῆς δόξης τοῦ μακαρίου (blessed) θεοῦ, ὅ (which) ἐπιστεύθην (was entrusted) ἐγώ (1 Tim. 1:11).

a. Is τὸ εὐαγγέλιον nominative or accusative in case? How can you be sure? (4.8.b, 8.1, 8.4, and 10.1)

b. In what use is μακαρίου? What is the significance of this use? (6.3, 6.4.a, and 22.1) What relationship exists between an adjective and the noun it modifies? (6.2)

c. Locate ὅ. (27.1 and 27.3.a)

CASE: **acc.**   PART OF SPEECH: **rel. prn.**
NUMBER: **sing.**   FUNCTION IN THE SENTENCE: **do.** of ἐπιστεύθην
GENDER: **neut.**   LEXICAL FORM: ὅς, ἥ, ὅ

17. οἱ πονηροὶ ἐσώθησαν ὅτι ἐδιδάχθησαν τὴν ὁδὸν τοῦ Χριστοῦ.

a. Are each of the augments of ἐσώθησαν and ἐδιδάχθησαν syllabic or temporal? Explain your answer. (3.1, 11.1, 12.2.b.1, 17.1 and 17.2)

b. Why does ὁδόν have a feminine article? (5.3 and 7.1)

18. καὶ εἶδον τοὺς νεκρούς (the dead), . . . καὶ ἐκρίθησαν οἱ νεκροὶ ἐκ τῶν γεγραμμένων (things written) ἐν τοῖς βιβλίοις (Rev. 20:12).

a. In what use is the adjective νεκρούς in this sentence? How about νεκροί? What is the significance of this use? (6.1, 6.3, and 6.4.c)

b. Parse γεγραμμένων. (3.1, 23.1, and 23.3)

PART OF SPEECH: **VERB**	TENSE: **perf.**	CASE: **gen.**
STEM: γραμ-	VOICE: **pass.**	NUMBER: **pl.**
LEXICAL FORM: γράφω	VERBAL FORM: **part.**	GENDER: **masc.**
CONNECTING VOWEL: **NONE**	PART. SIGN: -μεν-	ENDING: -ων

c. γεγραμμένων is an example of the substantive use of a participle. As an adjective the participle may function as a substantive and, in this way, resemble a noun. (See 20.7.b.2)

19. ἐγενήθης μαθητὴς τοῦ κυρίου ὅτι ἡ ἀγάπη αὐτοῦ ἐγνώσθη σοί.

a. Why is the predicate nominative (μαθητὴς) of ἐγενήθης in the nominative case? (9.4 and 11.1)

b. Explain the metamorphosis from γινώσκω to ἐγνώσθη. (3.1, 17.1, and 17.2)

20. καὶ ὁ διάβολος (devil) . . . ἐβλήθη εἰς τὴν λίμνην (lake) τοῦ πυρὸς (fire) . . . (Rev. 20:10).

a. Is the augment of ἐβλήθη syllabic or temporal? Explain your answer. (12.2.b)

b. List all of the factors that identify λίμνην as an accusative case noun. (See 4.6, 5.3, 8.1, and 8.4 of the textbook and 17.1 of the workbook.)

c. Locate πυρὸς. (See 17.1 of the workbook and 18.1 and 18.3 of the textbook.)

PART OF SPEECH: **NOUN**	FUNCTION IN THE SENTENCE: **descrip.** of λίμνην	
CASE: **gen.**	GENDER: **neut.**	DECLENSION: **3rd**
NUMBER: **sing.**	LEXICAL FORM: πῦρ	

LESSON 18: Third Declension: Liquid and Mute Stem Noouns

18.1.a Supplemental vocabulary:

δίδωμι - I give (29.1)
ἐκεί - there (28.5) (adv.)
ἐξουσίαζω - I have authority over
οὐδείς, (οὐθείς), οὐδεμία, οὐδέν - no
  one, nothing (27.1)

ὁμοίως - likewise (adv.)
σῶμα, σώματος, τό - body (19.1)
σωτήρ, σωτῆρος, ὁ - Savior
ὥσπερ - just as (adv.)
ὥστε - so that (adv.)

18.1.b Notice that the vocabulary defines αἰών as "age." εἰς τὸν αἰῶνα is an idiom that is commonly translated as "forever," and εἰς τοὺς αἰῶνας καὶ αἰώνων is an idiom that is commonly translated "forever and ever."

18.2.a The first declension has _____ sets of endings: _____ of these are feminine and _____ is masculine. (5.4)

18.2.b The second declension has _____ sets of endings: one for masculine nouns and the other for neuter nouns. (The student should be aware that there are a few feminine second declension nouns that follow the second declension masculine endings.)

18.2.c The primary difference between the first and the second declensions is that, in the first declension, the predominant vowel sound in the ending is a(n) ___ sound and, in the second declension, it is a(n) ___ sound.

18.2.d By what characteristics are third declension nouns recognized?

18.2.e How is the stem of third declension nouns located?

18.2.f The first and second declension nouns are generally built on the nominative case; however, the third declension nouns are based on the _____ singular form.

18.2.g Review the four things one must know in order to form the third declension?

18.2.h Normally the nominative and genitive singular forms of third declension nouns are listed in the vocabulary.

18.2.i The third inflected form of the plural changes when the _____ of the third declension noun ends with a consonant. This is a result of the combination of the final consonant with ___ of the ____ ending. Note the following changes:

π, β, or ___ + σι = ψι   ___, δ, or θ drops off leaving σι

κ, γ, or χ + ___ = ξι   ν drops off leaving ____

18.2.j Because two consonants are lost in the case of ντ, the preceding vowel _____.

18.2.k What rule must be followed with regard to the form used in the accusative singular?

18.2.l The vocative form in the singular is either the _____ or the same form as the _____ . In the plural, it is always the same as the _____ .

18.3.a LIQUID NOUNS: Nouns ending in one of the liquid consonants ___ or ___ are mostly masculine with a few feminine.

18.3.b How do you decline a third declension noun that ends in a liquid consonant?

18.3.c Some liquid nouns experience vowel gradation. Explain.

18.3.d Note that the accent of third declension liquid noun πατήρ, shifts in an irregular manner. What rule of noun accent does this violate? (See workbook, section 2.7)

18.4.a Mute nouns are those whose stems end in a(n) _____ _____ .
18.4.b Mute nouns are either masculine or feminine and are alike in endings except for the _____ _____ .

18.5 EXERCISES:

1. ἐλπίδα οὐκ ἔχομεν ὅτι οὐ γινώσκομεν τὸν κύριον.

a. Locate ἐλπίδα. (18.1 and 18.2)

PART OF SPEECH: FUNCTION IN THE SENTENCE:

CASE: GENDER: DECLENSION:

NUMBER: LEXICAL FORM:

b. What affect does the order of the object, negative particle, and verb, ἐλπίδα οὐκ ἔχομεν, have on the translation of this sentence? Explain. (4.7) Is this a matter of accidence or syntax? (7.2)

c. Is ὅτι a coordinating or a subordinating conjunction? Explain the significance of your answer. (13.3.a)

2. ἡ γυνὴ τοῦ ἰδίου σώματος (body) οὐκ ἐξουσιάζει (has authority over) ἀλλὰ ὁ ἀνήρ, ὁμοίως (likewise) δὲ καὶ ὁ ἀνὴρ τοῦ ἰδίου σώματος οὐκ ἐξουσιάζει ἀλλὰ ἡ γυνή   (1 Cor. 7:4).

a. Locate σώματος. (19.1 and 19.3.b)

PART OF SPEECH: **NOUN**   FUNCTION IN THE SENTENCE: **descrip.** of τοῦ ἰδίου
CASE: **gen.**   GENDER: **neut.**   DECLENSION: **3rd**
NUMBER: **sing.**   LEXICAL FORM: σῶμα

c. Compare ἀλλὰ with δὲ. (See 9.1, 9.5, and 12.1 of the textbook and 12.1.c of the workbook.)

3. οἱ πιστοὶ μαθηταὶ ἐκήρυξαν τὸ εὐαγγέλιον ἐν τῇ νυκτὶ καὶ ἐν τῇ ἡμέρᾳ.

a. Dissect and parse ἐκήρυξαν. (9.1 and 15.2)

PART OF SPEECH: AUGMENT   STEM:

TENSE: PERSON: ENDING:

VOICE:	NUMBER:	CONNECTING VOWEL:
MOOD:	LEXICAL FORM:	SUBJECT:

b. Is ἐκήρυξαν constative, ingressive, or culminative? What is the significance of this type of aorist? (15.3.a)

c. Is νυκτὶ dative, locative, or instrumental? What about ἡμέρᾳ? How can you be sure? (4.5.e, 7.5, 18.1, and 18.4) Does the preposition help in identifying the case? How? (8.1 and 8.4)

4. καὶ ὅτε εἶδον αὐτόν, ἔπεσα πρὸς τοὺς πόδας αὐτοῦ ὡς νεκρός (Rev. 1:17).

a. What part of speech is ὅτε? What is the significance of this part of speech? (See 12.1.b of the workbook and 18.1 of the textbook.)

b. Is εἶδον a first singular or a third plural second aorist active indicative verb? (2.1, 16.1, and 16.2) How can you be sure? (7.5)

5. ὥστε (so that) ἡμεῖς ἀπὸ τοῦ νῦν οὐδένα (no one) οἴδαμεν (we know) κατὰ σάρκα (2 Cor. 5:16).

a. ἀπὸ τοῦ νῦν is an idiom where νῦν is used as an adjective with an article. This idiom is best translated "from now" or "henceforth" (Aland, *GNT UBS4, Dictionary*, p. 122; Robertson, p. 83; and Robertson and Davis, p. 246-247).

b. Locate οὐδένα. (27.1 and 27.3.f)

PART OF SPEECH: **neg. prn.**	FUNCTION IN THE SENTENCE: **do.** of οἴδαμεν	
CASE: **acc.**	GENDER: **masc.**	DECLENSION: **N/A**
NUMBER: **sing.**	LEXICAL FORM: οὐδείς	

c. Parse οἴδαμεν. (23.1 and 23.2.d)

PART OF SPEECH: **VERB**	TENSE: **perf.**	PERSON: **1st**
SUBJECT: **(1st pl.)**	VOICE: **act.**	NUMBER: **pl.**
STEM: οἴδ-	MOOD: **indic.**	LEXICAL FO RM: οἶδα

6. ἐκεῖνος ἐξῆλθεν εὐθύς. ἦν δὲ νύξ (John 13:30).

a. Parse ἦν. (9.1, 9.4, and 12.2.d)

PART OF SPEECH:	TENSE:	PERSON:
SUBJECT:	VOICE:	NUMBER:
STEM:	MOOD:	LEXICAL FORM:

b. What mandates νύξ as nominative case? (11.1, 18.1, and 18.4)

7. ὁ νόμος διὰ Μωϋσέως ἐδόθη (was given), ἡ χάρις καὶ ἡ ἀλήθεια διὰ Ἰησοῦ Χριστοῦ ἐγένετο (John 1:17).

a. What is the significance of the (¨) in Μωϋσέως? (2.5)

b. Explain why the ending of ἀλήθεια differs from the definite article? (5.1, 5.3, and 5.4.a.1)

c. What use of the imperfect tense is ἐγένετο? What is the significance of this use? (11.1, 12.3.c, and 13.2)

8. αὕτη ἐστὶν ἡ ἀγγελία τῆς ἀληθείας· ὁ θεός ἐστιν ἀγαθὸς καὶ οἱ υἱοὶ αὐτοῦ μένουσιν ἐν αὐτῷ εἰς τοὺς αἰῶνας τῶν αἰώνων.

a. What type of pronoun is αὕτη? (10.1 and 10.2.a) What use is αὕτη in this sentence? What is the significance of this use? (10.3.a)

b. What is the use of the adjective ἀγαθὸς in this sentence? What is the significance of this use? (6.1, 6.3, and 6.4.b)

c. Why is εἰς τοὺς αἰῶνας τῶν αἰώνων translated "for ever and ever" rather than "into/to/in the ages and of ages?" (See 18.1.b of the workbook.)

9. ἐν ἀρχῇ ἦν ὁ λόγος, καὶ ὁ λόγος ἦν πρὸς τὸν θεόν, καὶ θεὸς ἦν ὁ λόγος (John 1:1).

a. Locate λόγος. (2.1 and 4.8.a)

PART OF SPEECH: FUNCTION IN THE SENTENCE:

CASE: GENDER: DECLENSION:

NUMBER: LEXICAL FORM:

b. Is the first use of καὶ a coordinating or a subordinating conjunction? How about the second use of καὶ? What is the significance of the use of this type of conjunction? (13.3.a)

c. Why is θεὸς the predicate nominative of the second occurrence of ἦν? Why not have θεόν? (4.1, 4.8.a, 9.4, and 12.2)

10. ὁ κύριος διδάσκει ὅτι ὁ θεός ἐστιν ὁ πατὴρ ἀγαθῶν ἀνθρώπων.

a. Is ἐστιν necessary to convey the message of this sentence? (9.4) Why is πατὴρ the predicate nominative of ἐστιν? (9.4, 18.1, and 18.3) What identifies πατὴρ as nominative case in this sentence? (4.3)

b. Locate πατήρ. (18.1 and 18.3)

PART OF SPEECH: FUNCTION IN THE SENTENCE:

CASE: GENDER: DECLENSION:

NUMBER: LEXICAL FORM:

c. What use is the adjective ἀγαθῶν in this sentence? What is the significance of this use? (6.1, 6.3, and 6.4.a)

11. καὶ ἦν ἡ μήτηρ τοῦ Ἰησοῦ ἐκεῖ (there) (John 2:1).

a. What is the subject of ἦν? On what do you base your answer? (3.3, 9.1, 9.4, and 12.2)

b. Locate Ἰησοῦ. (12.1)

PART OF SPEECH: FUNCTION IN THE SENTENCE:

CASE: GENDER: DECLENSION:

NUMBER: LEXICAL FORM:

c. What part of speech is ἐκεῖ? What is the significance of this part of speech? (See 18.1.1 and 28.5 of the textbook and 12.1.b of the workbook.)

12. ὁ θεός ἐστιν ὁ ἄρχων τῆς βασιλείας αὐτοῦ.

a. What is the object of ἐστιν? Explain the case the object is in. (7.5, 9.1, and 9.4)

b. Why is the nominative singular masculine article used with ἄρχων, which has the appearance as a genitive plural noun? (4.3, 18.1, and 18.2)

c. Locate βασιλείας. (5.1 and 5.4.a)

PART OF SPEECH: FUNCTION IN THE SENTENCE:

CASE: GENDER: DECLENSION:

NUMBER: LEXICAL FORM:

13. ἀπεκρίθη οὖν αὐτῷ ὁ ὄχλος, Ἡμεῖς ἠκούσαμεν ἐκ τοῦ νόμου ὅτι ὁ Χριστὸς μένει εἰς τὸν αἰῶνα (John 12:34).

a. What is the significance of the use of ἀπεκρίθη as used in this sentence? (11.1, 11.4.d, 17.1, and 17.2)

b. What is the significance of ἐκ τοῦ νόμου following ἠκούσαμεν? (2.1, 11.6, 15.1, and 15.2)

c. Explain the translation of εἰς τὸν αἰῶνα. (18.1)

14. χάρις καὶ εἰρήνη ἀπὸ θεοῦ πατρὸς καὶ Χριστοῦ Ἰησοῦ τοῦ σωτῆρος (Savior) ἡμῶν (Titus 1:4).

a. Locate χάρις. (18.1 and 18.4)

PART OF SPEECH: FUNCTION IN THE SENTENCE:

CASE: GENDER: DECLENSION:

NUMBER: LEXICAL FORM:

b. Is θεοῦ genitive or ablative in case? (4.4, 4.8.a, and 7.1) On what do you base your answer? (7.5, 8.1, and 8.4)

c. Locate σωτῆρος. (See 18.1.a of the workbook and 18.3 of the textbook.)

PART OF SPEECH: FUNCTION IN THE SENTENCE:

CASE: GENDER: DECLENSION:

NUMBER: LEXICAL FORM:

15. ὁ δὲ δοῦλος οὐ μένει ἐν τῇ οἰκίᾳ εἰς τὸν αἰῶνα, ὁ υἱὸς μένει εἰς τὸν αἰῶνα (John 8:35).

a. Why is δὲ the second word of this sentence in Greek, but is translated as the first word of this sentence? What is the significance of this phenomenon? (See 9.1 and 9.5 of the textbook and 9.5.b of the workbook.)

b. Explain the spelling of οὐ as used in this sentence compared to the optional spellings of this word. What is the significance of this word in this sentence? (9.1 and 9.5)

c. Is οἰκίᾳ dative, locative, or instrumental in case? (5.3, 5.4.a.1, 8.1, 8.4, and 18.1) What is the significance of this case? (4.5.e)

16. ὥσπερ (just as) γὰρ ἡ γυνὴ ἐκ τοῦ ἀνδρός, οὕπως καὶ ὁ ἀνὴρ διὰ τῆς γυναικός (1 Cor. 11:12).

a. Why is γὰρ the second word of the Greek sentence, but is translated as if it was the first word? What is the significance of this phenomenon? (See 9.5 and 10.1 of the textbook and 10.1.b of the workbook.)

b. List the adverbs in this sentence. What is the significance of adverbs? (See 12.1.2 and 18.1.a of the workbook and 18.1 of the textbook.)

c. Locate γυναικός. (5.3, 6.1, 8.4, 18.1, and the paradigm at the back of the textbook.

PART OF SPEECH: FUNCTION IN THE SENTENCE:

CASE: GENDER: DECLENSION:

NUMBER: LEXICAL FORM:

17. διὰ τοῦ θανάτου τοῦ υἱοῦ βλέπομεν τὴν ἀγάπην τοῦ πατρός.

     a. Is διὰ translated "through" or "because of" in this sentence? On what do you base your answer? (8.1 and 8.4)

     b. Dissect and parse βλέπομεν. (2.1 and 3.3)

PART OF SPEECH: AUGMENT   STEM:

TENSE: PERSON: ENDING:

VOICE: NUMBER: CONNECTING VOWEL:

MOOD: LEXICAL FORM: SUBJECT:

     c. Locate ἀγάπην. (5.1 and 5.4.a.3)

PART OF SPEECH: FUNCTION IN THE SENTENCE:

CASE: GENDER: DECLENSION:

NUMBER: LEXICAL FORM:

18. ἡ οὖν Μαριὰμ (Mary) ὡς ἦλθεν ὅπου (where) ἦν ᾽Ιησοῦς ἰδοῦσα (when she beheld) αὐτὸν ἔπεσεν αὐτοῦ πρὸς τοὺς πόδας (John 11:32).

     a. Is ἦλθεν constative, ingressive, or culminative? What is the significance of this type of aorist? (15.3.b)

b. Is the augment of ἔπεσεν temporal or syllabic? Explain. 12.2.a, 16.1, and 16.3)

19. ἡ ἀγγελία τῆς ἐκκλησίας φέρει ἀγάπην, ἀλήθειαν, χάριν, καὶ ἐλπίδα.

a. Is ἀγγελία translated as "angel/messenger" or "message"? (2.1, 5.4.a.1, and 18.1) How can you be sure? (5.3 and 7.5)

b. How can you be sure that ἐκκλησίας is genitive singular feminine rather than accusative plural feminine? (5.3)

c. ἀγάπην, ἀλήθειαν, χάριν, and ἐλπίδα are accusative singular feminine nouns. Why do each of these nouns have different endings? (5.1, 5.4.a.1, 5.4.a.3, 18.1, and 18.4)

20. ἔργα τῶν χειρῶν σού εἰσιν οἱ οὐρανοί (Heb. 1:10).

a. Is ἔργα or οὐρανοί the subject of εἰσιν? On what do you base your answer? (4.8.a and b, 7.5, 9.1, 9.4, 10.1, and 11.1)

b. Why is the ν necessary with εἰσιν in this sentence? (3.3.f and 9.4)

LESSON 19: Third Declension: Vowel Stem and Neuter Nouns

19.1 Supplemental vocabulary:

βασιλεύω - I reign, rule,
  possess legal right
γραμματεύς, ὁ - scribe (21.1)
δάκρυ, δάκρους, τό - a tear
Ἰακώβ, ὁ - Jacob
μέγας, μεγάλη, μέγα - great (adj.) (28.1)

Νικόδημος, -ου, ὁ - Nicodemus
νυνί - now (adv.)
πᾶς, πᾶσα, πᾶν - all (adj.) (28.1)
Φαρισαίος, ὁ - a Pharisee (24.1)
τρεῖς (m/f), τρία (n) - three (adj.)

19.2 Three classes of nouns have stems which end in a vowel. Noun stems ending in ___ are feminine; stems ending in ____ are masculine; and nouns ending in ___ can be any gender.

19.2.a.1 The ι stem nouns are _____ in gender. In the ι stem nouns, ___ replaces the final ι in some cases. The forms in the _____ and _____ plural are the result of the contraction of εες and εας respectively.

19.2.a.2 Additional facts concerning the inflection of this class of third declension nouns:

    1. Find the stem by striking off the ς in the nominative singular.

    2. The genitive singular is ως rather than ος.

    3. ε unites with ι ending in dative (etc.) singular to form a diphthong.

    4. The accent of the genitive/ablative singular and plural is irregular and stands on the antepenult even with a long ultima. (See section 2.7 of the workbook for the rule violated by this occurrence.)

19.2.b.1 The ευ stem nouns are _____ in gender. In the ευ stem the _____ is dropped when the ending begins with a vowel. The forms in the _____ and _____ plural are the result of the contraction of εες and εας respectively.

19.2.b.2 Additional facts concerning the inflection of this class of third declension nouns:

    1. The stem is found by deleting the ς from the nominative singular form.

    2. The genitive singular is ως rather than ος.

    3. ε unites with ι ending in dative (etc.) singular to form a diphthong.

19.2.c The inflection of this class of third declension nouns is regular. In this class, the stem is also found by deleting the ς from the nominative singular form. Most υ stem nouns are _____; however, a few are _____ and one is _____.

19.3 Two groups of third declension neuter nouns derive their stem from the _____ _____ form. All the nouns whose stems end in ____ have their genitive/ablative singular ending in -ους. Nouns whose stems end in ατ will have their genitive singular ending in _____.

19.3.a The forms of the third declension nouns ending in ες changes radically. Why does this noun change so radically? (The textbook lists both the original forms and the resulting forms. The original forms do not occur in the New Testament; therefore, the Greek New Testament student should concentrate on the resulting form. The original forms <u>do</u> exist in classical Greek.)

19.3.b.1 In ατ stem third declension nouns, the endings are added to the stem, which is found in the _____ _____. Delete the ος of this case, and the stem remains.

19.3.b.2 Note the loss of the ____ in the nominative, accusative, and vocative singular form. Also note the loss of the τ before _____ in the dative plural form.

19.4 EXERCISES:

1. ἦν δὲ ἄνθρωπος ἐκ τῶν Φαρισαίων (Pharisees), Νικόδημος (Nicodemus) ὄνομα αὐτῷ, ἄρχων τῶν Ἰουδαίων· οὗτος ἦλθεν πρὸς αὐτὸν νυκτός (John 3:1-2).

a. Is ἄνθρωπος the subject or the predicate nominative of ἦν? Explain. (7.5, 9.4, and 12.2.d)

b. Locate ὄνομα. (19.1 and 19.3.b)

PART OF SPEECH: FUNCTION IN THE SENTENCE:

CASE: GENDER: DECLENSION:

NUMBER: LEXICAL FORM:

c. Is ἦλθεν constative, ingressive, or culminative? Explain the significance of this type of aorist. (11.1, 15.1, and 15.3.b)

2. οἱ μαθηταὶ τοῦ κυρίου ἔφαγον ἄρτον καὶ ἰχθύας καὶ στάχυας ἐν τῇ πόλει.

a. Parse ἔφαγον. (9.1, 16.1, and 16.2)

PART OF SPEECH: TENSE: PERSON:

SUBJECT: VOICE: NUMBER:

STEM: MOOD: LEXICAL FORM:

b. ἰχθύας is a vowel stem noun. What does the statement "vowel stem noun" mean? (19.2)

c. List the factors that identify πόλει as a locative noun. (5.3, 7.5, 8.1, 8.4, 19.1, and 19.2.a)

3. Χριστὸς ἐκήρυσσεν τὸ εὐαγγέλιον τοῖς ὄχλοις, καὶ οἱ ἀρχιερεῖς ἔπεμπον τοὺς δούλους ἀκούειν αὐτόν.

a. Is the augment of ἐκήρυσσεν syllabic or temporal? Explain the difference between the syllabic and temporal augments. (12.2.b) Is ἐκήρυσσεν descriptive, repeated/iterate, or inceptive (12.3.a)? What is significant about this type of imperfect tense verb? (12.3.a)

b. Dissect and parse ἔπεμπον. (3.1 and 12.2.a)

PART OF SPEECH: AUGMENT: STEM:

TENSE: PERSON: ENDING:

VOICE: NUMBER: CONNECTING VOWEL:

MOOD: LEXICAL FORM: SUBJECT:

c. Parse ἀκούειν. (2.1 and 3.3)

PART OF SPEECH: TENSE: PERSON:

SUBJECT: VOICE: NUMBER:

STEM: MOOD: LEXICAL FORM:

4. αὐτὸς ὑμᾶς βαπτίσει ἐν πνεύματι ἁγίῳ καὶ πυρί (Matt. 3:11).

a. Is αὐτὸς necessary in this sentence? Why or why not? What is the significance of the presence of αὐτὸς in this sentence? (9.1, 9.2, and 9.3.b)

b. What is the function of the tense of βαπτίσει? Explain. (14.3.a)

c. Locate πνεύματι. (19.1 and 19.3.b)

PART OF SPEECH: FUNCTION IN THE SENTENCE:

CASE: GENDER: DECLENSION:

NUMBER: LEXICAL FORM:

5. ὁ θεὸς ἔχει τὴν δύναμιν κρίσεως ἐν τῷ κόσμῳ καὶ ἐν τῷ οὐρανῷ.

a. Locate κρίσεως. (19.1 and 19.2.a)

PART OF SPEECH: FUNCTION IN THE SENTENCE:

CASE: GENDER: DECLENSION:

NUMBER: LEXICAL FORM:

b. Is the phrase ἐν τῷ κόσμῳ καὶ ἐν τῷ οὐρανῷ dative, locative, or instrumental in nature? Explain your answer. (4.5.e, 7.5, 8.1, and 8.4)

6. οἱ ἱερεῖς γινώσκουσιν τὸν νόμον, ἀλλ᾽ οὐ μένουσιν ἐν τῷ θελήματι τοῦ θεοῦ.

a. Is ἀλλ' a coordinating or a subordinating conjunction? What is the significance of the type of conjunction? (12.1 and 13.3.a)

b. Why does elision occur with ἀλλ' in this sentence? (2.5)

c. What is the significance of the placement of οὐ in this sentence? (9.1, 9.5, and 9.6) Why is οὐ used instead of οὐκ? (9.1)

7. καὶ εἶπεν αὐτοῖς, Τοῦτο τὸ γένος ἐν οὐδενὶ (nothing) δύναται ἐξελθεῖν εἰ μὴ ἐν προσευχῇ (prayer) (Mark 9:29).

a. Explain the change in form from the present active indicative λέγω to its second aorist active indicative form εἶπεν. (3.1, 16.1, 16.2, and 16.4)

b. Explain the use of τὸ with γένος. (4.3, 19.1, and 19..3.a)

c. Locate οὐδενὶ. (27.1 and 27.3.f)

PART OF SPEECH: **neg. prn.**   FUNCTION IN THE SENTENCE: **obj.of ἐν**
CASE: **inst.**   GENDER: **neut.**   DECLENSION: **N/A**
NUMBER: **sing.**   LEXICAL FORM: οὐδέν

8. ὁ Ἰησοῦς . . . εἶπεν . . . τοῦτό ἐστιν τὸ σῶμά μου (Matt. 26:26).

a. Is τοῦτό in the substantive or predicate use? (10.1, 10.2, and 10.3.a) What is the significance of this use? (6.4.c)

b. Why does τοῦτό have two accents in the phrase τοῦτό ἐστιν? (9.6.b)

c. Why does σῶμά have two accents in the phrase σῶμά μου? (9.6.b)

9. γινώσκομεν καὶ τὸ θέλημα καὶ τὴν ἀγάπην τοῦ θεοῦ.

a. Parse γινώσκομεν. (3.1 and 3.3)

PART OF SPEECH: TENSE: PERSON:

SUBJECT: VOICE: NUMBER:

STEM: MOOD: LEXICAL FORM:

b. How is the coordinating conjunction καὶ used in this sentence? What is the significance of this use? (13.3.d)

c. Locate θέλημα. (19.1 and 19.3.b)

PART OF SPEECH: FUNCTION IN THE SENTENCE:

CASE: GENDER: DECLENSION:

NUMBER: LEXICAL FORM:

10. καὶ βασιλεύσει (he shall rule) ἐπὶ τὸν οἶκον Ἰακὼβ (Jacob) εἰς τοὺς αἰῶνας καὶ τῆς βασιλείας αὐτοῦ οὐκ ἔσται τέλος (Luke 1:33).

a. What tense is βασιλεύσει? On what do you base your answer? (See 14.2 of the textbook and 19.1 of the workbook.) What is the significance of the tense function of βασιλεύσει in this sentence? (14.3.a)

b. How is ἐπὶ best translated in this sentence? (8.1) How are you able to determine your answer? (4.1, 4.3, 4.8.a, 7.5, and 8.4)

c. Explain why the ending of βασιλείας differs from the ending of its accompanying definite article. (5.1, 5.3, and 5.4.a.1)

11. ἐν τῷ ὀνόματι τοῦ Χριστοῦ ἔχομεν ἐλπίδα τῆς ζωῆς.

a. Locate ὀνόματι. (19.1 and 19.3.b)

PART OF SPEECH: FUNCTION IN THE SENTENCE:

CASE: GENDER: DECLENSION:

NUMBER: LEXICAL FORM:

b. Does τοῦ Χριστοῦ express possession or separation? (4.5.b) What case does this describe? (7.5)

c. Is ἐλπίδα the direct object or the predicate nominative of ἔχομεν? (7.4.c) On what do you base your answer? (18.2)

12. τὸ αἷμα Ἰησοῦ τοῦ υἱοῦ αὐτοῦ καθαρίζει ἡμᾶς ἀπὸ πάσης (every) ἁμαρτίας (1 John 1:7).

a. αἷμα is the subject of καθαρίζει. Could a nominative plural form αἷμα also serve as the subject of καθαρίζει? Why or why not? (10.4)

b. Parse καθαρίζει. (3.3 and 13.1)

PART OF SPEECH: TENSE: PERSON:

SUBJECT: VOICE: NUMBER:

STEM: MOOD: LEXICAL FORM:

c. Does ἀπὸ express the genitive or ablative case function? (8.1) Does this case express posses-sion or separation? (8.1 and 8.4)

13. οἱ πονηροὶ μένουσιν ἐν τῷ σκότει τῆς ἁμαρτίας, οἱ δὲ πιστοὶ ἀκούουσιν τὰ ῥήματα τοῦ κυρίου καὶ γίνονται ἀγαθοὶ μαθηταί.

a. Locate ἁμαρτίας. (5.1, 5.3, and 5.4.a.1)

PART OF SPEECH: FUNCTION IN THE SENTENCE:

CASE: GENDER: DECLENSION:

NUMBER: LEXICAL FORM:

b. Parse γίνονται. (11.1 and 11.3)

PART OF SPEECH: TENSE: PERSON:

SUBJECT: VOICE: NUMBER:

STEM: MOOD: LEXICAL FORM:

c. Is ἀγαθοὶ an attributive, predicative, or substantive adjective? What function does this use of the adjective serve? (6.1, 6.3, and 6.4.a)

14. νυνὶ (now) δὲ μένει πίστις, ἐλπίς, ἀγάπη, τὰ τρία (three) ταῦτα· μείζων (the greatest) δὲ τούτων ἡ ἀγάπη (1 Cor. 13:13).

a. Does μένει portray continuous or punctiliar action. Explain the difference. (3.1 and 3.2.a)

b. Compare and contrast πίστις, ἐλπίς, and ἀγάπη as much as possible. (5.1, 5.4.a.3, 18.1, 18.2, 19.1, and 19.2.a)

c. What use is μείζων in? (6.4.c, 28.1, 28.2.b, and 28.3) What about τούτων? (10.1, 10.2.a, and 10.3.a) Explain the significance of the use of these words. (μείζων is a nominative singular masculine/feminine adjective.)

15. λέγω γὰρ ὑμῖν ὅτι πολλοὶ (many) προφῆται καὶ βασιλεῖς ἠθέλησαν ἰδεῖν ἃ (what) ὑμεῖς βλέπετε καὶ οὐκ εἶδαν (they did see) (Luke 10:24).

 a. Why is γὰρ the second word of the sentence, but is translated into English as the first word of the sentence? (See 9.5 and 10.1 of the textbook and 10.1.b of the workbook.)

 b. Is ἠθέλησαν constative, ingressive, or culminative? Explain the significance of this type of aorist. (3.1, 15.1, and 15.3.a)

 c. Explain the significance of ὑμεῖς in this sentence. (9.1, 9.2, and 9.3.b)

16. λήμψεσθε δύναμιν ἀπὸ τοῦ θεοῦ καὶ ἔσεσθε οἱ μαθηταὶ αὐτοῦ.

 a. Dissect and parse λήμψεσθε. (3.1, 14.1, and 14.4)

PART OF SPEECH: AUGMENT: STEM:

TENSE: PERSON: ENDING:

VOICE: NUMBER: CONNECTING VOWEL:

MOOD: LEXICAL FORM: SUBJECT:

 b. Locate δύναμιν. (19.1 and 19.2.a)

PART OF SPEECH: FUNCTION IN THE SENTENCE:

CASE: GENDER: DECLENSION:

NUMBER: LEXICAL FORM:

c. What is the antecedent of αὐτοῦ? On what do you base your answer? (9.1, 9.2, and 9.3.a)

17. τῇ γὰρ χάριτι ἐστε σεσωσμένοι (were saved) διὰ πίστεως· καὶ τοῦτο οὐκ ἐξ ὑμῶν, θεοῦ τὸ δῶρον (Eph. 2:8).

a. Is χάριτι dative, locative, or instrumental? Explain the significance of this case. (4.5.f, 7.5, 8.1, 8.4, 18.1, and 18.4)

b. Is διὰ translated as "through" or "because of" in this sentence? In what case is διὰ translated? What confirms your answer? (7.5, 8.1, and 8.4)

c. Why is the verb of being omitted in the phrase θεοῦ τὸ δῶρον? (9.4) Since the verb of being should be present in the phrase θεοῦ τὸ δῶρον, why must one conclude that δῶρον is nominative singular neuter rather than accusative singular neuter? (9.4)

18. ἔρχονται πρὸς αὐτὸν οἱ ἀρχιερεῖς καὶ οἱ γραμματεῖς (scribes) καὶ οἱ πρεσβύτεροι (Mark 11:27).

a. What is the subject of ἔρχονται? On what do you base your answer? (See 4.3, 4.5.a, 4.8.a, 7.1, 11.1, 11.3, and 21.1 of the textbook and 19.1 of the workbook.)

b. What affect does the late appearance of the subject of ἔρχονται have on the translation of this sentence? Explain. (4.7)

c. What part of speech is πρεσβύτεροι? (7.1) In what use is πρεσβύτεροι in this sentence? What is the significance of this use? (6.3 and 6.4.c)

19. χάρις ὑμῖν καὶ εἰρήνη ἀπὸ θεοῦ πατρὸς ἡμῶν καὶ κυρίου Ἰησοῦ Χριστοῦ (Gal. 1:3).

a. Does ἀπὸ θεοῦ express possession or separation? (4.8.a and 7.1) What case defines this answer? (4.5 and 7.5)

b. Locate κυρίου. (4.1, 4.8.a, and 7.5)

PART OF SPEECH: FUNCTION IN THE SENTENCE:

CASE: GENDER: DECLENSION:

NUMBER: LEXICAL FORM:

20. καὶ ταύτην τὴν φωνὴν ἡμεῖς ἠκούσαμεν ἐξ οὐρανοῦ . . . ὄντες (while we were) ἐν τῷ ἁγίῳ ὄρει (2 Pet. 1:18).

a. Is the presence of ἡμεῖς necessary in this sentence? What is the significance of the presence of ἡμεῖς in this sentence? (3.3, 9.1, 9.2, and 9.3.b)

b. Is the augment of ἠκούσαμεν syllabic or temporal? Explain the difference between these two types of augments. (3.1, 12.2.a, 15.1, and 15.2)

c. Is ὄρει dative, locative, or instrumental? Explain your answer. (7.5, 19.1, and 19.3.a) How does the preposition help determine your answer? (8.1 and 8.4) What is the significance of this case? (4.5.e)

LESSON 20: Present and Future Participles

20.1 Supplemental vocabulary.

ἐπεί - since (adv.)

ἔθνος, ἔθνους, τό - nation
 (pl. Gentiles) (21.1)

οὐχί - not (emphatic form of
 οὐχ) (31.1)

φρονέω - I think

20.2.a The present active participle is declined like a _____ _____ _____ _____
noun in the masculine and neuter forms and like a _____ _____ ___ noun in the feminine forms.

20.2.b Explain the process of forming a present active participle.

20.2.c What irregular phenomenon occurs in the accenting of participles?

20.3 The forms of εἰμί are identical to the present active participle of λύω if the _____ is
removed.

20.4.a The characteristic sign of the present middle and passive participle is the infix _____,
which is added to the stem by means of the connecting vowel ___.

20.4.b The masculine and neuter present middle/passive participles are declined like masculine
and neuter nouns of the _____ _____, and the feminine is declined like a noun ending
in ___ in the _____ _____.

20.4.c Explain the process of forming a present middle and passive participle.

20.5 A ___ is inserted after the verb stem to distinguish a future active and middle participle from
a present active and middle participle.

20.6.a The participle is a _____ _____ since it has characteristics of verbs and
adjectives. The participle is built on the _____ stem and has endings like a(n) adjective.

20.6.b Review the verbal and adjectival qualities of a participle:

20.7.a.1 What four tenses have participles?

20.7.a.2 How does the voice and tense of participles compare and contrast to the voice and tense of other verbal forms?

20.7.a.3 Match the following:

___ The present participle   ___ The aorist and perfect participle
___ The future participle   ___ Adverbial use of the participle
___ Temporal participle

     A. indicate(s) action subsequent to the action of the main verb.
     B. tells the time of the main verb.
     C. indicate(s) action antecedent to the action of the main verb.
     D. demonstrates the verbal aspect and expresses when, how, why, on what condition, by what means, or under what conditions an action took place.
     E. indicate(s) action simultaneous with the action of the main verb.

20.7.b.1 The participle, when used like an adjective, agrees with the noun it modifies in
_____, _____, and _____.

20.7.b.2 In what three adjectival ways may a participle be used?

20.7.b.3 Match the following:

___ The attributive use   ___ The predicative use
___ The periphrastic construction   ___ The substantive use

     A. In this manner, the participle may function as a noun.
     B. In this manner, the participle may be used as a modifier. When the participle is in this use (immediately after the article), it is translated as a relative clause.
     C. This is the use of a finite verb with the participle in a compound tense form. Frequently this finite verb is εἰμί.
     D. In this use (without the article), the participle is translated in an adverbial sense. This type of participle completes the meaning of a statement.

20.7.c.1 No translation appears with the participle forms because so many variations occur in the New Testament. How must you translate the participle?

20.7.c.2 When the participle is used adverbially:

___ the present tense is translated as   A. "when" or "after"
___ the aorist tense is translated as   B. "before"
___ the future tense is translated as   C. "while" or "as"

20.8 EXERCISES:

1. οὐχὶ (not) ταῦτα ἔδει παθεῖν τὸν Χριστὸν καὶ εἰσελθεῖν εἰς τὴν δόξαν αὐτοῦ; (Luke 24:26).

a. Parse ἔδει. δεῖ is an impersonal verb used only in the third person singular. It takes the accusative and infinitive. (20.1)

PART OF SPEECH: **VERB**   TENSE: **imp.**   PERSON: **3rd**
SUBJECT: **(3rd sing.)**   VOICE: **act.**   NUMBER: **sing.**
STEM: ἔδ-   MOOD: **impers.**   LEXICAL FORM: δεῖ

b. What case is Χριστὸν in? (4.8.a and 7.1) What is the function of Χριστὸν in this sentence? (3.3.b and 31.4.a)

c. Why does δόξαν have a different ending than its definite article? (5.1, 5.3, and 5.4.a.1)

2. ταῦτα εἶπον τοῖς εἰσερχομένοις εἰς τὴν πόλιν.

a. What use is the demonstrative pronoun ταῦτα in and how should this word be translated? (10.1, 10.2.a, and 10.3.a)

b. Locate πόλιν. (19.1 and 19.2.a)

PART OF SPEECH: FUNCTION IN THE SENTENCE:

CASE: GENDER: DECLENSION:

NUMBER: LEXICAL FORM:

3. εἰσερχόμενος εἰς τὴν ἐκκλησίαν ἔλεγεν τὴν παραβολὴν ὑμῖν.

a. Is εἰσερχομένος verbal or adjectival in this sentence? What is the significance of this type of participle and how is this participle translated in this sentence based on its type? (11.1, 20.4, and 20.7.a)

b. Why is the participle εἰσερχομένος translated as past tense? (20.7.a)

c. Is ἔλεγεν a descriptive, iterate, or inceptive imperfect. Explain the significance of this type of imperfect. (3.1, 12.2.a, and 12.3.c)

4. εἶπεν τῷ Πέτρῳ . . . σκάνδαλον εἶ ἐμοῦ, ὅτι οὐ φρονεῖς (you are thinking) τὰ τοῦ θεοῦ ἀλλὰ τὰ (the things) τῶν ἀνθρώπων (Matt. 16:23).

a. Explain the change in stem from the present active indicative third singular form λέγει to the second aorist active indicative third singular form εἶπεν. (3.1, 3.3, 16.1, 16.2, and 16.4)

b. Is τῷ translated in the phrase εἶπεν τῷ Πέτρῳ? Why or why not? (7.4.a)

c. The two occurrences of the definite article τὰ are accusative plural neuter. These two definite articles are in the substantive use and are translated as "the things." (See 4.1, 4.3 and 30.3)

5. αἱ ἐκκλησίαι αἱ λυόμεναι ὑπὸ τοῦ πονηροῦ ἄρχοντος δοξάζονται ὑπὸ τοῦ κυρίου.

a. Is ὑπὸ translated "by" or "under" in the first occurrence in this sentence? How about the second occurrence? How can you be sure? (8.1 and 8.4)

b. What use is the adjective πονηροῦ in this sentence? What is the significance of this use in this sentence? (6.1, 6.3, and 6.4.a)

c. Parse δοξάζονται. (9.1 and 11.3)

PART OF SPEECH: TENSE: PERSON:

SUBJECT: VOICE: NUMBER:

STEM: MOOD: LEXICAL FORM:

6. οἱ λαμβάνοντες τὴν χάριν τοῦ θεοῦ σώζονται.

a. Dissect and parse λαμβάνοντες. (3.1 and 20.2)

PART OF SPEECH: TENSE: CASE:

STEM: VOICE: NUMBER:

LEXICAL FORM: VERBAL FORM: GENDER:

CONNECTING VOWEL: PART. SIGN: ENDING:

b. Is τοῦ θεοῦ genitive or ablative? (4.5.b, 4.8.a, and 7.1) How can you be sure? (7.5)

c. Parse σώζονται. (11.1 and 11.3)

PART OF SPEECH: TENSE: PERSON:

SUBJECT: VOICE: NUMBER.

STEM: MOOD: LEXICAL FORM:

7. παράκλητον ἔχομεν πρὸς τὸν πατέρα Ἰησοῦν Χριστὸν δίκαιον (1 John 2:1).

a. Locate παράκλητον. (4.3, 4.8.a, and 20.1)

PART OF SPEECH: FUNCTION IN THE SENTENCE:

CASE: GENDER: DECLENSION:

NUMBER: LEXICAL FORM:

b. Why does πατέρα have a different ending than its definite article τὸν? (4.3, 18.1, and 18.3)

c. Most versions of the New Testament translate the adjective δίκαιον as attributive in the phrase Ἰησοῦν Χριστὸν δίκαιον. This phrase agrees in case, number, and gender with παράκλητον which Ἰησοῦν Χριστὸν δίκαιον describes. Notice that, in English, a definite article is supplied with δίκαιον; however, the Greek does not supply the definite article in order to stress quality and essence. (See 30.5 of the textbook.)

8. διδάσκομεν τὰ γραφόμενα ἐν τῷ βιβλίῳ τῆς ζωῆς.

a. Dissect and parse γραφόμενα. (3.1 and 20.4)

PART OF SPEECH: TENSE: CASE:

STEM: VOICE: NUMBER:

LEXICAL FORM: VERBAL FORM: GENDER:

CONNECTING VOWEL: PART. SIGN: ENDING:

b. What use is γραφόμενα in this sentence? What is the significance of this use in this sentence? (20.7.b.3)

c. Is the object of ἐν (βιβλίῳ) dative, locative, or instrumental? (4.8.b, 7.5. 8.1, 8.4 and 13.1) What is the significance of this case? (4.5.e)

9. τοῦτό ἐστιν τὸ πνεῦμα τὸ σῷζον ὑμᾶς καὶ καθαρίζον ὑμᾶς ἀπὸ τῶν ἁμαρτιῶν ὑμῶν.

a. What is the use of the demonstrative pronoun τοῦτό? What is the significance of this use? (10.1, 10.2.a, and 10.3.a)

b. What type of construction is the combination of ἐστιν with the participles σῷζον and καθαρίζον? (9.1, 9.4, 11.1, 13.1, and 20.7.b.3) What is the use of these participles in this sentence? (20.7.b.1)

c. ἀπὸ τῶν ἁμαρτιῶν expresses the ablative case. (8.1) Is ὑμῶν genitive or ablative? (4.5.b, 7.5, 9.1, and 9.2)

10. ἐν αὐτῷ ζωὴ ἦν, καὶ ἡ ζωὴ ἦν τὸ φῶς τῶν ἀνθρώπων (John 1:4).

a. Is ἐν αὐτῷ locative or instrumental? (7.5, 8.1, 8.4, 9.1, and 9.2) What is the significance of this case? (4.5.e)

b. Parse the first occurrence of ἦν. (9.1 and 12.2.d) Note that this verb does not have voice since it is a verb showing state of being rather than action. (9.4)

PART OF SPEECH: TENSE: PERSON:

SUBJECT: VOICE: NUMBER:

STEM: MOOD: LEXICAL FORM:

c. Is ἀνθρώπων genitive or ablative plural masculine? (4.1, 4.5.b, and 4.8.a) How can you be sure? (7.5)

11. ὁ λέγων ὅτι ἔχει κοινωνίαν (fellowship) μετὰ τοῦ θεοῦ ἀλλὰ μένει ἐν τῷ σκότει ἁμαρτίας ἐστὶν ψεύστης.

   a. Is ὅτι a coordinating or a subordinating conjunction? What is the significance of the type of conjunction? (13.3.a)

   b. Is μετὰ translated "with" or "after" in this sentence? How can you be sure? (7.5, 8.1, and 8.4)

   c. According to rule 9.4, the predicate nominative of a verb of being is a nominative singular substantive (noun phrase). Why does this sentence have ἐστὶν ψεύστης? (20.1 and 5.4.b)

12. ὁ θεὸς φῶς ἐστιν καὶ σκοτία ἐν αὐτῷ οὐκ ἔστιν οὐδεμία (not at all) (1 John 1:5).

a. Why is ὁ θεὸς the subject of ἐστιν rather than φῶς? (4.8.a, 7.1, and 7.5)

   b. Is καὶ a coordinating or a subordinating conjunction? What is the significance of the type of conjunction? (13.3.a)

   c. What is the antecedent of αὐτῷ? On what do you base your answer? (9.1, 9.2, and 9.3.a)

13. ἦσαν ἐν τῷ οἴκῳ τῷ λυομένῳ.

a. Locate οἴκῳ . (4.1 and 4.8.a)

PART OF SPEECH: FUNCTION IN THE SENTENCE:

CASE: GENDER: DECLENSION:

NUMBER: LEXICAL FORM:

b. Is λυομένῳ a verbal or adjectival participle? (3.1 and 20.7.b) What is the significance of the use of this participle? (20.7.b.1)

14. ἐν τοῖς ὀφθαλμοῖς αὐτοῦ ὁ ἀπόστολος εἶδεν τὰς χεῖρας τοῦ κυρίου μετὰ τὴν ἀνάστασιν.

a. Is ἐν locative or instrumental in this sentence? How can you be sure? (7.5, 8.1, and 8.4)

b. What is unusual about the placement of the noun that αὐτοῦ is associated with? On what do you base your answer? (9.1, 9.2, and 9.3.b)

c. Is αὐτοῦ genitive singular, ablative singular, or accusative plural feminine? (5.1 and 5.4.a.1) How can you be sure? (5.3 and 7.5)

15. ὑμεῖς ἐκ τοῦ πατρὸς τοῦ διαβόλου ἐστὲ . . . οὐκ ἔστιν ἀλήθεια ἐν αὐτῷ . . . . ψεύστης ἐστὶν καὶ ὁ πατὴρ αὐτοῦ (John 8:44).

a. Is ὑμεῖς necessary in this sentence? Why or why not? What is the significance of the presence of ὑμεῖς in this sentence? (9.1, 9.2, and 9.3.b)

b. Explain why πατρὸς has the definite article τοῦ in this sentence? (4.3, 18.1, and 18.3)

c. Locate ψεύστης. (5.4.b and 20.1)

PART OF SPEECH: FUNCTION IN THE SENTENCE:

CASE: GENDER: DECLENSION:

NUMBER: LEXICAL FORM:

16. οἱ ὄντες υἱοὶ τοῦ θεοῦ ὀφείλουσιν μένειν ἐν τῷ λόγῳ αὐτοῦ.

a. Dissect and parse ὄντες. (9.1 and 20.3)

PART OF SPEECH: TENSE: CASE:

STEM: VOICE: NUMBER:

LEXICAL FORM: VERBAL FORM: GENDER:

CONNECTING VOWEL: PART. SIGN: ENDING:

b. Parse μένειν. (3.1 and 3.3)

PART OF SPEECH: TENSE: PERSON:

SUBJECT: VOICE: NUMBER:

STEM: MOOD: LEXICAL FORM:

c. What is the antecedent of αὐτοῦ? On what do you base your answer? (9.1, 9.2, and 9.3.a)

17. εἴδομεν τὸν ἀπόστολον ὄντα ἐν τῇ ἐκκλησίᾳ.

a. Is εἴδομεν constative, ingressive, or culminative? What is the significance of this type of aorist? (15.3.a)

b. What use is ὄντα in the phrase τὸν ἀπόστολον ὄντα? What is the significance of this use? (4.1, 4.8.a, 6.4.b, 9.1, 20.7.a)

c. Locate ἐκκλησίᾳ. (5.1 and 5.4.a.1)

PART OF SPEECH: FUNCTION IN THE SENTENCE:

CASE: GENDER: DECLENSION:

NUMBER: LEXICAL FORM:

18. ἀκούοντα δὲ τὰ ἔθνη (Gentiles) ἔχαιρον καὶ ἐδόξαζον τὸν λόγον τοῦ κυρίου (Acts 13:48).

a. What use is ἀκούοντα in this sentence? What is the significance of this use in this sentence? (2.1, 20.2, and 20.7.a)

b. Is ἔθνη nominative or accusative plural neuter noun? (See 19.3.a and 21.1 of the textbook and 20.1 of the workbook.) How can you be sure? (7.5) What function is ἔθνη in this sentence? (4.5.a)

c. Are ἔχαιρον and ἐδόξαζον descriptive, iterative, or inceptive? (7.1, 9.1, and 12.4) What is the significance of this type of aorist? (12.3.b)

19. οἱ πονηροὶ ἄνθρωποι ψεύδονται ἕως τῆς ἡμέρας ἐκείνης ὅταν ὁ κύριος ἔρχεται.

a. What part of speech is πονηροὶ? (6.1 and 6.2) In what use is πονηροὶ in this sentence? What is the significance of this use? (6.4.a)

b. In what voice is ψεύδονται? How about ἔρχεται? In what special use is this voice? (11.1, 11.3, and 20.1) What is the significance of this use? (11.4.d)

c. In what use is the demonstrative pronoun ἐκείνης? (10.1, 10.2.b, and 10.3.b) Compare the use of ἐκείνης in the phrase τῆς ἡμέρας ἐκείνης with the adjective in the same use. (6.4.b and 10.3.b)

20. εἶπεν δὲ Μαριὰμ πρὸς τὸν ἄγγελον, Πῶς ἔσται τοῦτο, ἐπεὶ (since) ἄνδρα οὐ γινώσκω; (Luke 1:34).

a. Explain the ending of Μαριὰμ? (20.1) How can you be sure of the case of Μαριὰμ? (7.5)

b. What part of speech is ἐπεί? (See 20.1 of the workbook.) What is the significance of this part of speech? (See 12.1.b of the workbook.)

c. Locate ἄνδρα. (7.5, 18.1, and the end of the textbook.)

PART OF SPEECH: **NOUN**   FUNCTION IN THE SENTENCE: **do.** of γινώσκω
CASE: **acc.**   GENDER: **masc.**   DECLENSION: **2nd**
NUMBER: **sing.**   LEXICAL FORM: ἀνήρ

LESSON 21: Aorist Active and Middle Participles

21.1 Supplemental vocabulary.

ἀνέρχομαι - I come up, I go up
ἀνίστημι - I rise up, I leave (29.1)
γεννάω - I bear, give birth to (30.1)
Δαυίδ, ὁ - David (25.1)
δέσμιος, ὁ - prisoner
δίδωμι - I give, I grant (29.1)
ἐάν - if (24.1)
ἑαυτοῦ, -ῆς, -οῦ - of himself, herself, itself (27.1)
ἐγγύς - near (adv.)

εἰ μή - except
ἐκεῖ - there, in that place (25.1)
ὁράω - I see (26.1)
ὅς, ἥ, ὅ - who, which, what (27.1)
πᾶς, πᾶσα, πᾶν - all, every (28.1)
προνοέω - I try to do
τίς, τί - who? what? (27.1)
τις, τι - one, someone, something (27.1)
χάριν - for the sake of, by reason of (prep. with the genitive) (31.1)

21.2.a Like the aorist indicative, the aorist participle builds on the _____ stem. The aorist participle does not have a(n) _____.

21.2.b Review the four component parts of the first aorist active participle using λύω as the model.

21.2.c The forms of the aorist middle and the aorist passive participle are entirely different. The middle has the same aorist stem as the active _____. Add to this stem the middle participle infix _____ and the endings (_____ _____ for the masculine and neuter and the _____ _____ for the feminine).

21.2.d The first aorist middle participle is identical to the present middle and passive participle, except for the substitution of ____ for the connecting vowel ____.

21.2.e The second aorist stem uses the _____ _____ stem. The forms of the second aorist middle participle are identical to those of the present participle, except for the _____ and the _____.

21.3.a The two primary concerns of verbs are _____ and _____ _____ _____.

21.3.b Although participles are verbal in nature, the time of action is not absolute with them, but relates to the time of action of the _____ _____. The _____, therefore, which indicates action in past time, is absent in participles.

21.3.c The time in aorist participles indicates action _____ to the action of the main verb.

21.3.d _____ in the aorist participle indicates the relation of the subject to the action as it does in any other verb form.

21.3.e Remember that the translation of the aorist participle requires a variety of English helping verbs or clauses; therefore, no single translation is correct.

21.3.f In the sentence ὁ ἄνθρωπος εἰπὼν ταῦτα βλέπει τὸν κύριον, the participle εἰπὼν is in the _____ use. This sentence is translated, "The man who said these things is seeing the Lord." The participle in this use is translated as a relative clause. (20.7.b.1)

21.3.g In the sentence εἰποῦσα ταῦτα ἐξῆλθεν ἐκ τοῦ οἴκου, there is no article used with the participle, therefore, the participle εἰποῦσα is in the _____ use. Generally the participle used substantively has the article preceding it; therefore, the lone standing participle is considered to agree with the unexpressed subject of the main verb and is translated as in the predicate use, adverbially. This sentence is translated, "When she had said these things, she went out of the house." (20.7.b.2)

21.3.h The sentence ὁ ἄνθρωπος ὁ εἰπὼν ταῦτα ἦλθεν εἰς τὸν οἶκον presents the participle εἰπὼν in the _____ use. This sentence is translated, "The man who had said these things went into the house." The participle used in this use is translated as a relative clause. (20.7.b.1)

21.3.i The sentence ἡ εἰποῦσα ταῦτα ἦλθεν εἰς τὸν οἶκον presents the participle εἰποῦσα in the _____ use. This sentence is translated, "The woman who had said these things went into the house." The participle in this use is translated as a relative clause. (20.7.b.2)

21.4 EXERCISES:

1. ἐξελθὼν ἐκ τοῦ οἴκου ταῦτα εἶπεν.

   a. Dissect and parse ἐξελθὼν. (12.1 and 21.2)

PART OF SPEECH: TENSE: CASE:

STEM: VOICE: NUMBER:

LEXICAL FORM: VERBAL FORM: GENDER:

CONNECTING VOWEL: PART. SIGN: ENDING:

   b. Is οἴκου genitive singular masculine or ablative singular masculine? What role does the preposition ἐκ have in identifying the case of οἴκου? (4.1, 4.5.c, 8.1, and 8.4)

2. πισταί εἰσιν αἱ δεξάμεναι τοὺς ἀποστόλους τοὺς διωκομένους.

a. In what use is the adjective πισταί in the above sentence? What is the significance of this use? Is the appearance of εἰσιν necessary in this sentence? Why or why not? (6.1, 6.3, 6.4.b, and 9.4)

b. Dissect and parse διωκομένους. (20.4 and 21.1)

PART OF SPEECH: TENSE: CASE:

STEM: VOICE: NUMBER:

LEXICAL FORM: VERBAL FORM: GENDER:

CONNECTING VOWEL: PART. SIGN: ENDING:

c. Does the case, number, and gender of the article τοὺς have to agree with the case, number, and gender of the participle διωκομένους? Explain. (6.2, 6.4.a, and 20.6)

3. ὁ μὴ ἰδὼν τὸν πρόσωπον τοῦ κυρίου οὐκ ἐπίστευσεν εἰς αὐτόν.

a. In what use is the participle ἰδὼν in this sentence? What is the significance of this use? (20.7.b.2)

b. Parse ἐπίστευσεν. (12.1 and 15.2)

PART OF SPEECH: TENSE: PERSON:

SUBJECT: VOICE: NUMBER:

STEM: MOOD: LEXICAL FORM:

4. ἔτι ὢν ἐν τῇ ὁδῷ ὁ κύριος εἶπεν ταῦτα τοῖς ἐξελθοῦσιν ἐκ τοῦ οἴκου καὶ πορευομένοις μετ' αὐτοῦ πρὸς τὴν πόλιν.

a. Why does the second declension noun ὁδῷ take the feminine article τῇ? (4.4, 5.3 and 7.1)

b. Is ταῦτα in the substantive or predicate use in this sentence? (10.1, 10.2.a, and 10.3.a) How does this use affect the translation? (6.4.c and 10.3.a)

c. Why is μετά spelled μετ' in this sentence? What is the significance of this spelling? (2.5)

5. κηρύσσομεν περὶ τοῦ σώσαντος ἡμᾶς καὶ καθαρίσαντος ἡμᾶς ἀπὸ τῶν ἁμαρτιῶν ἡμῶν.

a. Is περὶ best translated "about, concerning" or "around, about" in this sentence? What determines the translation of this preposition? (8.1 and 8.4)

b. Dissect and parse καθαρίσαντος. (13.1 and 21.2)

PART OF SPEECH: TENSE: CASE:

STEM: VOICE: NUMBER:

LEXICAL FORM: VERBAL FORM: GENDER:

CONNECTING VOWEL: PART. SIGN: ENDING:

c. What is the antecedent of the first occurrence of ἡμᾶς in this sentence? What about the second occurrence of ἡμᾶς? What about ἡμῶν? (7.5, 9.1, 9.2, and 9.3.a)

6. οὗτός ἐστιν ὁ ἄρτος ὁ ἐκ τοῦ οὐρανοῦ καταβαίνων. . . . (John 6:50).

a. In what use is the demonstrative pronoun οὗτός? What is the significance of this use? (10.1, 10.2.a, and 10.3.b)

b. Is the verb of being ἐστιν necessary in οὗτός ἐστιν ὁ ἄρτος? Why or why not? (9.1, 9.4, 10.1, 10.2.a, and 10.3.b)

c. Dissect and parse καταβαίνων. (9.1 and 20.2)

PART OF SPEECH: TENSE: CASE:

STEM: VOICE: NUMBER:

LEXICAL FORM: VERBAL FORM: GENDER:

CONNECTING VOWEL: PART. SIGN: ENDING:

7. συναγαγόντες οἱ μαθηταὶ ἐδόξασαν τὸ ὄνομα τοῦ αἰωνίου θεοῦ.

a. In what use is συναγαγόντες in this sentence? What is the significance of the participle in this use? (20.7.a)

b. Dissect and parse ἐδόξασαν. (9.1, 15.1, and 15.2)

PART OF SPEECH: TENSE: CASE:

STEM: VOICE: NUMBER:

LEXICAL FORM: VERBAL FORM: GENDER:

CONNECTING VOWEL: PART. SIGN: ENDING:

c. Locate ὄνομα. (19.1 and 19.3.b)

PART OF SPEECH: FUNCTION IN THE SENTENCE:

CASE: GENDER: DECLENSION:

NUMBER: LEXICAL FORM:

8. πάντες (all) γὰρ ὑμεῖς υἱοὶ φωτός ἐστε καὶ υἱοὶ ἡμέρας (1 Thess. 5:5).

a. What is the relationship of ὑμεῖς and the first occurrence of υἱοί in this sentence? What about ὑμεῖς and the second occurrence of υἱοί? (9.1 and 9.4) Is the verb ἐστε necessary in this sentence? Why or why not? (9.4)

b. Is ἡμέρας genitive singular feminine, ablative singular feminine, or accusative plural feminine? (4.5.b, 5.1 and 5.4.a.1) How can you be sure? (7.5)

9. οὗτοί εἰσιν οἱ κηρύξαντες τὸ εὐαγγέλιον τῆς ἀγάπης, ἀλλ' ἐκεῖνοί εἰσιν οἱ διώξαντες τοὺς πιστεύοντας αὐτό.

a. Write the two periphrastic constructions in this sentence. What is the significance of these constructions? (20.7.b.3)

b. Is the verb of being necessary in the phrase οὗτοί εἰσιν οἱ κηρύξαντες? Why or why not? How about the phrase ἐκεῖνοί εἰσιν οἱ διώξαντες? Why or why not? (6.4.b, 9.1, 9.4, 10.1, 10.2.b, 10.3.b, and 20.7.b.3)

c. Locate ἐκεῖνοί. (10.1 and 10.2.b)

CASE: PART OF SPEECH:

NUMBER: FUNCTION IN THE SENTENCE:

GENDER: LEXICAL FORM:

10. μὴ δεξάμενοι σημεῖον ἀπὸ τοῦ Ἰησοῦ, οἱ ὄχλοι ἀπῆλθον εἰς τὴν πόλιν.

a. Does the participle δεξάμενοι have an adjectival or verbal function in this sentence? What is the significance of the use of this participle in this sentence? Explain. (20.7.a)

b. Does the participle δεξάμενοι describe action antecedent, simultaneous, or subsequent to the action of the main verb? (20.7.a.1) Explain the relationship of time of the action of the main verb and the time of the action of the participle? (20.7.a and 21.3)

c. Locate πόλιν. (19.2.a and 20.1)

PART OF SPEECH: FUNCTION IN THE SENTENCE:

CASE: GENDER: DECLENSION:

NUMBER: LEXICAL FORM:

11. ἀπεκρίθη Ἰησοῦς, Ἀμὴν ἀμὴν λέγω σοι, ἐὰν (if) μή τις (one) γεννηθῇ (is born) ἐξ ὕδατος καὶ πνεύματος, οὐ δύναται εἰσελθεῖν εἰς τὴν βασιλείαν τοῦ θεοῦ (John 3:5).

a. Why is μή used rather than οὐ to negate γεννηθῇ? (9.1, 9.5, and 21.1)

b. Locate ὕδατος. (18.2 and 21.1)

PART OF SPEECH: FUNCTION IN THE SENTENCE:

CASE: GENDER: DECLENSION:

NUMBER: LEXICAL FORM:

c. What part of speech is εἰσελθεῖν? What is the significance of this part of speech? (12.1 and 16.2)

12. ἀλλὰ τί (what) λέγει; Ἐγγύς (near) σου τὸ ῥῆμά ἐστιν ἐν τῷ στόματί σου καὶ ἐν τῇ καρδίᾳ σου, τοῦτ' ἔστιν τὸ ῥῆμα τῆς πίστεως ὅ (which) κηρύσσομεν (Rom. 10:8).

a. Are the two appearances of ἐν associated with the locative or instrumental case in this sentence? How can you be sure? (4.5.e, 7.5, 8.1, and 8.4)

b. Why does elision occur with τοῦτο in this sentence? (2.5)

c. Parse κηρύσσομεν. (3.3 and 9.1)

PART OF SPEECH: TENSE: PERSON:

SUBJECT: VOICE: NUMBER:

STEM: MOOD: LEXICAL FORM:

13. καὶ ἀποκριθεὶς (when he answered) ὁ Ἰησοῦς ἔλεγεν διδάσκων ἐν τῷ ἱερῷ, Πῶς λέγουσιν οἱ γραμματεῖς ὅτι ὁ Χριστὸς υἱὸς Δαυίδ (David) ἐστιν; (Mark 12:35).

a. Dissect and parse ἀποκριθεὶς. (11.1 and 22.2)

PART OF SPEECH: **VERB**	TENSE: **1 aor.**	CASE: **nom.**
STEM: ἀποκριθ-	VOICE: **pass.-dep.**	NUMBER: **sing.**
LEXICAL FORM: ἀποκρίνομαι	VERBAL FORM: **part.**	GENDER: **masc.**
CONNECTING VOWEL: -ο-	PART. SIGN: -θ-	ENDING: -μαι

b. Does ἀποκριθεὶς have a verbal or an adjectival use in this sentence? Specify the significance of the use of ἀποκριθεὶς in this sentence? (20.7.a) How about διδάσκων? Specify the significance of the use of διδάσκων in this sentence? (20.7.a)

c. Locate γραμματεῖς. (19.2.b and 21.1)

PART OF SPEECH: FUNCTION IN THE SENTENCE:

CASE: GENDER: DECLENSION:

NUMBER: LEXICAL FORM:

14. προνοοῦμεν (we try to do) γὰρ καλὰ οὐ μόνον ἐνώπιον κυρίου ἀλλὰ καὶ ἐνώπιον ἀνθρώπων (2 Cor. 8:21).

a. Why is γὰρ the second word of this sentence translated as the first word of this sentence? (See 9.5 and 10.1 of the textbook and 10.1.b of the workbook.)

b. What kind of conjunction ἀλλὰ? What is the significance of the type of conjunction? (12.1 and 13.3.a)

c. Is ἀνθρώπων genitive or ablative in case? (4.1 and 4.8.a) What is the significance of this case? (4.5.c) On what do you base your answer? (7.5)

15. καὶ τὴν πόλιν τὴν ἁγίαν Ἰερουσαλὴμ καινὴν εἶδον καταβαίνουσαν ἐκ τοῦ οὐρανοῦ ἀπὸ τοῦ θεοῦ (Rev. 21:2).

a. In what use is the adjective ἁγίαν in the phrase τὴν πόλιν τὴν ἁγίαν? What is the significance of this use? (6.1, 6.3, and 6.4.a) In what other way might this phrase be written in Greek to demonstrate the same use? (6.4.a)

b. Locate οὐρανοῦ . (4.8.a and 11.1)

PART OF SPEECH: FUNCTION IN THE SENTENCE:

CASE: GENDER: DECLENSION:

NUMBER: LEXICAL FORM:

c. Does ἀπὸ express possession or separation? What case is this preposition associated with? (4.5.c, 8.1, and 8.4)

16. ἀνῆλθεν (he went up) δὲ εἰς τὸ ὄρος Ἰησοῦς καὶ ἐκεῖ (there) ἐκάθητο μετὰ τῶν μαθητῶν αὐτοῦ (John 6:3).

a. Is ἀνῆλθεν constative, ingressive, or culminative? What is the significance of this type of aorist? (15.3.b, 16.1, and 16.2)

b. What is the case function of Ἰησοῦς in this sentence? Why is this word problematic? (4.5.a and 12.1) How can you be sure of the function of Ἰησοῦς in this sentence? (7.5)

c. What voice is ἐκάθητο in? (13.2 and 21.1) What is the significance of the voice of ἐκάθητο? (11.4.d)

17. τούτου χάριν (for this reason) ἐγὼ Παῦλος ὁ δέσμιος (prisoner) τοῦ Χριστοῦ Ἰησοῦ ὑπὲρ ὑμῶν τῶν ἐθνῶν (Eph. 3:1).

a. What part of speech is χάριν? (See 21.1 of the workbook.) What is the significance of this part of speech? (See 12.1.b of the workbook.)

b. How can you be sure that ὑμῶν does not express possession? (9.1, 9.2, and 9.3.d)

c. Explain the translation of ἐθνῶν in this sentence? (4.8.b and 21.1)

18. ἄρξησθε (do not begin) λέγειν ἐν ἑαυτοῖς (yourselves), Πατέρα ἔχομεν τὸν Ἀβραάμ. λέγω γὰρ ὑμῖν ὅτι δύναται ὁ θεὸς ἐκ τῶν λίθων τούτων ἐγεῖραι τέκνα τῷ Ἀβραάμ (Luke 3:8)

a. What part of speech is λέγειν? What is the significance of this part of speech? (3.1 and 3.3.b)

b. Locate ἑαυτοῖς. (27.1 and 27.3.e)

PART OF SPEECH: **rfx. prn.**   FUNCTION IN THE SENTENCE: **obj. of** ἐν
CASE: **loc.**   GENDER: **masc.**   PERSON: **2nd**
NUMBER: **pl.**   LEXICAL FORM: ἑαυτοῦ

c. Why is the middle/passive form of the verb δύναται translated as active in voice? Explain this phenomenon. (11.4.d)

19. ἀναστὰς (after he arose and left) δὲ ἀπὸ τῆς συναγωγῆς εἰσῆλθεν εἰς τὴν οἰκίαν Σίμωνος (Luke 4:38).

a. What case is συναγωγῆς in this sentence? (5.4.a.3 and 21.1) How can you be sure of the case of συναγωγῆς? (7.5, 8.1, and 8.4) What is the significance of this case? (4.5.c)

b. What is the significance of the construction of the compound verb εἰσῆλθεν followed by εἰς? Is the double appearance of εἰς translated twice? (8.1, 8.4, and 8.6)

20. μηδὲ δίδοτε (give) τόπον τῷ διαβόλῳ (Eph. 4:27).

a. What kind of conjunction is μηδέ? (13.3.a and 21.1) How is this conjunction used in this sentence? What is the significance of the use of this conjunction? (13.3.e)

b. Parse δίδοτε. (25.2 and 29.1)

PART OF SPEECH: **VERB**   TENSE: **pres.**   STEM: διδ-
PERSON: **2nd**   VOICE: **act.**   SUBJECT: **(2nd pl.)**
NUMBER: **pl.**   MOOD: **imper.**   LEXICAL FORM: δίδωμι

c. Is διαβόλῳ dative, locative, or instrumental? (4.8.a and 20.1) How can you be sure? What is the significance of this case? (4.5.d)

LESSON 22: Aorist Passive Participles

22.1 Supplemental vocabulary.

'Ασία, ἡ - Asia   οἶδα - I know (23.1)
ζητέω - I seek (26.1)   ὀργή, ἡ - wrath
καθαρός, -ά, όν - clean, pure (adj.)   'Ραββί, ὁ - Rabbi indeclinable
μαθητεύω - I make a disciple   φύσις, φύσεως, ἡ - essence, nature
μᾶλλον - more, all the more (adv.) (28.1)

22.2.a Like the aorist passive indicative, the aorist passive participle builds on the _____ _____ stem. The aorist participle does not have a(n) _____.

22.2.b The endings used for the aorist passive participle are the _____ _____ for the masculine and neuter and the _____ _____ for the feminine. The feminine aorist passive participle endings follow the noun stems ending in ε, ι, or ρ. (See 5.4.a.)

22.2.c Review the four component parts of the aorist passive participle.

22.3 The second aorist passive participle is formed like the first aorist passive participle except for the omission of the _____.

22.4.a The aorist passive participle expresses action _____ to the action of the main verb, similar to other aorist participles.

22.4.b The passive voice indicates that the subject _____ the action.

22.4.c The kind of action of the aorist passive participle is _____ based on whether the participle is adjectival or verbal. (20.7)

22.5.a The _____ _____ consists of a participle and a substantive which are in the genitive case and are indirectly connected to the main part of the sentence.

22.5.b In the genitive absolute construction the _____ of the main verb is different from the substantive used with the participle.

22.5.c In the sentence εἰπόντες ταῦτα οἱ ἀπόστολοι ἀπῆλθον, what prevents the genitive absolute construction?

22.5.d In the sentence εἰπόντων ταῦτα τῶν μαθητῶν οἱ ἀπόστολοι ἀπῆλθον, what allows for the genitive absolute construction?

22.5.e In the sentence λέγοντος αὐτοῦ ταῦτα ἀπῆλθον, what allows for the genitive absolute construction?

22.5.f In the sentence εἶδον αὐτὸν λέγοντα ταῦτα, what prevents the genitive absolute construction?

22.6 Greek has an idiom where the subject of the sentence is in the _____ case and the verb appears as a(n) _____. Some grammars call this phenomenon the _____ of general reference, but in practice, it is a subject _____.

22.7 EXERCISES:

1. περὶ δὲ τῶν χρόνων καὶ τῶν καιρῶν, ἀδελφοί, οὐ χρείαν ἔχετε ὑμῖν γράφεσθαι (1 Thess. 5:1).

a. Why is δὲ translated as the first word of this sentence and it is the second word of the sentence? (9.1 and 9.5)

b. How can you know the gender of χρόνων and καιρῶν respectively? (4.3, 4.6, and 22.1)

c. What case is ἀδελφοί in? (2.1 and 4.8.a) On what do you base your answer? (7.5) What is the significance of this case? (4.5.h)

2. εἰσελθόντων τῶν μαθητῶν εἰς τὸ πλοῖον, ὁ κύριος ἀπῆλθεν εἰς τὸ ὄραν.

a. How is the participle εἰσελθόντων used in this sentence? What is the significance of this use? (11.1 and 20.7.b.1 and 3)

b. Dissect and parse ἀπῆλθεν. (12.1, 16.1, and 16.2)

PART OF SPEECH:	TENSE:	PERSON:
SUBJECT:	VOICE:	NUMBER:
STEM:	MOOD:	LEXICAL FORM:

3. πορευθέντες οὖν μαθητεύσατε (make disciples) πάντα (all) τὰ ἔθνη, βαπτίζοντες αὐτοὺς εἰς τὸ ὄνομα τοῦ πατρὸς καὶ τοῦ υἱοῦ καὶ τοῦ ἁγίου πνεύματος . . . (Matt. 28:19).

a. Parse μαθητεύσατε. (See 22.1 of the workbook and 25.2 of the textbook.)

PART OF SPEECH: **VERB**	TENSE: **1 aor.**	PERSON: **2nd**
SUBJECT: **(2nd pl.)**	VOICE: **act.**	NUMBER: **pl.**
STEM: μαθητευ	MOOD: **imp.**	LEXICAL FORM: μαθητεύω

b. In what use is πάντα used in this sentence. Explain the significance of this use. (6.4.a, 28.1, and 28.2.a) This adjective does not follow the regular pattern as previously studied. Note that when this adjective is in the predicate use, it is translated as being attributive, (πάντα, ἔθνη - "all the nations"

4. Ἰησοῦς ἦλθεν καὶ ἐδίδαζεν εἰς μέσον τῶν λαῶν.

a. Is ἦλθεν constative, ingressive, or culminative? (15.3.b, 16.1, and 16.2) How about ἐδίδαζεν? (15.1, 15.2, or 15.3.a) What is the significance of these two types of aorist? (15.3.a and b)

b. List the elements that identify ἐδίδαζεν as an aorist tense verb. (3.1, 15.1, and 15.2)

5. ἀποκριθεὶς δὲ ὁ Πέτρος εἶπεν τῷ Ἰησοῦ, Κύριε, καλόν ἐστιν ἡμας ὧδε εἶναι (Matt. 17:4).

a. Why are the articles ὁ and τῷ not translated in the phrase ὁ Πέτρος εἶπεν τῷ Ἰησοῦ? (7.4.a)

b. Is τῷ Ἰησου used as dative, locative, or instrumental in this sentence? How can you be sure? (4.5.d, 7.5, and 20.1 footnote 1)

c. In what use is the adjective καλόν in the above sentence? What is the significance of this use? (6.1, 6.3, and 6.4.b) The student should be aware that it is possible for a substantive adjective to be the compliment of the subject expressed by a verb ending. See also 3.3 and 7.5. Is the appearance of ἐστιν necessary in this sentence? Why or why not? (6.4.b, 9.1, and 9.4)

6. αὕτη ἐστὶν ἡ σωτηρία ἡ κηρυχθεῖσα ἐν τῷ κόσμῳ ὑπὸ τῶν ἰδότων Ἰησοῦν.

a. Is the verb ἐστὶν necessary in this sentence? Why or why not? (7.5, 9.1, 9.4, 10.1, 10.2.a, and 10.3.b)

b. Explain how the time of the participle κηρυχθεῖσα is translated in conjunction with the time of the main verb. (20.7.a)

c. Is the participle ἰδότων used as attributive, predicative, or substantive in this sentence? Explain the significance of this use. Is this participle used as verbal or adjectival? (20.7.b.1)

7. Ἀμὴν ἀμὴν λέγω ὑμῖν ὅτι ὁ τὸν λόγον μου ἀκούων καὶ πιστεύων τῷ πέμψαντί με ἔχει ζωὴν αἰώνιον καὶ εἰς κρίσιν οὐκ ἔρχεται . . . (John 5:24).

a. Dissect and parse πέμψαντί. (3.1 and 21.2)

PART OF SPEECH: TENSE: CASE:

STEM: VOICE: NUMBER:

LEXICAL FORM: VERBAL FORM: GENDER:

CONNECTING VOWEL: PART. SIGN: ENDING:

b. Locate αἰώνιον. (18.1 and 18.4)

PART OF SPEECH: FUNCTION IN THE SENTENCE:

CASE: GENDER: DECLENSION:

NUMBER: LEXICAL FORM:

c. What is the significance of the use of οὐκ in this sentence? (9.1 and 9.5)

8. ἐλθόντος τοῦ ἁγίου πνεύματος ἐπ' αὐτοὺς ἔλαβον δύναμιν.

a. Identify the genitive absolute in this sentence and explain the significance of this construction. (21.2 and 22.g)

b. In what use is the adjective ἁγίου in the above sentence? What is the significance of this use? (6.1, 6.3, and 6.4.a)

c. Locate δύναμιν. (19.1 and 19.2.a)

PART OF SPEECH: FUNCTION IN THE SENTENCE:

CASE: GENDER: DECLENSION:

NUMBER: LEXICAL FORM:

9. μακάριοι οἱ πτωχοὶ τῷ πνεύματι, ὅτι αὐτῶν ἐστιν ἡ βασιλεία τῶν οὐρανῶν (Matt. 5:3).

a. In what use is the adjective μακάριοι in the above sentence? What is the significance of this use? (See 6.3, 6.4.b, and 22.1 of the textbook and 17.1 and 22.1 of the workbook.) Is the appearance of ἐστιν necessary in this sentence? Why or why not? (6.4.b, 9.1, and 9.4)

b. What type of clause does ὅτι introduce? What is the significance of this type of clause. (13.3.a) Based on the identification of this type of clause, is this a compound or a complex sentence? (7.4.d)

10. ταῦτα εἰπὼν βλεπότων αὐτῶν ἀνελήμφθη (he was taken up) ἀπὸ τῶν ὀφθαλμῶν αὐτῶν εἰς οὐρανόν.

a. In what use is the demonstrative pronoun ταῦτα in this sentence? How is the demonstrative pronoun in translated with the adjective in this use? (6.4.c, 10.1, 10.2.a, and 10.3.a)

b. Is εἰπὼν used adverbally or ajectivally? What is the sinificance of this use? (20.7.a and b.3)

c. Why must οὐρανόν be in the accusative case? (8.1 and 8.4)

11. καὶ ἐλθόντων πρὸς τὸν ὄλον προσῆλθεν (came to) αὐτῷ ἄνθρωπος . . . (Matt. 17:14).

a. Identify the genitive absolute in this sentence and explain the significance of this construction. (21.2 and 22.5)

b. Dissect and parse προσῆλθεν. (11.1 and 16.2)

PART OF SPEECH: AUGMENT: STEM:

TENSE: PERSON: ENDING:

VOICE: NUMBER: CONNECTING VOWEL:

MOOD: LEXICAL FORM: SUBJECT:

12. μακάριός ἐστιν ὁ ἰδὼν τὴν σωτηρίαν τοῦ θεοῦ ἐν τῷ μέσῳ τῷ λαῷ αὐτοῦ.

a. In what use is the adjective μακάριός in the above sentence? What is the significance of this use? (See 6.3, 6.4.b, and 22.1 of the textbook and 17.1 of the workbook.) Is the appearance of ἐστιν necessary in this sentence? Why or why not? (6.4.b, 9.1, and 9.4)

b. Dissect and parse ἰδὼν. (See 16.1, 16.3, 21.2 and 21.1 of the workbook.)

PART OF SPEECH: TENSE: CASE:

STEM: VOICE: NUMBER:

LEXICAL FORM: VERBAL FORM: GENDER:

CONNECTING VOWEL: PART. SIGN: ENDING:

13. μακάριοι οἱ καθαροὶ (the pure) τῇ καρδίᾳ, ὅτι αὐτοὶ τὸν θεὸν ὄψονται (they will see) (Matt. 5:8).

a. Is τῇ καρδίᾳ in the dative, locative, or instrumental case in this sentence? What is the significance of this case? (4.5.e, 5.1, and 5.4.a.1)

b. What type of clause does ὅτι introduce? What is the significance of this type of clause. (13.3.a) Based on the identification of this type of clause, is this a compound or a complex sentence? (7.4.d)

c. Parse ὄψονται. (See 14.2 of the textbook and 21.1 of the workbook.)

PART OF SPEECH: TENSE: PERSON:

SUBJECT: VOICE: NUMBER:

STEM: MOOD: LEXICAL FORM:

14. Πέτρος δὲ καὶ Ἰωάννης ἀνέβαινον εἰς τὸ ἱερὸν ἐπὶ τὴν ὥραν τῆς προσευχῆς (of prayer) (Acts 3:1).

a. Is the augment of ἀνέβαινον a syllabic or a temporal augment? Explain. (12.2.b) Why is this compound verb spelled ἀνέβαινον rather than ἀναέβαινον? (12.2.c)

b. Why does the ending of ὥραν differ from the ending of its definite article τὴν? (5.1, 5.3, 5.4.a.1, and 22.1)

15. διὰ τοῦτο οὖν μᾶλλον (all the more) ἐζήτουν (they were seeking) αὐτὸν οἱ Ἰουδαῖοι ἀποκτεῖναι, ὅτι οὐ μόμον ἔλυεν τὸ σάββατον, ἀλλὰ καὶ πατέρα ἴδιον ἔλεγεν τὸν θεὸν . . . (John 5:18).

a. Is the antecedent of αὐτὸν stated in this sentence? What can you know for certain about the antecedent of αὐτὸν? (9.1, 9.2, and 9.3.a)

b. Is ἀλλὰ a coordinating or a subordinating conjunction? What is the significance of this type of conjunction? (12.1 and 13.3.a)

c. What is the significance of the tense of ἔλεγεν? (3.1, 12.2.a, and 12.3.c)

16. καὶ εἰσῆλθεν πάλιν εἰς τὴν συναγωγήν (Mark 3:1).

a. Is εἰσῆλθεν constative, ingressive, or culminative? What is the significance of this type of aorist? (15.3.b, 16.1, and 16.2)

b. What part of speech is πάλιν? (7.1) What is the significance of this part of speech? (12.1.b of the workbook)

17. Νῦν ἀπολύεις τὸν δοῦλόν σου, . . . κατὰ τὸ ῥῆμά σου ἐν εἰρήνῃ (Luke 2:29).

a. What is the significance of the tense, voice, and mood of ἀπολύεις? (2.1, 3.2.a, b, and c, and 22.1)

b. What elements identify the case and function of ῥῆμά? (4.3, 7.5, 8.1, 8.4, 19.1, and 19.3.b)

c. What case is εἰρήνῃ in? (5.1 and 5.4.a.3) How can you be sure? (7.5, 8.1, and 8.4) What is the significance of this case? (4.5.e)

18. ἀσπάζονται ὑμᾶς αἱ ἐκκλησίαι τῆς ᾽Ασίας (of Asia) (1 Cor. 16:19).

a. Parse ἀσπάζονται. (11.3 and 22.1)

PART OF SPEECH: TENSE: PERSON:

SUBJECT: VOICE: NUMBER:

STEM: MOOD: LEXICAL FORM:

b. What is the significance of the voice of ἀσπάζονται? Explain. (11.3, 11.4.d, and 22.1)

c. Why does the ending of the definite article τῆς differ from the ending of ᾿Ασίας? (See 5.1, 5.3, and 5.4.a.1 of the textbook and 22.1 of the workbook.)

19. ἤμεθα τέκνα φύσει (by nature) ὀργῆς (of wrath) ὡς καὶ οἱ λοιποί (Ephesians 2:3).

a. Parse ἤμεθα. (9.1 and 12.3.d)

PART OF SPEECH: TENSE: PERSON:

SUBJECT: VOICE: NUMBER:

STEM: MOOD: LEXICAL FORM:

b. What is the function of τέκνα in this sentence? (4.8.a, 9.1, and 9.4) How can you be sure? (7.5)

c. Locate φύσει. (See 19.2.a of the textbook and 22.1 of the workbook.)

20. λέγοντες αὐτοῦ ταῦτα εἶδον τὴν ἀλήθειαν τῆς ἀγάπης τοῦ θεοῦ.

a. Does the participle λέγοντες have an adjectival or verbal function in this sentence? What is the significance of the use of this participle in this sentence? Explain. (11.1, 20.7.a, and 22.3)

b. Locate ἀλήθειαν. (5.1 and 5.4.a.1)

PART OF SPEECH: FUNCTION IN THE SENTENCE:

CASE: GENDER: DECLENSION:

NUMBER: LEXICAL FORM:

LESSON 23: The Perfect and Pluperfect Tenses

23.1.a Supplemental vocabulary.

ἀνίστημι - I raise, bring to life (29.1)
ἀντίριστος, ὁ - antichrist (29.1)
δωρεάν - without cost, freely (adv)
εἰ μή - except
εὐαγγελίζω – I preach (25.1)
ζάω - I live (26.1)
ἤδη - already (adv.) (25.1)
λαλέω - I speak (26.1)
ναί - yes

ὅς, ἥ, ὅ - who, which, what (27.1)
οὐδείς - no one (27.1)
οὔπω - not yet (adv.) (30.1)
παράπτωμα, παραπτώματος, τό - sin, false step, transgression
πᾶς, πᾶσα, πᾶν - all, every (adj.) (28.1)
πλανάω - I deceive (27.1)
πληρόω - I fill, fulfill, complete (26.1)
τις, τι - someone, something (rfx. prn.) (27.1)
τρίτος, -η, -ον - third (adj.) (31.1)

23.1.b What is the unusual fact concerning the verb forms βεβάπτισμαι, ἐγήγερμαι, εὐηγγέλισμαι, and σέσωσμαι?

23.2 What three features distinguish the perfect tense?

1.   2.   3.

23.2.a.1 The most obvious feature of the perfect tense is the _____ of the stem.

23.2.a.2 Reduplication is usually achieved by _____ the original consonant and inserting a(n) ___ between the two.

23.2.a.3.1 The perfect active of λύω is ___ (reduplication) + ___ (stem) + ___ (tense sign) + ___ (ending).

23.2.a.3.2 Verbs that begin with ___, ___, or ___ are reduplicate with the corresponding smoother consonants ___, ___, ___ respectively.

23.2.a.3.3 Verbs that begin with a vowel or a diphthong _____ the vowel in order to reduplicate.

23.2.a.3.4 Verbs that begin with two consonants, a double consonant, or a(n) ___ often reduplicate by adding ___ to the front of the stem, which resembles an augment.

23.2.a.3.5 With compound verbs, the reduplication comes between the _____ and the _____ and looks like an augment.

23.2.b.1 The tense sign of the perfect is ___ .

23.2.b.2 _____ _____ do not use the tense sign.

23.2.b.3 Sometimes the verb stem changes when it ends in a _____. If the stem ends in ___, ___, or ___ the consonant is dropped before κ in the perfect.

23.2.c The endings of the perfect active are similar to the _____ _____ _____ and those of the perfect middles and passive are similar to the _____ _____ and _____.

23.2.d.1 Sawyer points out that all verbs do not follow the guidelines for forming the perfect tense. How can you be certain of the correct form?

23.2.d.2 In the lexicon, the _____ principal part is the perfect active, and the _____ principal part is the perfect middle and passive.

23.3.a.1 What four components does the perfect active participle contain?

1.   3.

2.   4.

23.3.a.2 The masculine and the neuter perfect active participles use the _____ declension endings and the feminine uses the _____ declension endings like those whose stem end in ι.

23.3.a.3 The perfect active participle of λύω is ___ (reduplication) + ___ (stem) + ___ (tense sign) + ___ masculine/neuter or ___ feminine (the connecting syllable) + ___ (ending).

23.3.a.4 What is unusual concerning the masculine and neuter nominative singular perfect active participle?

23.3.b.1 The perfect middle and passive participle uses the _____ declension ending for the masculine and neuter and the _____ declension ending for the feminine.

23.3.b.2 The perfect middle/passive participle of λύω is ___ (reduplication) + ___ (stem) + ___ (tense sign of the middle/passive) + ___ (ending).

23.3.b.3 Compare and contrast the similarity of the present middle/passive participle and the perfect middle/passive participle. (20.4)

23.4.a The perfect tense stands for _____ action which has been completed and stands completed in the _____.

23.4.b What three ideas does the perfect tense convey?

1.   2.   3.

23.4.c This perfected action may be illustrated in two ways: _____ or _____. (See 3.2.a.)

23.4.d Sometimes the perfect can be translated correctly by the English _____ tense.

23.4.e The _____ voice demonstrates the true nature of the perfect tense better than the active when translated into English.

23.5.a Explain the significance of the use of the pluperfect tense.

23.5.b Unlike the perfect tense, the pluperfect is a true past tense and is used only in the _____ mood.

23.5.c The pluperfect is formed on the _____ stem.

23.5.d A(n) _____ is often used in addition to the reduplication, but in New Testament Greek, sometimes it is missing.

23.5.e The pluperfect active of λύω consists of ___ (augment) + ___ (reduplication) + ___ (sign of the perfect) + ___ the pluperfect ending.

23.6 οἶδα is a second perfect verb in form but has a(n) _____ meaning and is translated this way in English.

23.5 EXERCISES:

1. εἰ γὰρ νεκροὶ οὐκ ἐγείρονται, οὐδὲ Χριστὸς ἐγήγερται (1 Cor. 15:16).

a. Is εἰ a conditional particle or the present active second singular form of εἰμί? (See 9.1 and 9.4 of the textbook and 23.1.b of the workbook.)

b. How does οὐκ affect the translation of ἐγείρονται? (9.1 and 9.5)

2. καὶ σκοτία ἤδη (now) ἐγεγόνει καὶ οὔπω (not yet) ἐληλύθει πρὸς αὐτοὺς ὁ Ἰησοῦς . . . (John 6:17).

a. Dissect and parse ἐγεγόνει. (11.1 and 23.5)

PART OF SPEECH: DUPLICATION: STEM:

TENSE: PERSON   TENSE SIGN: **NOT USED WITH THIS VERB**

VOICE: NUMBER: ENDING:

MOOD: LEXICAL FORM: SUBJECT:

b. What part of speech is οὔπω? (23.1.a of the workbook) What is the significance of this part of speech? (28.4)

c. Locate Ἰησοῦς. (20.1)

PART OF SPEECH: FUNCTION IN THE SENTENCE:

CASE: GENDER: DECLENSION:

NUMBER: LEXICAL FORM:

3. καὶ εἶπεν αὐτοῖς ὅτι Οὕτως γέγραπται παθεῖν τὸν Χριστὸν καὶ ἀναστῆναι (to rise) ἐκ νεκρῶν τῇ τρίτῃ (third) ἡμέρᾳ . . . (Luke 24:46).

a. Is ὅτι a coordinating or a subordinating conjunction? What is the significance of the type of conjunction? (13.3.a)

b. Parse γέγραπται. (3.1 and 23.2)

PART OF SPEECH: TENSE: PERSON:

SUBJECT: VOICE: NUMBER:

STEM: MOOD: LEXICAL FORM:

c. Is τρίτη attributive, predicative, or substantive? On what can you base your answer? (See 23.1.a of the workbook and 6.3, 6.4.a, and 31.1 of the textbook.)

4. λέγει αὐτῷ, Ναὶ (yes) κύριε, ἐγὼ πεπίστευκα ὅτι σὺ εἶ ὁ Χριστὸς ὁ υἱὸς τοῦ θεοῦ ὁ εἰς τὸν κόσμον ἐρχόμενος (John 11:27).

a. Locate κύριε. (4.8.a and 7.1)

PART OF SPEECH: FUNCTION IN THE SENTENCE:

CASE: GENDER: DECLENSION:

NUMBER: LEXICAL FORM:

b. Is this sentence a compound sentence or a complex sentence? Explain the difference between compound and complex sentences. (7.4.d)

5. ἀκηκόαμεν τὴν ἀλήθειαν καὶ ἐγνώκαμεν ὅτι ἀπὸ θεοῦ ἐστίν.

a. Why does the perfect tense verb ἀκηκόαμεν take an augment when the perfect tense usually does not take one? (23.2.a.3)

b. Parse ἐστίν. (9.1 and 9.4)

PART OF SPEECH: TENSE: PERSON:

SUBJECT: VOICE: **NO VOICE**   NUMBER:

STEM: MOOD: LEXICAL FORM:

6. ἐγὼ ἐλήλυθα ἐν τῷ ὀνόματι τοῦ πατρός μου, καὶ οὐ λαμβάνετέ με (John 5:43).

a. Is the presence of ἐγὼ necessary in this sentence? Why or why not? (9.1, 9.2, and 9.3.b)

b. Is τοῦ πατρός genitive or ablative singular masculine? (4.3, 4.5.b, 18.1, and 18.4) How can you be sure? (7.5)

7. τὰ τέκνα τοῦ θεοῦ γεγόνατε.

a. How can you be sure of the case of τὰ τέκνα since this form could be two different cases. (7.5)

b. What effect does the late order of the subject and verb have on the translation of this sentence? Explain. (4.7)

8. ἦλθεν ὁ Ἰησοῦς εἰς τὴν Γαλιλαίαν κηρύσσων τὸ εὐαγγέλιον τοῦ θεοῦ καὶ λέγων ὅτι Πεπλήρωται (has been fulfilled) ὁ καιρὸς καὶ ἤγγικεν ἡ βασιλεία τοῦ θεοῦ (Mark 1:14-15).

a. Why is the definite article not translated in ἦλθεν ὁ Ἰησοῦς? (7.4)

b. Why is there a movable ν completing the verb ἤγγικεν? (3.3.f)

9. ταῦτα εἶπεν ὁ Ἰησοῦς πρὸς τοὺς πεπιστευκότας εἰς αὐτόν.

   a. Is πρὸς best translated in this sentence as "for," "at," or "to/toward"? (8.1) How can you be sure? (7.5 and 8.4)

   b. Dissect and parse πεπιστευκότας. (12.1 and 23.2)

PART OF SPEECH:	DUPLICATION:	STEM:
TENSE:	PERSON	TENSE SIGN:
VOICE:	NUMBER:	ENDING:
MOOD:	LEXICAL FORM:	SUBJECT:

   c. What is the antecedent of αὐτόν? How can you be sure? (7.5, 9.1, and 9.3.a)

10. περὶ δὲ τῆς ἡμέρας ἐκείνης ἢ τῆς ὥρας οὐδεὶς (no one) οἶδεν, οὐδὲ οἱ ἄγγελοι ἐν οὐρανῷ οὐδὲ ὁ υἱός, εἰ μὴ (except) ὁ πατήρ (Mark 13:32).

   a. What kind of demonstrative pronoun is ἐκείνης? What is the significance of this kind of demonstrative pronoun? (10.1 and 10.2.b) In what use is the demonstrative pronoun ἐκείνης in this sentence? What is the significance of this use? (10.3.b)

   b. Does οὐδὲ function as a simple connective, emphatic, or correlative in this sentence? Explain the difference in these three uses. (13.1 and 13.3.e)

   c. Note that εἰ μὴ is an idiom that is translated "except." (See 21.1 of the workbook.)

11. οἱ βεβαπτισμένοι μαθηταί εἰσιν ἐν τῇ ἐκκλησίᾳ.

a. Why is the phrase οἱ βεβαπτισμένοι μαθηταί εἰσιν not a periphrastic construction? Explain. (20.7.b.3)

b. Is the object of ἐν (ἐκκλησίᾳ) dative, locative, or instrumental? (7.5 and 8.1) What is the significance of this case? (4.5.e)

12. καὶ τοῦτό ἐστιν τὸ (πνεῦμα) τοῦ ἀντιρίστου (antichrist), ὅ (which) ἀκηκόατε ὅτι ἔρχεται, καὶ νῦν ἐν τῷ κόσμῳ ἐστὶν ἤδη (1 John 4:3).

a. The translator should note that in the New Testament text the definite article τὸ stands substantively for τὸ πνεῦμα. This is the predicate nominative of ἐστιν. (9.4)

b. Dissect and parse ἔρχεται. (7.5, 9.3, and 12.1)

PART OF SPEECH: DUPLICATION: STEM:

TENSE: PERSON   TENSE SIGN:

VOICE: NUMBER: ENDING:

MOOD: LEXICAL FORM: SUBJECT:

c. Locate κόσμῳ. (4.8.a and 7.1)

PART OF SPEECH: FUNCTION IN THE SENTENCE:

CASE: GENDER: DECLENSION:

NUMBER: LEXICAL FORM:

13. ὁ δὲ ἀποκριθεὶς εἶπεν, Γέγραπται, οὐκ ἐπ᾽ ἄρτῳ μόνῳ ζήσεται (shall live) ὁ ἄνθρωπος, ἀλλ᾽ ἐπὶ παντὶ (every) ῥήματι ἐκπορευομένῳ διὰ στόματος θεοῦ (Matt. 4:4).

a. Dissect and parse ἀποκριθείς. (11.1 and 22.3)

PART OF SPEECH:	TENSE:	CASE:
STEM:	VOICE:	NUMBER:
LEXICAL FORM:	VERBAL FORM:	GENDER:
CONNECTING VOWEL:	PART. SIGN:	ENDING:

b. Locate ῥήματι. (19.1 and 19.3.b)

PART OF SPEECH: FUNCTION IN THE SENTENCE:

CASE: GENDER: DECLENSION:

NUMBER: LEXICAL FORM:

c. Is διά translated "through" or "because of" in this sentence? On what do you base your answer? (7.5, 8.1, and 8.4)

14. οἱ ἐξεληλυθότες ἐκ τοῦ σκότους εἰς τὸ φῶς ἔγνωκαν ὅτι ὁ θεός ἐστιν ἀγάπη.

a. What use is ἐξεληλυθότες in this sentence? What is the significance of this use in this sentence? (20.7.b.2)

b. Why does the preposition ἐκ occur after the participle with which it is compounded to? How does this effect the translation of the compound participle and the preposition? (8.1 and 8.4)

c. How may the translator distinguish between the subject and the predicate nominative of ἐστιν? (7.5 and 9.4)

15. δωρεάν (without cost) τὸ τοῦ θεοῦ εὐαγγέλιον εὐηγγελισάμην (I preached) ὑμῖν (2 Cor. 11:7).

a. Locate θεοῦ. (4.8.a and 7.1)

PART OF SPEECH: FUNCTION IN THE SENTENCE:

CASE: GENDER: DECLENSION:

NUMBER: LEXICAL FORM:

b. Is τὸ εὐαγγέλιον nominative or accusative singular neuter? How can you be sure? (4.3, 4.8.b, 7.5, and 11.1)

c. Is the augment of εὐηγγελισάμην syllabic or temporal? (3.1 and 12.2.b) What tense stem is the imperfect built on? (12.2)

16. καὶ ἔχει ἐπὶ τὸ ἱμάτιον . . . αὐτοῦ ὄνομα γεγραμμένον· βασιλεὺς βασιλέων καὶ κύριος κυρίων (Rev. 19:16).

a. Is ἱμάτιον nominative or accusative singular neuter? (4.8.b and 10.1) On what do you base your answer? (7.5, 8.1, and 8.4)

b. List the occurrences of paranomasia in this sentence? What is paranomasia? (See lesson 6 sentence 17.b of the workbook.)

c. Does γεγραμμένον have a verbal or adjectival use? What is the significance of this use? (20.7.b, 23.1, and 23.3.b) In what use is γεγραμμένον in this sentence? What is the significance of this use? (20.7.b.1)

17. ἡ πίστις ὑμῶν ἡ πρὸς τὸν θεὸν ἐξελήλυθεν, ὥστε μὴ χρείαν ἔχειν ἡμᾶς λαλεῖν (to say) τι (anything) (1 Thess. 1:8).

a. Why is the definite article τὸν not translated in the phrase πρὸς τὸν θεὸν? (7.4.a)

b. List the elements that identify ἐξελήλυθεν as a perfect tense verb. (23.1, 23.2.a, and b)

c. What parts of speech are ἔχειν and λαλεῖν? What is the significance of this part of speech? (3.1, 3.3.b, and 26.1)

18. ἀποκριθεὶς δὲ ὁ ᾽Ιησοῦς εἶπεν αὐτοῖς, Πλανᾶσθε (you deceive yourselves) μὴ εἰδότες (perf. act. part. of οἶδα) τὰς γραφὰς μηδὲ τὴν δύναμιν τοῦ θεοῦ (Matt. 22:29).

a. How can you be sure that ἀποκριθεὶς is not a present active indicative second person singular verb? (7.5, 11.1, 11.3, 11.4.d, 12.1, and 21.2)

b. Dissect and parse εἶπεν. (3.1, 16.1, and 16.2)

PART OF SPEECH: AUGMENT: STEM:

TENSE: PERSON: ENDING:

VOICE: NUMBER: CONNECTING VOWEL:

MOOD: LEXICAL FORM: SUBJECT:

c. Is γραφὰς genitive singular feminine, ablative singular feminine, or accusative plural feminine? (5.1 and 5.4.a.3) On what do you base your answer? (5.3)

19. ὃ ἐὰν (whatever) δήσῃς (you might bind) ἐπὶ τῆς γῆς ἔσται δεδεμένον ἐν τοῖς οὐρανοῖς, καὶ ὃ ἐὰν λύσῃς (you might loose) ἐπὶ τῆς γῆς ἔσται λελυμένον ἐν τοῖς οὐρανοῖς (Matt. 16:19).

a. In what use is δεδεμένον in the phrase ὃ ἐὰν δήσῃς ἐπὶ τῆς γῆς ἔσται δεδεμένον? What construction is the participle in this sentence? What is the significance of this construction? (20.7.b.3)

b. Dissect and parse δεδεμένον. (23.1 and 23.3.b)

PART OF SPEECH: REDUPLICATION: STEM:

TENSE: PERSON: TENSE SIGN:

VOICE: NUMBER: ENDING:

MOOD: LEXICAL FORM: SUBJECT:

c. Is οὐρανοῖς dative, locative, or instrumental plural masculine? (4.3, 4.5.e, 4.8.a, and 11.1) On what do you base your answer? (7.5, 8.1, and 8.4)

20. καὶ ὄντας ἡμᾶς νεκροὺς τοῖς παραπτώμασιν (sins) . . . χάριτί ἐστε σεσῳσμένοι (Eph. 2:5).

a. Is ὄντας verbal or adverbial? What is the significance of this use of the participle and specifically what is this type of participle called? (20.7.a)

b. In what use is the adjective νεκροὺς in the phrase ὄντας ἡμᾶς νεκροὺς? What is the significance of this use? (6.1, 6.3, and 6.4.b)

c. What elements identify the tense and verbal form of σεσῳσμένοι? (11.1, 23.1, 23.2, and 23.3.b)

LESSON 24: Subjunctive Mood

24.1 Supplemental vocabulary:

ἀγαπάω - I love (28.1)
δίδωμι - I give (29.1)
εἷς, μία, ἕν - one (27.1)
ἐλεύθερος, -α, -ον - free, in a
  state of freedom (adj.)
καταλύω - I destroy (intensive)
νομίζω - I think
ὅπου - where (adv) (24.1)

περισσεύω - I exceed
πλείων, -ον - more (a comparative of
  πολύς) (28.1)
ποτήριον, τό - cup
πύλη, ἡ - gate
σπόρος, ὁ - seed
τρέχω - I progress

24.2.a _____ expresses the relation of the action of the verb to reality.

24.2.b In translating verbs, one must discern whether the action of a verb is actually taking place or potential. This question introduces two basic moods in any language: the _____ and the _____.

24.2.c There are four moods in the New Testament with the _____ mood expressing real action and the _____, _____, and _____, moods expressing potential action.

24.2.d The matter of real or potential action is considered from the perspective of the _____ or _____.

24.2.e Action which is viewed by the speaker as real is expressed by the _____ mood.

24.2.f The potential moods express action which is viewed by the speaker or writer as _____, contingent upon certain conditions.

24.2.g The moods state the action in varying degrees from reality:

_____ is the mood of moderate contingency, where the action is not really taking place, but is objectively possible.

_____ is the mood that expresses action which is volitionally possible and involves the exercise of the will. One person is trying to exert influence on another to produce action.

_____ is the mood that expresses action really taking place.

_____ is the mood is strong contingency and expresses action not taking place but which is subjectively possible.

24.3.a The subjunctive mood appears almost exclusively in the New Testament in the _____ and the _____ tenses.

24.3.b.1 The connecting vowel ___/___ replaces the connecting vowel ___/___ of the indicative mood.

24.3.b.2 All subjunctive tenses use the endings of the _____ _____ and there is no _____ even in the aorist. This is because _____ of action is lost in the subjunctive and _____ of action is the key factor.

24.3.b.3 The irregular accent of the aorist passive is the result of the contraction of ____ with ___/___.

24.3.b.4 How is the present subjunctive of εἰμί formed?

24.3.c Subjunctives either use the _____ endings or the _____ and _____ endings.

24.4.a.1 Since the subjunctive expresses action which is not a reality but is _____ _____, this means that, in the mind of the speaker or writer, there is a good possibility of the action taking place.

24.4.a.2 The fulfillment is expected in the _____, and thus the subjunctive is closely related to the _____ indicative.

24.4.a.3 The future indicative describes what _____ take place and the subjunctive describes what ____ take place. The words _____ or _____ often appear in translating subjunctives.

24.4.b.1 The _____ of action is the important difference in the various tenses in the subjunctive and not the _____ of action.

24.4.b.2 The major difference in the kind of action of New Testament subjunctives is _____ or _____.

24.4.b.3 The time of the verb in the subjunctive is dependent upon _____ _____ _____ as in the _____.

24.4.c The subjunctive has a variety of meanings:

The _____ subjunctive is used to express a rhetorical question where no answer is expected or a real question which expects an answer.

The subjunctive is used to express _____ _____. This construction employs the double negative οὐ μή, which is much stronger than οὐ alone with the indicative.

The _____ subjunctive is the use of the second person aorist subjunctive to express a negative entreaty or command.

The New Testament contains a variety of uses where the subjunctive is the verb of a _____ _____ clause. These subjunctives express _____ and are clauses in _____ _____. _____ clauses are final and indicate the purpose of the main clause of a sentence.

The _____ subjunctive is the use of the first person plural to exhort others to join in the action.

24.5 Conditional sentences comprise two clauses, a _____ _____ clause (the _____) and the _____ clause (the _____). There are four classes of conditional clauses:

_____ class condition is the probable future condition. The conjunction ἐάν appears with the subjunctive in the protasis and any form is need in the apodosis. It expresses what will probably take place, subject to the condition being fulfilled.

_____ class condition affirms the reality of the condition. It is expressed with εἰ and the indicative mood in the protasis and almost any mood or tense in the apodosis.

_____ class condition is the possible future condition. It is expressed with εἰ and the optative mood in the protasis and the optative mood in the apodosis.

_____ class condition is the contrary to fact condition. The secondary or past tenses of the indicative mood are used. It is expressed with εἰ and the indicative mood in the protasis and ἄν and the indicative mood in the apodosis.

24.6 EXERCISES:

1. τὸ λοιπὸν προσεύχεσθε (**imperative**, pray), ἀδελφοί, περὶ ἡμῶν, ἵνα ὁ λόγος τοῦ κυρίου τρέχῃ (might make progress) καὶ δοξάζηται καθὼς καὶ πρὸς ὑμᾶς (2 Thess. 3:1)

a. Is ἵνα a coordinating or a subordinating conjunction? What is the significance of the type of conjunction? (13.3.a and 24.1)

b. Is τρέχῃ a dative/locative/instrumental singular feminine noun or present active subjunctive third person singular verb? (See 24.1 of the workbook and 24.3.c.1 of the textbook.)

c. Is agency expressed with the verb δοξάζηται? On what do you base your answer? (9.1, 11.5, and 24.3.c.1)

2. οὕτως καὶ ἡ πίστις, ἐὰν μὴ ἔχῃ ἔργα, νεκρά ἐστιν (Jas. 2:17).

a. Locate πίστις. (19.1 and 19.2.a)

PART OF SPEECH: FUNCTION IN THE SENTENCE:

CASE: GENDER: DECLENSION:

NUMBER: LEXICAL FORM:

b. What class condition is this sentence? Explain the significance of this class condition. (24.5.c)

c. What is the significance of the ἐὰν μὴ construction? (24.4.c.4)

3. Ἄγωμεν καὶ ἡμεῖς ἵνα ἀποθάνωμεν μετ᾽ αὐτοῦ (John 11:16).

a. Why is the connecting vowel of Ἄγωμεν and ἀποθάνωμεν an ω instead of o? (24.3.b.1)

b. What use of the subjunctive are Ἄγωμεν and ἀποθάνωμεν? What is the significance of this use? (24.4.c.1)

c. Is ἡμεῖς necessary in this sentence? (3.3, 9.1, and 9.2) What is the significance of ἡμεῖς in this sentence? (9.3.b)

4. λέγω γὰρ ὑμῖν ὅτι ἐὰν μὴ περισσεύσῃ (exceed) ὑμῶν ἡ δικαιοσύνη πλεῖον (more than) τῶν γραμματέων καὶ Φαρισαίων, οὐ μὴ εἰσέλθητε εἰς τὴν βασιλείαν τῶν οὐρανῶν (Matt. 5:20).

a. What class condition does ἐὰν μὴ περισσεύσῃ express? On what do you base your answer? What is the significance of this condition? (24.5.c)

b. Why is the ending of βασιλείαν, -αν and the article is τὴν? Why is the word not spelled βασιλείην? (5.1, 5.3, and 5.4.a.2)

c. What function does the preposition perform in εἰσέλθητε? Is the preposition εἰς translated twice in the phrase εἰσέλθητε εἰς? (See 8.4 of the textbook and 8.4.c of the workbook.)

5. ἐὰν εἴπωμεν ὅτι κοινωνίαν ἔχομεν μετ᾽ αὐτοῦ καὶ μένωμεν ἐν ἁμαρτίᾳ, ψευδόμεθα (See 1 John 1:6.).

a. What class condition does ἐὰν εἴπωμεν express? On what do you base your answer? What is the significance of this condition? (24.5.c)

b. How can you be sure that ἔχομεν is in the indicative mood rather than the subjunctive mood? (3.3 and 24.3.b.1)

c. Dissect and parse ψευδόμεθα. (11.3, 11.4.d, and 20.1)

PART OF SPEECH: AUGMENT: STEM:

TENSE: PERSON: ENDING:

VOICE: NUMBER: CONNECTING VOWEL:

MOOD: LEXICAL FORM: SUBJECT:

6. καὶ ἔλεγεν, Οὕτως ἐστὶν ἡ βασιλεία τοῦ θεοῦ ὡς ἄνθρωπος βάλῃ τὸν σπόρον (seed)
ἐπὶ τῆς γῆς (Mark 4:26).

a. Dissect and parse ἔλεγεν. (3.1 and 12.2.a)

PART OF SPEECH: AUGMENT: STEM:

TENSE: PERSON: ENDING:

VOICE: NUMBER: CONNECTING VOWEL:

MOOD: LEXICAL FORM: SUBJECT:

b. Is τοῦ θεοῦ genitive or ablative? (4.8.a and 7.1) On what do you base your answer? (7.5)
What is the significance of this case? (4.5.b)

c. How do you determine the gender of σπόρον? (4.3 and 4.6)

7. καὶ ἐὰν πορευθῶ καὶ ἑτοιμάσω τόπον ὑμῖν, πάλιν ἔρχομαι καὶ παραλήμψομαι ὑμᾶς
πρὸς ἐμαυτόν (myself), ἵνα ὅπου εἰμὶ ἐγὼ καὶ ὑμεῖς ἦτε (John 14:3).

a. Is the construction καὶ . . . καὶ simple connective conjunctions or correlative conjunctions?
Explain. (13.3.a and c)

b. Dissect and parse παραλήμψομαι. (8.1, 9.4.d, 14.1, and 14.2

PART OF SPEECH:	AUGMENT:	STEM:
TENSE:	PERSON:	ENDING:
VOICE:	NUMBER:	CONNECTING VOWEL:
MOOD:	LEXICAL FORM:	SUBJECT:

c. Is the presence of ἐγὼ necessary in the phrase εἰμὶ ἐγὼ ? Is ὑμεῖς necessary in the phrase ὑμεῖς ἦτε? Why or why not? (9.1, 9.2, and 9.3.b) What is the significance of the present of these pronouns in the nominative case? (9.3.c)

8. οἱ μὴ πιστεύοντες τὸ εὐγγέλιον οὐ μὴ σωθῶσιν ἐν τῇ δυνάμει αὐτοῦ.

a. What is the significance of μὴ in the phrase μὴ πιστεύοντες? (9.5 and 21.1)

b. What use is μὴ πιστεύοντες in this sentence? What is the significance of this use in this sentence? (20.7.b.2)

c. What is the subject of σωθῶσιν? On what do you base your answer? (4.5.a, 7.5, and 20.7.b.2)

9. μὴ νομίσητε (think) ὅτι ἦλθον καταλῦσαι (to destroy) τὸν νόμον ἢ τοὺς προφήτας (Matt. 5:17).

a. What is the use of the subjunctive νομίσητε? Explain. (See 24.3.c.1 and 24.4.c.2 of the textbook and 24.1 of the workbook.)

b. Is ἤ a coordinating or a subordinating conjunction? What is the significance of this type of conjunction? (13.1 and 13.3.a)

c. Why does προφήτας have a masculine definite article? (4.3, 5.1, and 5.4.b.2)

10. εἰ ἐκήρυξας τὸ εὐαγγέλιον, οἱ ἂν ἁμαρτωλοὶ ἐπίστευσαν.

a. What mood does the particle εἰ indicate that the verb is? (24.1)

b. Dissect and parse ἐκήρυξας. (9.1 and 15.2)

PART OF SPEECH: AUGMENT: STEM:

TENSE: PERSON: ENDING:

VOICE: NUMBER: CONNECTING VOWEL:

MOOD: LEXICAL FORM: SUBJECT:

c. What class condition does this sentence express? On what do you base your answer? What is the significance of this condition? (24.5.b)

11. καὶ αὕτη ἐστὶν ἡ ἐντολὴ αὐτοῦ, ἵνα πιστεύωμεν τῷ ὀνόματι τοῦ υἱοῦ αὐτοῦ Ἰησοῦ Χριστοῦ (1 John 3:23).

a. What factors indicate that πιστεύωμεν is a subjunctive mood verb? (10.1, 24.1, 24.3.b and c)

b. The antecedent of both appearances of αὐτοῦ is not listed in this sentence? What can be known for certain about the antecedent of the two occurrences of αὐτοῦ? (9.1, 9.2, and 9.3.a)

c.   Locate ὀνόματι. (19.1 and 19.3.b)

PART OF SPEECH: FUNCTION IN THE SENTENCE:

CASE: GENDER: DECLENSION:

NUMBER: LEXICAL FORM:

12. εἰσήλθομεν εἰς τὴν ἐκκλησίαν ἵνα ἀκούσωμεν τὸν λόγον τοῦ θεοῦ τὸν κηρυσσόμενον.

a. What use of the subjunctive is εἰσήλθομεν? What is the significance of this use? (24.4.c.1)

b. What use is κηρυσσόμενον in this sentence? What is the significance of this use in this sentence? (20.7.b.1)

13. εἶπεν αὐτοῖς ὁ Ἰησοῦς, Εἰ ὁ θεὸς πατὴρ ὑμῶν ἦν ἠγαπᾶτε (you love) ἂν ἐμέ, ἐγὼ γὰρ ἐκ τοῦ θεοῦ ἐξῆλθον (John 8:42).

a. Is αὐτοῖς dative, locative, or instrumental? (9.1 and 9.2) How can you be sure? (7.5)

b. Note that ἠγαπᾶτε is a contract verb from the form ἀγαπάω. (See 24.1 of the workbook and lesson 28 of the textbook.)

c. What class condition does this sentence express? On what does one base their answer? What is the significance of this condition? (24.5.a)

14. ταῦτα ἔγραψα ὑμῖν ἵνα εἰδῆτε ὅτι ζωὴν ἔχετε αἰώνιον, τοῖς πιστεύουσιν εἰς τὸ ὄνομα τοῦ υἱοῦ τοῦ θεοῦ (1 John 5:13).

a. Dissect and parse ἔγραψα. (3.1 and 15.2)

PART OF SPEECH: AUGMENT: STEM:

TENSE: PERSON: ENDING:

VOICE: NUMBER: CONNECTING VOWEL:

MOOD: LEXICAL FORM: SUBJECT:

b. Does ἵνα introduce a main clause or a subordinate clause? Explain. (13.3.a, 24.1, and 24.4.c)

c. How can you be sure that ὄνομα is accusative singular neuter rather than nominative singular neuter? (8.1 and 8.4)

15. καὶ γὰρ ἐν ἑνὶ (one) πνεύματι ἡμεῖς πάντες (all) εἰς ἓν (one) σῶμα ἐβαπτίσθημεν, εἴτε Ἰουδαῖοι εἴτε Ἕλληνες (Greeks) εἴτε δοῦλοι εἴτε ἐλεύθεροι (free people) (1 Cor. 12:13).

a. How does the preposition ἐν help in the identification of the case of πνεύματι? (8.1, 19.1, and 19.3.b)

b. What voice is ἐβαπτίσθημεν in? (7.1, 15.1, and 17.2) What is the significance of the voice of ἐβαπτίσθημεν in this sentence? (11.5)

c. How can you be sure of the case of σῶμα? (4.6, 7.5, 8.1, 8.4, 19.1, and 19.3.b)

16. διὸ καὶ Ἰησοῦς, ἵνα ἁγιάσῃ διὰ τοῦ ἰδίου αἵματος τὸν λαόν, ἔξω τῆς πύλης (gate) ἔπαθεν (Heb. 13:12).

a. What effect does the order of Ἰησοῦς and its verb ἔπαθεν have on the translation of this sentence? (4.7)

b. What part of speech is ἰδίου? In what use is ἰδίου? What is the significance of this use? (6.3, 6.4.a, and 9.1)

c. Explain the change in spelling from the present tense to the aorist form ἔπαθεν. (16.1 and 16.2)

17. τέλος γὰρ νόμου Χριστὸς εἰς δικαιοσύνην παντὶ τῷ πιστεύοντι (Rom. 10:4).

a. Why is τέλος γὰρ νόμου Χριστὸς translated as if ἐστιν is present, though it is not? (6.4.b, 7.1, 7.5, 9.4, and 19.1)

b. Is νόμου genitive or ablative singular masculine? (4.1 and 4.8.a) How can you be sure? (7.5) What is the significance of this case? 4.5.b)

c. Is πιστεύοντι a verbal or an adjectival participle. (20.7.b) In what use is this participle? What is the significance of this use? (20.7.b.2)

18. οὐ δύνασθε ποτήριον (cup) κυρίου πίνειν (to drink) καὶ ποτήριον δαιμονίων (1 Cor. 10:21).

a. What part of speech is οὐ ? Why is οὐ not in the form of οὐκ or οὐχ in this sentence? (9.1) What is the significance of this word? (9.5)

b. Is ποτήριον nominative or accusative singular neuter? (4.8.b and 24.1) On what do you base your answer? (7.5) What is the significance of this case? (4.5.g)

c. What part of speech is πίνειν? What is the significance of this part of speech? (3.3 and 21.1)

19. εἶπεν οὖν πάλιν αὐτοῖς, . . . ὅπου ἐγὼ ὑπάγω ὑμεῖς οὐ δύνασθε ἐλθεῖν (John 8:21).

a. What kind of aorist is εἶπεν? What is the significance of this kind of aorist? (15.3.b, 16.1 and 16.2)

b. What part of speech is ὅπου? (24.1) What is the significance of this part of speech? See 12.1.b of the workbook.)

c. What is the significance of the voice of δύνασθε? (11.3, 11.4.d, and 13.1)

20. καὶ αὕτη ἐστὶν ἡ μαρτυρία, ὅτι ζωὴν αἰώνιον ἔδωκεν (he gave) ἡμῖν ὁ θεός, καὶ αὕτη ἡ ζωὴ ἐν τῷ υἱῷ αὐτοῦ ἐστιν (1 John 5:11).

a. Is the subject of the first occurrence of ἐστὶν, αὕτη or μαρτυρία? (5.4.a.1, 9.1, 9.4, 10.1, 10.2.a, 10.3.a, and 24.1) How can you be sure? (4.5.a, 7.5, and 9.4)

b. How can you be sure that αὕτη is a near demonstrative pronoun and not a third personal pronoun? (9.1, 9.2, 10.1, and 10.2.a)

c. Note that αἰώνιον is an accusative singular feminine adjective that modifies ζωὴν. (6.3, 6.4.a, and 21.1)

LESSON 25: Imperative Mood

25.1 Supplemental vocabulary:

ἀνάθεμα, τό - a curse (accursed)
ἄφρων, -ονος, ὁ, ἡ - unwise, fool,
  inconsiderable (adj.)
δάκτυλος, ὁ - finger
ἐμαυτοῦ, -ῆς (gen.) - of myself (27.1)
ἐνεργής, -έος, -οῦς, ὁ, ἡ - active,
  effective, efficient, energetic (adj.)
ἐξουθενέω - I despise
ἐπίγνωσις, -εως, ἡ - knowledge

θερίζω - I reap
Ἰουδαία, ας, ἡ - Judea
μνημονεύω - I remember
μυριάς, -άδος, ἡ - ten thousand
Μωσῆς or Μωϋσῆς, ὁ - Moses (18.1)
ὅς, ἥ, ὅ - who, which, what (27.1)
πᾶς. πᾶσα, πᾶν - all, every (adj.) (28.1)
πλευρά, ἡ - side
προσλαμβάνω - I receive
σιωπάω - I keep silent

25.2.a In the Greek language, only the _____ and the _____ tenses use the imperative mood.

25.2.b.1 How is the imperative moods normally formed?

25.2.b.2 The only exception to question 25.2.b.1 above is the second person singular of εἰμί which has a _____ _____.

25.2.c The second plural imperative of all forms is identical to the _____ _____ _____ forms.

25.2.d From the second plural form you can determine the _____ _____ and _____ _____ with the exception of the εἰμί forms. Change the ___ to ___ in the third singular and to _____ in the third plural.

25.2.e Sometimes variant endings for the _____ _____ occur. You must learn the second singular endings _____.

25.3.a In both Greek and English the imperative mood expresses a _____.

25.3.b In English only the _____ person is used in the imperative mood and the implied subject is _____. Greek has forms for both the _____ and _____ persons.

25.3.c No forms for the _____ person occur since the _____ _____ expresses the idea of an imperative.

25.3.d Translate the _____ person into the usual English command with _____ implied. With the _____ person, you normally use the word _____ to express this idea.

25.3.e The difference between the present imperative and the aorist imperative is _____ ___ _____ and not _____. Based on this, the aorist has no _____.

25.3.f Explain the difference between the kind of action of the present imperative and the aorist imperative.

25.3.g Review the primary uses of the imperative mood. (25.3)

25.3.h Note that the _____ _____ is similar to the _____ _____.

25.4.a The endings for the second plural indicative and imperative are identical; therefore, only the _____ of the sentence will indicate which mood is intended.

25.4.b The aorist indicative will have a(n) _____ to distinguish it from the imperative.

25.5 EXERCISES:

1. καὶ ἔλεγεν, Ὃς (the one who) ἔχει ὦτα ἀκούειν ἀκουέτω (Mark 4:9).

a. Locate ὦτα. (19.2.c and 25.1)

PART OF SPEECH: FUNCTION IN THE SENTENCE:

CASE: GENDER: DECLENSION:

NUMBER: LEXICAL FORM:

b. What is the significance of ἀκούειν? (3.3.b) Locate the verbal elements of this word such as tense, voice, verbal form, and lexical form. (2.1 and 3.3)

c. Dissect and parse ἀκουέτω. (2.1 and 25.2)

PART OF SPEECH: AUGMENT: STEM:

TENSE: PERSON: ENDING:

VOICE: NUMBER: CONNECTING VOWEL:

MOOD: LEXICAL FORM: SUBJECT:

2. καὶ ἰδοὺ ἔσῃ σιωπῶν (silent) καὶ μὴ δυνάμενος λαλῆσαι (to speak) ἄχρι ἧς (that) ἡμέρας γένηται ταῦτα (Luke 1:20).

a. Parse ἔσῃ. (9.1 and 14.5)

PART OF SPEECH: TENSE: PERSON:

SUBJECT: VOICE: NUMBER:

STEM: MOOD: LEXICAL FORM:

b. What kind of construction is ἔσῃ σιωπῶν καὶ μὴ δυνάμενος? What is the significance of this construction? (20.7.b.3)

c. Locate ἧς. (27.1 and 27.3.a)

PART OF SPEECH: **rel. prn.**   FUNCTION IN THE SENTENCE: **obj.** of ἄχρι
CASE: **gen.**   GENDER: **fem.**   DECLENSION: **N/A**
NUMBER: **sing.**   LEXICAL FORM: ἥ

3. καὶ ἰδοὺ φωνὴ ἐκ τῶν οὐρανῶν λέγουσα, Οὗτός ἐστιν ὁ υἱός μου ὁ ἀγαπητός (Matt. 3:17).

a. Is οὐρανῶν genitive or ablative in case? (4.8.a, 8.1 and 11.1) What is the significance of the case of this phrase in this sentence? (4.5.c) Does the preposition ἐκ suggest agency or separation? (8.1 and 8.4)

b. Why must the verb of being ἐστιν be inserted in the phrase Οὗτός ἐστιν ὁ υἱός? (9.1, 9.2, 9.3.b, 10.1, 10.2.a, and 10.3.b)

c. Is ἀγαπητός in the attributive, predicative, or substantive use? On what do you base your answer? (6.1, 6.3, and 6.4.a)

4. ἀλλὰ καὶ ἐὰν ἡμεῖς ἢ ἄγγελος ἐξ οὐρανοῦ εὐαγγελίζηται [ὑμῖν] παρ᾽ ὃ (what) εὐηγγελισάμεθα ὑμῖν, ἀνάθεμα (cursed) ἔστω (Gal. 1:8).

a. List the factors which indicate that εὐαγγελίζηται is a subjunctive mood verb. (24.1 and 24.3.c.2)

b. Dissect and parse εὐηγγελισάμεθα. (15.2 and 23.1)

PART OF SPEECH: AUGMENT: STEM:

TENSE: PERSON: ENDING:

VOICE: NUMBER: CONNECTING VOWEL:

MOOD: LEXICAL FORM: SUBJECT:

c. What is unusual concerning the number of the subject of ἔστω in comparison of this mood in Greek with the normal usage of this mood in English? (25.3) What other mood function does the translation of this verb resemble? (24.4.c.1)

5. πίνετε τὸ ὕδωρ τῆς ζωῆς καὶ ἐσθίετε τὸν ἄρτον τῆς ζωῆς.

a. Are πίνετε and ἐσθίετε indicative, subjunctive, or imperative in mood? (25.2) Explain the significance of this mood. (25.3)

b. Why must ὕδωρ be accusative rather than the nominative subject? (3.3.c, 9.1, 9.2, 9.3.b, and 25.2)

c. Is τῆς ζωῆς genitive or ablative? (5.4.a.2 and 7.1) How are you able to determine the case usage of the noun in this sentence? (7.5) What is the significance of this case usage? (4.5.b)

6. καὶ ὑπὲρ αὐτῶν ἐγὼ ἁγιάζω ἐμαυτόν (myself), ἵνα ὦσιν καὶ αὐτοὶ ἡγιασμένοι ἐν ἀληθείᾳ (John 17:19).

a. Locate ἐμαυτόν. (27.1 and 27.3.e)

PART OF SPEECH: **rfx. prn.**   FUNCTION IN THE SENTENCE: **do.** of ἡγιασμένοι
CASE: **acc.**   GENDER: **N/A**   DECLENSION: **N/A**
NUMBER: **sing.**   LEXICAL FORM: ἐμαυτοῦ

b. List the factors which indicate that ὦσιν is a subjunctive mood verb. (24.1 and 24.3.b.4)

c. Dissect and parse ἡγιασμένοι. (23.3.b and 24.1)

PART OF SPEECH: AUGMENT: STEM:

TENSE: PERSON: ENDING:

VOICE: NUMBER: CONNECTING VOWEL:

MOOD: LEXICAL FORM: SUBJECT:

7. εἰ ὁ ἄνθρωπος πιστεύει εἰς Χριστόν, βαπτισθήτω.

a. How can you be sure that πιστεύει is an indicative mood verb? (24.1)

b. What class condition sentence is the above sentence? What is the significance of this class condition? (24.5.a)

c. What is unusual concerning the number of the subject of βαπτισθήτω in comparison of this mood in Greek with the normal usage of this mood in English? (25.3)

8. ὅ (what) γὰρ ἐὰν σπείρῃ ἄνθρωπος, τοῦτο καὶ θερίσει (will reap) (Gal. 6:7).

a. Locate ὅ. (4.1, 27.1 and 27.3)

PART OF SPEECH: **rel. prn.**   FUNCTION IN THE SENTENCE: **do.** of σπείρῃ
CASE: **acc.**   GENDER: **neut.**   DECLENSION: **N/A**
NUMBER: **sing.**   LEXICAL FORM: ὅ

b. Define the function of the subjunctive mood in σπείρῃ and the significance of this type of subjunctive. (24.4.c)

c. How can you be sure that τοῦτο is the subject θερίσει? Does the subject of σπείρῃ help in determining the subject of θερίσει? (7.5)

9. ἀποκριθεὶς δὲ ὁ Σίμων (Simon) Πέτρος εἶπεν, Σὺ εἶ ὁ Χριστὸς ὁ υἱὸς τοῦ θεοῦ τοῦ ζῶντος (living) (Matt. 16:16).

a. What is the significance of Σὺ in the phrase Σὺ εἶ ὁ Χριστὸς? (9.1, 9.2, and 9.3.c.3)

b. What use is the participle ζῶντος in the phrase τοῦ θεοῦ τοῦ ζῶντος? (20.7.b.1) Note that the participle translates more as an adjective than a participle in this use. What is the significance of the use of the participle ζῶντος? (6.4.a and 20.7.b.1)

10. μετὰ ταῦτα ἦλθεν ὁ Ἰησοῦς καὶ οἱ μαθηταὶ αὐτοῦ εἰς τὴν Ἰουδαίαν (Judea) γῆν καὶ ἐκεῖ . . . ἐβάπτιζεν (John 3:22).

  a. Is the demonstrative pronoun ταῦτα in the predicate or substantive use in this sentence? (10.1, 10.2.a, and 10.3.a)

  b. Ἰησοῦς and μαθηταὶ are the subjects of the third singular verb ἦλθεν. Robertson identified this phenomenon as the singular verb with the first subject, which is a common phenomenon in the New Testament (Robertson, p. 405).

  c. Ἰουδαίαν is a noun taking on the character of an attributive adjective in the phrase τὴν Ἰουδαίαν γῆν. A literal translation is "into the Judea land;" however, most translate this phrase as "the land of Judea."

11. ὁ ἐσθίων τὸν μὴ ἐσθίοντα μὴ ἐξουθενείτω (despise), ὁ δὲ μὴ ἐσθίων τὸν ἐσθίοντα μὴ κρινέτω, ὁ θεὸς γὰρ αὐτὸν προσελάβετο (has received) (Rom. 14:3).

  a. What use is ἐσθίων in this sentence? What is the significance of this use in this sentence? (20.7.b.2)

  b. What kind of imperative mood verbs are ἐξουθενείτω and κρινέτω? (25.3) What is unusual concerning the number of the subjects of ἐξουθενείτω and κρινέτω in comparison of this mood in Greek and the normal usage of this mood in English? (25.3)

  c. List the postpositive words in this sentence? What is the significance of postpositive words? (See 9.5 and 10.1 of the textbook and 10.1.b of the workbook.)

12. Φέρε τὸν δάκτυλόν (finger) σου ὧδε καὶ ἴδε τὰς χεῖράς μου καὶ φέρε τὴν χεῖρά σου καὶ βάλε εἰς τὴν πλευράν (side) μου . . . (John 20:27).

a. What does the mood of the two occurrences of φέρε suggest in this sentence? (25.3)

b. Is χείράς genitive singular feminine, ablative singular feminine, or accusative plural feminine? How can you be sure? (5.3)

c. What case is used with εἰς in this sentence? What are the variant translations of εἰς? (8.1) How can you know which translation of εἰς is best used in this sentence?

13. εἶπεν οὖν αὐτοῖς ὁ Ἰησοῦς, Ἀμὴν ἀμὴν λέγω ὑμῖν, ἐὰν μὴ φάγητε τὴν σάρκα τοῦ υἱοῦ τοῦ ἀνθρώπου καὶ πίητε αὐτοῦ τὸ αἷμα, οὐκ ἔχετε ζωὴν . . . (John 6:53).

a. Parse εἶπεν. (3.1, 16.1, and 16.2)

PART OF SPEECH: TENSE: PERSON:

SUBJECT: VOICE: NUMBER:

STEM: MOOD: LEXICAL FORM:

b. How do ἐὰν μὴ determine that φάγητε and πίητε are not indicative mood verbs? What mood(s) is/are these verbs? (21.1 and 24.1)

c. Locate σάρκα. (18.1 and 18.4)

PART OF SPEECH: FUNCTION IN THE SENTENCE:

CASE: GENDER: DECLENSION:

NUMBER: LEXICAL FORM:

14. λέγει δὲ Ἀβραάμ, Ἔχουσι Μωϋσέα καὶ τοὺς προφήτας· ἀκουσάτωσαν αὐτῶν (Luke 16:29).

a. λέγει is present active indicative third singular verb in form; however, it is translated as a past tense verb. This phenomenon, called a historical present, is a past event that is viewed with the vividness of a present occurrence (Dana and Mantey, p. 185).

b. What is the ¨ in Μωϋσέα called? What is the significance of this diacritical mark? (2.3)

15. πορευόμενοι δὲ κηρύσσετε λέγοντες ὅτι Ἤγγικεν ἡ βασιλεία τῶν οὐρανῶν (Matt. 10:7).

a. Is κηρύσσετε indicative or imperative in mood? (25.2) How can you determine whether κηρύσσετε in indicative or imperative in mood? (25.4)

b. What kind of conjunction is ὅτι? (13.3.a) What kind of clause does this conjunction introduce? What is the significance of this type of clause? (13.3.a and 24.c.5)

c. Parse Ἤγγικεν. (23.1 and 23.2)

PART OF SPEECH: TENSE: PERSON:

SUBJECT: VOICE: NUMBER:

STEM: MOOD: LEXICAL FORM:

d. Robertson classified words such as οὐρανῶν as an idiomatic plural. This is phenomenon where abstract substantives are plural, yet they are translated into English as singular (Robertson, p. 408).

16. καὶ ἀποκριθεὶς ὁ Ἰησοῦς λέγει αὐτοῖς, Ἔχετε πίστιν θεοῦ (Mark 11:22).

a. How can Ἰησοῦς be the subject of ἀποκριθεὶς when ἀποκριθεὶς appears to be a present active indicative second singular verb? (3.3, 12.1, 20.1, and 22.2)

b. Note if ἀποκριθεὶς was a present active indicative second singular verb the accent would be on the penult, ἀποκρίθεις. Why is it impossible for ἀποκριθεὶς to be present active indicative second singular verb? (11.1 and 11.3)

c. How can you determine whether Ἔχετε is in the indicative or imperative mood? (2.1, 7.5, and 25.4)

17. μνημόνευε (remember) Ἰησοῦν Χριστὸν ἐγηγερμένον ἐκ νεκρῶν, ἐκ σπέρματος Δαυίδ, κατὰ τὸ εὐαγγέλιόν μου (2 Tim. 2:8).

a. What is the use of the mood of μνημόνευε? (See 25.2, 25.3, and 26.3 of the textbook and 25.1 of the workbook.)

b. What elements identify the tense the verbal form ἐγηγερμένον? (3.1, 23.1, 23.2, and 23.3)

c. What elements identify εὐαγγέλιόν as an accusative case noun? (4.3, 4.8.a, 8.1, 8.4, and 10.1)

18. εἶπεν δὲ αὐτῷ ὁ θεός, Ἄφρων (fool), ταύτῃ τῇ νυκτὶ τὴν ψυχήν σου ἀπαιτοῦσιν (they are demanding) ἀπὸ σοῦ (Luke 12:20).

a. In what use is ταύτῃ in the phrase ταύτῃ τῇ νυκτὶ? (10.1, 10.2.a, and 10.3.b) What is unusual about this use of the demonstrative pronoun compared with an adjective in the same use? (6.4.a and 10.3.b) What is the significance of this use? (10.3.b)

b. Parse ἀπαιτοῦσιν. (3.3 of the textbook and 25.1 of the workbook)

PART OF SPEECH: TENSE: PERSON:

SUBJECT: VOICE: NUMBER:

STEM: MOOD: LEXICAL FORM:

19. Ἰδοὺ ἦλθεν κύριος ἐν ἁγίαις μυριάσιν (with ten thousand) αὐτοῦ (Jude 14).

a. Is ἦλθεν constative, ingressive, or culminative? What is the significance of this type of aorist? (15.3.b, 16.1, and 16.2)

b. Locate μυριάσιν. (19.2.c and 25.1)

PART OF SPEECH: FUNCTION IN THE SENTENCE:

CASE: GENDER: DECLENSION:

NUMBER: LEXICAL FORM:

20. ὅπως ἡ κοινωνία τῆς πίστεώς σου ἐνεργὴς (effective) γένηται ἐν ἐπιγνώσει (knowledge) παντὸς (all) ἀγαθοῦ τοῦ ἐν ἡμῖν εἰς Χριστόν (Philem. 6).

a. What part of speech is ὅπως? (25.1) What is the significance of this part of speech? (12.1.b of the workbook)

b. Explain why σου does not have an accent? (9.1, 9.2, and 9.6.b)

c. Locate παντὸς. (28.1 and 28.2.a)

PART OF SPEECH: **adj.**   FUNCTION: **MODIFIES** ἀγαθοῦ
CASE: **gen.**   GENDER: **neut.**   DECLENSION: **3rd**
NUMBER: **sing.**   LEXICAL FORM: πᾶν

LESSON 26: Contract Verbs

26.1 Supplemental vocabulary:

ἀλλήλων - of one another (gen.) (27.1)

ἀναγέλλω - I proclaim, announce

ἐμός, -ή, -όν - my, mine (pos. adj.)
  (27.3.g)

ἑώρακα - I have seen (perfect
  active indicative of ὁράω

ἡμέτερος, -α, ον - our

Ἰουδαία, ας, ἡ - Judea

κέρδος, ὁ - gain

ὅστις, ἥτις, ὅτι - who, what (ind rel.
  prn.) (27.1)

οὐδείς, (οὐθείς), οὐδεμία - no one,
  nothing, (usually with the indicative mood)
  (neg. prn.) (27.1)

τίς, τί - who, what (int. prn.) (27.1)

26.2.a Contract verbs are a special class of verbs with the stems ending in ___, ___, and ___. These vowels are the contract vowels.

26.2.b Contract verbs add the same endings as other ___ _____, but when the final stem vowel (___, ___, or ___) comes into contact with a connecting vowel, the two vowels contract into a _____ _____ or _____.

26.2.c Contraction takes place only in the _____ and the _____ tenses since the _____ and the _____ tenses take the tense sign σ and the _____ tense takes the tense sign κ.

26.3. Review how to identify the vocabulary form of contract verbs.

26.4.a.1. Review the principles of contraction with the vowel contracting with a vowel.

26.4.a.2. Review the principles of contraction with the vowel contracting with a diphthong.

2.4.b Review the contract chart of vowels.

26.4.c Review the three rules apply to the accent of contract verbs.

26.5 Review models of contract verbs.

26.6.1 Verbs whose stems end in a liquid consonant (___, ___, ___, ___) are called liquid verbs.

26.6.2 In the future active and middle indicative and the future active and middle infinitive, liquid verbs drop the ___ and add a(n) ___ and behave like _____ _____.

26.7 EXERCISES:

1. τί (why) δέ με καλεῖτε, Κύριε κύριε, καὶ οὐ ποιεῖτε ἃ (what) λέγω; (Luke 6:46).

a. Note τί is an interrogative pronouns and ἃ is a relative pronoun. (See 27.1 and 27.3.a)

b. Explain why καλεῖτε and ποιεῖτε are classified as contract verbs. (26.1 and 26.2)

c. Locate Κύριε. (4.8.a and 7.1)

PART OF SPEECH: FUNCTION IN THE SENTENCE:

CASE: GENDER: DECLENSION:

NUMBER: LEXICAL FORM:

2. καὶ μετὰ ταῦτα περιπάτει ὁ Ἰησοῦς ἐν τῇ Γαλιλαίᾳ· οὐ γὰρ ἤθελεν ἐν τῇ Ἰουδαίᾳ (Judea) περιπατεῖν, ὅτι ἐζήτουν αὐτὸν οἱ Ἰουδαῖοι ἀποκτεῖναι (John 7:1).

a. In what use is ταῦτα in this sentence? What is the significance of this use? (10.1, 10.2.a, and 10.3.a) Why is it impossible for ταῦτα to be in the attributive use in this sentence? (10.3.b)

b. Within the rules of grammar that Sawyer has covered up to this point, is it correct to assume that οἱ Ἰουδαῖοι is inclusive of the male gender only? Why or why not? (6.3, 6.4.c, and 7.1)

c. List the infinitives in this sentence. (3.3 and 15.2)

3. ἐμοὶ γὰρ τὸ ζῆν Χριστὸς καὶ τὸ ἀποθανεῖν κέρδος (gain) (Phil. 1:21).

a. Explain the position of γὰρ in this sentence and how this word is translated in English, verses its Greek position. (See 10.1 and page 45 and footnote 1 of Sawyer.)

b. Locate κέρδος. (26.1 of the workbook and 4.5.a, 4.8.a, 7.4.b, and 31.4.b of the textbook)

PART OF SPEECH: FUNCTION IN THE SENTENCE:

CASE: GENDER: DECLENSION:

NUMBER: LEXICAL FORM:

4. καὶ ἐν ταῖς ἡμέραις ἐκείναις ζητήσουσιν οἱ ἄνθρωποι τὸν θάνατον καὶ οὐ μὴ εὑρήσουσιν αὐτόν (Rev. 9:6).

a. Is ἐκείναις a near or a far demonstrative pronoun? Distinguish the significance between a near or a far demonstrative pronoun. (10.1 and 10.2.b) In what use is ἐκείναις and what is the significance of this use? (10.3.b)

b. Explain the significance of οὐ μὴ in this sentence. (9.1, 21.1, and 24.4.c.4)

5. Ὅ (that which) ἦν ἀπ᾽ ἀρχῆς, ὃ ἀκηκόαμεν ὃ ἑωράκαμεν (we have seen) τοῖς ὀφθαλμοῖς ἡμῶν, ὃ ἐθεασάμεθα καὶ αἱ χεῖρες ἡμῶν ἐψηλάφησαν περὶ τοῦ λόγου τῆς ζωῆς (1 John 1:1).

a. Note that the Greek does not supply the definite article in ἀπ᾽ ἀρχῆς. Why is it proper to translate this phrase "from the beginning?" (4.3 and 30.5)

b. Parse ἐψηλάφησαν. (15.2 and 26.1)

PART OF SPEECH: TENSE: PERSON:

SUBJECT: VOICE: NUMBER:

STEM: MOOD: LEXICAL FORM:

c. What cases may περὶ be used and how is this word translated in these cases? (8.1) What case is περὶ used with in this sentence? How can you determine the case περὶ is used with in this sentence? (7.5 and 8.4)

6. καὶ ἡ ζωὴ ἐφανερώθη, καὶ ἑωράκαμεν καὶ μαρτυροῦμεν καὶ ἀπαγγέλλομεν ὑμῖν τὴν ζωὴν τὴν αἰώνιον ἥτις (which) ἦν πρὸς τὸν πατέρα καὶ ἐφανερώθη ἡμῖν (1 John 1:2).

a. What is the significance of the voice of ἐφανερώθη in this sentence? (11.2 and 11.5.d)

b. Explain the procedure of contraction in μαρτυροῦμεν. (26.1, 26.4.a, and 26.5)

c. Is ἀπαγγέλλομεν a contract or a liquid verb? (25.1 and 26.6) Distinguish the difference between the two types of verbs. (26.4 and 26.6)

7. ὃ ἑωράκαμεν καὶ ἀκηκόαμεν, ἀπαγγέλλομεν καὶ ὑμῖν, ἵνα καὶ ὑμεῖς κοινωνίαν ἔχητε μεθ᾽ ἡμῶν, καὶ ἡ κοινωνία δὲ ἡ ἡμετέρα (our) μετὰ τοῦ πατρὸς καὶ μετὰ τοῦ υἱοῦ αὐτοῦ Ἰησοῦ Χριστοῦ (1 John 1:3).

a. What mood is ἵνα usually used with? (24.1) What kind of clause does ἵνα introduce? Explain the significance of this type of clause. (24.4.c.5)

b. Locate κοινωνίαν. (5.4.a and 18.1)

PART OF SPEECH: FUNCTION IN THE SENTENCE:

CASE: GENDER: DECLENSION:

NUMBER: LEXICAL FORM:

8. καὶ ταῦτα γράφομεν ἡμεῖς, ἵνα ἡ χαρὰ ἡμῶν ᾖ πεπληρωμένη (1 John 1:4).

a. Locate ταῦτα. (7.5, 11.1, and 11.2.a)

PART OF SPEECH: FUNCTION IN THE SENTENCE:

CASE: GENDER: DECLENSION:

NUMBER: LEXICAL FORM:

b. Why is ἡμεῖς not necessary in this sentence? What is the significance of ἡμεῖς in the phrase ταῦτα γράφομεν ἡμεῖς? (9.1, 9.2, and 9.3.b)

c. List the indicators that πεπληρωμένη is a subjunctive mood verb. (24.1 and 24.3.b.1)

9. καὶ ἔστιν αὕτη ἡ ἀγγελία ἥν (which) ἀκηκόαμεν ἀπ' αὐτοῦ καὶ ἀναγγέλλομεν (we proclaim) ὑμῖν, ὅτι ὁ θεὸς φῶς ἐστιν καὶ σκοτία ἐν αὐτῷ οὐκ ἔστιν οὐδεμία (not at all) (1 John 1:5).

a. How can you determine whether ἥν is the imperfect indicative third singular form of εἰμί or the accusative singular feminine relative pronoun? (9.1, 12.2.d, 27.1, and 27.27.3.a) What is the function of ἥν in this sentence? (27.27.3.a)

b. Dissect and parse ἀκηκόαμεν. (2.1, 23.1, and 23.2)

PART OF SPEECH: AUGMENT: STEM:

TENSE: PERSON: ENDING:

VOICE: NUMBER: CONNECTING VOWEL:

MOOD: LEXICAL FORM: SUBJECT:

c. Locate οὐδεμία. (27.1 and 27.3.f)

PART OF SPEECH: **neg. prn.**   FUNCTION: **pn.** of ἔστιν
CASE: **nom.**   GENDER: **fem.**   DECLENSION: **1st**
NUMBER: **sing.**   LEXICAL FORM: οὐδείς

10. ἐὰν εἴπωμεν ὅτι κοινωνίαν ἔχομεν μετ᾽ αὐτοῦ καὶ ἐν τῷ σκότει περιπατῶμεν, ψευδόμεθα καὶ οὐ ποιοῦμεν τὴν ἀλήθειαν·   (See 1 John 1:6.).

a. What class condition is this sentence? Explain the significance of this class condition. (24.5.c)

b. Locate σκότει. (19.1 and 19.3.a)

PART OF SPEECH: FUNCTION IN THE SENTENCE:

CASE: GENDER: DECLENSION:

NUMBER: LEXICAL FORM:

c. Explain why ποιοῦμεν is classified as a contract verb. (26.1 and 26.2)

11. ἐὰν δὲ ἐν τῷ φωτί περιπατῶμεν ὡς αὐτός ἐστιν ἐν τῷ φωτὶ, κοινωνίαν ἔχομεν μετ᾽ ἀλλήλων (one another) καὶ τὸ αἷμα Ἰησοῦ τοῦ υἱοῦ αὐτοῦ καθαρίζει ἡμᾶς ἀπὸ πάσης (every) ἁμαρτίας (1 John 1:7).

a. In what case is φωτί? (4.5.e, 19.3.b, and 20.1) How can you be sure? (7.5)

b. Identify and define the case function of Ἰησοῦ in this sentence? (4.5.b and 20.1)

c. In what case is ἁμαρτίας? (5.1 and 5.4.a.1) How can you be sure of the case of ἁμαρτίας? (7.5, 8.1, and 8.4)

LESSON 27: Pronouns

27.1 Supplemental Vocabulary: None

27.2 The pronoun stands for a (n) _____. Why are pronouns used in sentences?

27.3. Review the types and give examples of pronouns studied up to this point.

27.3.a.1 _____ pronouns are used to relate one substantive to another. Pronouns agree with their antecedent in gender and number, but case is determined by their function in a clause.

27.3.a.2 Often a _____ _____ is so closely related to its antecedent that it is attracted to the case of the antecedent though the case function might be different from the _____.

27.3.a.3 Sometimes the antecedent of a relative pronoun is not _____, but is _____.

27.3.a.4 The _____ _____ _____ ὅστις is rare except in the nominative. It is sometimes translated like the relative ὅ, but also as "whoever," especially when used with ἄν. This pronoun is so named because it is _____ _____, which includes the _____ _____ τις in its form.

27.3.b The interrogative pronoun means _____ or _____ and uses the third declension endings.

27.3.c The form of the _____ _____ is declined similar to that of the interrogative pronoun, except that it is enclitic.

27.3.d The _____ pronoun ἀλλήλων represents an interchange of action between the members of a plural subject.

27.3.e The _____ _____ ἐμαυτοῦ expresses the action of the subject upon itself. This pronoun provides a way other than the middle voice to express the reflexive idea. This pronoun does <u>not</u> appear in the nominative case.

27.3.f The _____ _____ are a combination of the numerical "one" combined with the negative particles οὐδέ and μηδέ.

27.3.g Greek numerals from five to ten are _____.

27.3.h The _____ pronoun is sometimes classified as a possessive adjective since it agrees in gender, number, and case with the noun it modifies.

27.4 EXERCISES:

1. ἐὰν εἴπωμεν ὅτι ἁμαρτίαν οὐκ ἔχομεν, ἑαυτοὺς πλανῶμεν (we deceive) καὶ ἡ ἀλήθεια οὐκ ἔστιν ἐν ἡμῖν. (1 John 1:8)

   a. List the indicators that εἴπωμεν is a subjunctive mood verb. (16.1 and 24.3.b.1)

   b. What is the significance of the reflexive pronoun ἑαυτοὺς? (27.1 and 27.3.e)

   c. Is ἡμῖν dative, locative, or instrumental? (9.1 and 9.2) How can you be sure? (8.1 and 8.4) What is the significance of this case? (4.5.e)

2. ἐὰν ὁμολογῶμεν τὰς ἁμαρτίας ἡμῶν, πιστός ἐστιν καὶ δίκαιος, ἵνα ἀφῇ (he might forgive) ἡμῖν τὰς ἁμαρτίας καὶ καθαρίσῃ ἡμᾶς ἀπὸ πάσης ἀδικίας. (1 John 1:9)

   a. What class condition is expressed in this sentence? What is the significance of this class condition? (24.5.c)

   b. What is the subject of ἐστιν? How can you determine that neither πιστός nor δίκαιος is the subject of ἐστιν? (7.5, 9.1, and 9.4)

   c. In what use are the adjectives πιστός and δίκαιος? What is the significance of this use? (6.1, 6.3, and 6.4.b)

3. ἐὰν εἴπωμεν ὅτι οὐχ ἡμαρτήκαμεν, ψεύστην ποιοῦμεν αὐτὸν καὶ ὁ λόγος αὐτοῦ οὐκ ἔστιν ἐν ἡμῖν. (1 John 1:10)

a. According to Dana and Mantey, "Some verbs require more than one object to complete their meaning." ψεύστην and αὐτὸν are direct and predicate objects of ποιοῦμεν, with αὐτὸν being the direct object (Dana and Mantey, p. 94).

b. Parse ποιοῦμεν. (26.1 and 26.2)

PART OF SPEECH: TENSE: PERSON:

SUBJECT: VOICE: NUMBER:

STEM: MOOD: LEXICAL FORM:

4. Τεκνία μου, ταῦτα γράφω ὑμῖν ἵνα μὴ ἁμάρτητε. καὶ ἐάν τις ἁμάρτῃ, παράκλητον ἔχομεν πρὸς τὸν πατέρα Ἰησοῦν Χριστὸν δίκαιον· (1 John 2:1)

a. What case is Τεκνία in this sentence? (4.8.b, 7.5, and 9.1) What is the significance of this case? (4.5.h)

b. What use is ταῦτα in conjunction with the phrase ταῦτα γράφω ὑμῖν? What is the significance of this use? (10.1, 10.2.a, and 10.3.a)

c. Is τις an interrogative or indefinite pronoun? How may one differentiate the two? Why is this pronoun usually used without an accent? (27.3.c)

5. καὶ αὐτὸς ἱλασμός ἐστιν περὶ τῶν ἁμαρτιῶν ἡμῶν, οὐ περὶ τῶν ἡμετέρων (ours) δὲ μόνον ἀλλὰ καὶ περὶ ὅλου τοῦ κόσμου. (1 John 2:2)

a. Is the presence of αὐτὸς necessary in this sentence? Why or why not? (9.1, 9.2, and 9.3.b) What is the significance of the presence of αὐτὸς in this sentence? (9.3.c)

b. Locate ἡμετέρων. (28.1 and 28.2)

PART OF SPEECH: **pos. adj.**   FUNCTION IN THE SENTENCE: **obj.** of the prep. περῳ
CASE: **gen.**   GENDER: **masc.**   DECLENSION: **N/A**
NUMBER: **pl.**   LEXICAL FORM: ἡμετέρος

c. Note that ὅλου is in the classical predicate use in the phrase ὅλου τοῦ κόσμου. This adjective is translated as "all" when in the predicate position and is translated as "whole" when in the attributive position. Compare ὅλου with the use of πᾶς in lesson 28.

6. καὶ ἐν τούτῳ γινώσκομεν ὅτι ἐγνώκαμεν αὐτόν, ἐὰν τὰς ἐντολὰς αὐτοῦ τηρῶμεν. (1 John 2: 3)

a. Parse ἐγνώκαμεν. (3.1 and 23.2)

PART OF SPEECH: TENSE: PERSON:

SUBJECT: VOICE: NUMBER:

STEM: MOOD: LEXICAL FORM:

b. Is ἐντολὰς genitive singular feminine, ablative singular feminine, or accusative plural feminine? (5.1 and 5.4.a.1) How can one be sure? (5.3) By what other means can you be sure of the case of ἐντολὰς? (7.5)

c. What class verb is τηρῶμεν? (26.1) What is the significance of this class of verbs? (26.2)

7. ὁ λέγων ὅτι Ἔγνωκα αὐτὸν καὶ τὰς ἐντολὰς αὐτοῦ μὴ τηρῶν, ψεύστης ἐστὶν καὶ ἐν τούτῳ ἡ ἀλήθεια οὐκ ἔστιν· (1 John 2:4)

a. What use is the participle λέγων in this sentence? What is the significance of this use in this sentence? (20.7.b.2)

b. What is the function of the perfect tense Ἔγνωκα? (23.4)

c. Locate ψεύστης. (5.4.b.2 and 20.1)

PART OF SPEECH: FUNCTION IN THE SENTENCE:

CASE: GENDER: DECLENSION:

NUMBER: LEXICAL FORM:

8. ὃς δ᾽ ἂν τηρῇ αὐτοῦ τὸν λόγον, ἀληθῶς ἐν τούτῳ ἡ ἀγάπη τοῦ θεοῦ τετελείωται, ἐν τούτῳ γινώσκομεν ὅτι ἐν αὐτῷ ἐσμεν. (1 John 2:5)

a. What classification of relative pronoun is ὅς in this sentence? Explain the significance and identifying feature of this relative pronoun. (27.1 and 27.3.a)

b. What three ideas does the perfect tense verb τετελείωται convey? (23.4)

c. What is the antecedent of the first occurrence of τούτῳ? What about the second occurrence of τούτῳ? (Note that these do not have the same antecedent.) What criteria does αὐτοῦ meet in association with its antecedent? (7.5, 9.1, 9.2, and 9.3.a)

9. ὁ λέγων ἐν αὐτῷ μένειν ὀφείλει καθὼς ἐκεῖνος περιεπάτησεν καὶ αὐτὸς [οὕτως] περιπατεῖν. (1 John 2:6)

a. Dissect and parse λέγων. (3.1 and 20.4)

PART OF SPEECH: TENSE: CASE:

STEM: VOICE: NUMBER:

LEXICAL FORM: VERBAL FORM: GENDER:

CONNECTING VOWEL: PART. SIGN: ENDING:

b. What use is ἐκεῖνος in this sentence? Explain the significance of this use. How should ἐκεῖνος be translated in the phrase καθὼς ἐκεῖνος περιεπάτησεν? (10.1, 10.2.b, 10.3.a)

c. Parse περιπατεῖν. (15.2 and 26.1)

PART OF SPEECH: TENSE: PERSON:

SUBJECT: VOICE: NUMBER:

STEM: MOOD: LEXICAL FORM:

LESSON 28: Irregular Adjectives and Adverbs

28.1 Supplemental vocabulary:

ἄρτι - at the present moment,
  now (adv. of time)
βίος, ὁ - life, means of living,
  sustenance

ἕως - while, as long as, until
  (conj. of time)

28.2 The examples of _____ in this lesson do not follow the regular pattern of declension.

28.2.a.1 The declension of πᾶς, πᾶσα, and πᾶν follows the _____ declension in the masculine and neuter gender and the _____ declension in the feminine gender.

28.2.a.2 MATCH THE FOLLOWING USES OF THE IRREGULAR ADJECTIVE:

___ "everyone who believes"   a. Predicate use with a noun: πᾶσα ἡ πόλις

___ "the whole city"   b. With a single anarthrous noun: πᾶσα πόλις

___ "all the city"   c. Attributive use with a noun: ἡ πᾶσα πόλις

___ "every city"   d. Predicate use with a participle: πᾶς ὁ πιστεύον

28.2.b The declension of μέγας, μεγάλη, μέγα and πολύς, πολλή, πολύ generally follows the _____ declension in the masculine and neuter, but in the nominative and accusative of these genders, they have some short, irregular forms.

28.2.c.1 The declension of ἀληθής, ἀληθές follows the _____ declension nouns γένος, γένους. The masculine and feminine have the same endings and the neuter has a separate set of endings.

28.2.c.2 The stem of the adjective ἀληθής, ἀληθές is _____. In most of its forms, the final ___ of the stem is dropped and the stem vowel ___ contracts with the ending.

28.3.a Review the three degrees of Greek adjectives. In terms of English usage of adjectives, define the distinction of these three degrees.

28.3.b When an adjective is regular it will add _____, _____, _____ to the stem for the comparative forms and _____, _____, _____ to the stem for the superlative.

28.3.c TRUE/FALSE: Superlative forms are plentiful in the New Testament; however, the superlative idea is also expressed by the comparative forms. Explain your answer.

28.3.d How can you determine the stem of irregular adjectives? Why is the location of the stem of irregular adjectives somewhat difficult?

28.4.a Adverbs are closely related to adjectives in _____ and _____.

28.4.b What ideas do adverbs in both Greek and English express?

28.4.c Adverbs have fixed forms and are not declined according to _____ and _____.

28.4.d Some adverbs are derived from the _____ _____ form of the adjective, substituting a ____ for the ____. Give an example of this phenomenon.

28.4.e Some adverbs ending in _____ will also form the comparative and superlative with the same endings adjectives use, _____ for the comparative and _____ for the superlative.

28.4.f Other adverbs reflect fixed endings in other cases of _____, _____, or _____. The endings of others appear to be unrelated to a _____ _____.

28.4.g How must one learn adverbs and why in this manner? With what ending do most adverbs end?

28.4.h Like prepositions, adverbs are used as _____ for nouns and verbs. (See 8.4 of the textbook.)

28.5 EXERCISES:

28.5.a Review the adverbs you have learned up to this point.

28.5.b Translate the following verses from 1 John 2:7-17 and answer the grammatical questions.

1. Ἀγαπητοί, οὐκ ἐντολὴν καινὴν γράφω ὑμῖν ἀλλ' ἐντολὴν παλαιὰν ἣν εἴχετε ἀπ' ἀρχῆς· ἡ ἐντολὴ ἡ παλαιά ἐστιν ὁ λόγος ὃν ἠκούσατε. (1 John 2:7)

a. What case is Ἀγαπητοί in this sentence? (4.8.a, 6.1, and 7.5) What is the significance of this case? (4.5.h)

b. What use is the adjective καινὴν in the phrase οὐκ ἐντολὴν καινὴν γράφω ὑμῖν? (6.1 and 6.3) What about the adjective παλαιὰν in the phrase ἀλλ' ἐντολὴν παλαιὰν ἣν? (6.3 and 28.1) What is the significance of this use? (6.4.a)

c. Is ἣν an imperfect form of εἰμί or a relative pronoun? (27.1 and 27.3.a) How can you be sure? (7.5, 12.2.d, and 27.3.a)

d. What is the use of λόγος in the phrase ἡ ἐντολὴ ἡ παλαιά ἐστιν ὁ λόγος? What is the significance of this use? (9.4)

2. πάλιν ἐντολὴν καινὴν γράφω ὑμῖν, ὃ ἐστιν ἀληθὲς ἐν αὐτῷ καὶ ἐν ὑμῖν, ὅτι ἡ σκοτία παράγεται καὶ τὸ φῶς τὸ ἀληθινὸν ἤδη φαίνει. (1 John 2:8)

a. Is ὃ a nominative singular masculine definite article or a nominative singular neuter relative pronoun? (27.1 and 27.3.a) How can you be sure? (4.3 and 27.3.a)

b. Is the presence of the verb of being ἐστιν necessary in the phrase ὃ ἐστιν ἀληθὲς? Why or why not? What is the significance of the presence of ἐστιν in this phrase? (9.4)

c. Is ἀληθινὸν a regular, a comparative, or a superlative adjective form? How can you be sure? What is the significance of this form? (28.1 and 28.3)

3. ὁ λέγων ἐν τῷ φωτὶ εἶναι καὶ τὸν ἀδελφὸν αὐτοῦ μισῶν ἐν τῇ σκοτίᾳ ἐστιν ἕως ἄρτι. (1 John 2:9)

     a. What use is λέγων in this sentence? What is the significance of this use in this sentence? (20.7.b.2)

     b. List all of the factors that you may consider in determining the case, number, and gender of φωτὶ. (4.3, 8.1, 8.4, 19.3.b, and 20.1)

     c. Is the phrase μισῶν ἐν τῇ σκοτίᾳ ἐστιν a periphrastic construction? On what do you base your answer? What is the significance of the periphrastic construction? (20.7.b.3)

4. ὁ ἀγαπῶν τὸν ἀδελφὸν αὐτοῦ ἐν τῷ φωτὶ μένει καὶ σκάνδαλον ἐν αὐτῷ οὐκ ἔστιν· (1 John 2:10)

     a. Transliterate this sentence. (1.1 and 1.4)

     b. How is ἐν translated in this sentence? What case is this preposition translated with in this sentence? On what do you base your answer? (7.5, 8.1, and 8.4)

     c. How can you determine that σκάνδαλον is a nominative case noun? (4.6, 4.8.b, 9.4, and 20.1)

5. ὁ δὲ μισῶν τὸν τὸν ἀδελφὸν αὐτοῦ ἐν τῇ σκοτίᾳ ἐστὶν καὶ ἐν τῇ σκοτίᾳ περιπατεῖ καὶ οὐκ οἶδεν ποῦ ὑπάγει, ὅτι ἡ σκοτία ἐτύφλωσεν τοὺς ὀφθαλμοὺς αὐτοῦ. (1 John 2:11)

a. Note the two similar forms: σκοτία "darkness" (12.1) and σκότος, σκότους "darkness" (19.1) as used in this sentence. The former is a nominative singular feminine first declension form whereas, the latter is a nominative singular neuter third declension form.

b. Dissect and parse οἶδεν. (23.1 and 23.2)

PART OF SPEECH: REDUPLICATION: STEM:

TENSE: PERSON: TENSE SIGN: **THIS VERB DOES NOT USE THE TENSE SIGN**

VOICE: NUMBER: ENDING:

MOOD: LEXICAL FORM: SUBJECT:

c. What part of speech is ποῦ? (28.1) What idea does this word express? (28.4)

d. Is the augment of ἐτύφλωσεν temporal or syllabic? (12.2.b.1) Explain the difference between the two kinds of augments. (12.2.b.1-2)

6. Γράφω ὑμῖν, τεκνία, ὅτι ἀφέωνται (are forgiven) ὑμῖν αἱ ἁμαρτίαι διὰ τὸ ὄνομα αὐτοῦ. (1 John 2:12)

a. How is διὰ translated in this sentence? On what do you base your answer? (8.1, 8.4, and 19.3.b)

b. Locate ὄνομα. (4.3, 19.1, and 19.3.b)

PART OF SPEECH: FUNCTION IN THE SENTENCE:

CASE: GENDER: DECLENSION:

NUMBER: LEXICAL FORM:

c. Is the antecedent of αὐτοῦ stated in this sentence? On what do you base your answer? (9.1, 9.2, and 9.3.a)

7. γράφω ὑμῖν, πατέρες, ὅτι ἐγνώκατε τὸν ἀπ' ἀρχῆς. γράφω ὑμῖν, νεανίσκοι, ὅτι νενικήκατε τὸν πονηρόν. (1 John 2:13)

a. In the phrase γράφω ὑμῖν, is ὑμῖν dative, locative, or instrumental? Explain the significance of this case in this sentence. (4.5.d, 7.5, 9.1, and 9.2)

b. Note that the occurrence of τὸν in the phrase ὅτι ἐγνώκατε τὸν ἀπ' ἀρχῆς is an example of the substantival use of the definite article and is translated as "the one." (See 30.3 of the textbook.)

c. Dissect and parse ἐγνώκατε. (3.1 and 23.2)

PART OF SPEECH:	REDUPLICATION:	STEM:
TENSE:	PERSON:	TENSE SIGN:
VOICE:	NUMBER:	ENDING:
MOOD:	LEXICAL FORM:	SUBJECT:

8. ἔγραψα ὑμῖν, παιδία, ὅτι ἐγνώκατε τὸν πατέρα. ἔγραψα ὑμῖν, πατέρες, ὅτι ἐγνώκατε τὸν ἀπ' ἀρχῆς. ἔγραψα ὑμῖν, νεανίσκοι, ὅτι ἰσχυροί ἐστε καὶ ὁ λόγος τοῦ θεοῦ ἐν ὑμῖν μένει καὶ νενικήκατε τὸν πονηρόν. (1 John 2:14)

a. Is the case function of ὑμῖν a matter of accidence or syntax? Explain. (7.2)

b. Locate πατέρα. (18.1 and 18.3)

PART OF SPEECH:	FUNCTION IN THE SENTENCE:	
CASE:	GENDER:	DECLENSION:
NUMBER:	LEXICAL FORM:	

9. Μὴ ἀγαπᾶτε τὸν κόσμον μηδὲ τὰ ἐν τῷ κόσμῳ. ἐάν τις ἀγαπᾷ τὸν κόσμον, οὐκ ἔστιν ἡ ἀγάπη τοῦ πατρὸς ἐν αὐτῷ· (1 John 2:15)

a. Why is Μὴ used to negate ἀγαπᾶτε rather than οὐκ? (9.1, 9.5, and 21.1)

b. In what use is the imperative verb ἀγαπᾶτε? (25.3.b) What is the significance of this use? (25.3)

c. Is τις an interrogative or an indefinite pronoun? On what do you base your answer? (27.3.c)

10. ὅτι πᾶν τὸ ἐν τῷ κόσμῳ, ἡ ἐπιθυμία τῆς σαρκὸς καὶ ἡ ἐπιθυμία τῶν ὀφθαλμῶν καὶ ἡ ἀλαζονεία τοῦ βίου, οὐκ ἔστιν ἐκ τοῦ πατρὸς ἀλλ' ἐκ τοῦ κόσμου ἐστίν. (1 John 2:16)

a. Is ὅτι a coordinating or a subordinating conjunction? What is the significance of this kind of conjunction? (13.3.a)

b. Locate πᾶν. (28.1 and 28.28.2.a)

PART OF SPEECH: FUNCTION IN THE SENTENCE:

CASE: GENDER: DECLENSION:

NUMBER: LEXICAL FORM:

c. How can you determine the gender of ὀφθαλμῶν? Why is the determination of the gender of ὀφθαλμῶν problematic? (4.3, 4.6, 4.8.a and 21.1)

d. Why does πατρὸς have a genitive/ablative definite article when this noun appears to be nominative singular masculine? (19.1 and 18.3)

11. καὶ ὁ κόσμος παράγεται καὶ ἡ ἐπιθυμία αὐτοῦ, ὁ δὲ ποιῶν τὸ θέλημα τοῦ θεοῦ μένει εἰς τὸν αἰῶνα. (1 John 2:17)

a. Dissect and parse παράγεται. (11.3 and 28.1)

PART OF SPEECH: AUGMENT: STEM:

TENSE: PERSON: ENDING:

VOICE: NUMBER: CONNECTING VOWEL:

MOOD: LEXICAL FORM: SUBJECT:

b. Locate ἐπιθυμία. (5.3, 5.4.a.1, and 22.1)

PART OF SPEECH: .   FUNCTION IN THE SENTENCE:

CASE: GENDER: DECLENSION:

NUMBER: LEXICAL FORM:

c. What is the subject of μένει? On what do you base your answer? (3.3, 7.5, and 20.7.b.2)

LESSON 29: Verbs of the μι Conjugation

29.1 Supplemental vocabulary:

ἐπαγγέλλω - I promise   χρίσμα, -ατος, τό - anointing

29.2.1 Verbs that are in the -ω conjugation are called the _____ conjugation. Why?

29.2.2 Verbs that are in the -μι conjugation are called the _____ conjugation. Why?

29.2.3 Why was it necessary for Sawyer to list all of the principle parts of the -μι conjugation verbs?

29.2.a and b Review the characteristics of -μι conjugation verbs that make them different from the -ω conjugation verbs.

29.2.c.1 Verbs of the -μι conjugation in the present active use a _____ vowel in the singular and a _____ vowel in the plural. Verbs of the -μι conjugation in the present middle/passive use a _____ vowel in the singular in the plural.

29.2.c.2 Verbs of the conjugation in the imperfect active use a _____ vowel in the singular and a _____ vowel in the plural. Verbs of the -μι conjugation in the imperfect middle/passive use a _____ vowel in the singular in the plural.

29.2.d When the alteration of long and short vowels occur, you know the basic stem vowel, which is ___ for δίδιωμι, ___ for ἵστημι, and ___ for τίθημι.

29.3 Review the paradigms of δίδιωμι, ἵστημι, and τίθημι.

29.4 EXERCISES:

1. Παιδία, ἐσχάτη ὥρα ἐστίν, καὶ καθὼς ἠκούσατε ὅτι ἀντίχριστος ἔρχεται, καὶ νῦν ἀντίχριστοι πολλοὶ γεγόνασιν, ὅθεν γινώσκομεν ὅτι ἐσχάτη ὥρα ἐστίν. (1 John 2:18)

a. ἐσχάτη ὥρα is translated as if a definite article is present. (Note 30.5 of the textbook.) The absence of the definite article emphasizes quality and essence.

b. Explain why ἔρχεται is translated as active voice, but is a middle form. (11.1, 11.3, and 11.4.d)

c. In what use is πολλοί? What is the significance of this use? (6.4.a, 28.1, and 28.2.b) How can you be sure of this use based on the absence of the definite article? (7.5)

2. ἐξ ἡμῶν ἐξῆλθαν ἀλλ' οὐκ ἦσαν ἐξ ἡμῶν· εἰ γὰρ ἐξ ἡμῶν ἦσαν, μεμενήκεισαν ἂν μεθ' ἡμῶν· ἀλλ' ἵνα φανερωθῶσιν ὅτι οὐκ εἰσὶν πάντες ἐξ ἡμῶν. (1 John 2:19)

a. What is the significance of the construction of the compound verb ἐξῆλθαν preceded by ἐξ? Is the double appearance of ἐξ (ἐκ) translated twice? (8.1, 8.4, and 8.6)

b. List the factors which confirm that μεμενήκεισαν is a perfect tense verb. (7.1 and 23.2.a and b)

c. List the factors which confirm that φανερωθῶσιν is a subjunctive mood verb. (24.1, 24.3.b.1, and 24.3.c.1)

3. καὶ ὑμεῖς χρῖσμα ἔχετε ἀπὸ τοῦ ἁγίου καὶ οἴδατε πάντες. (1 John 2:20)

a. What case is χρῖσμα in? (See 19.3.b of the textbook and 24.1 of the workbook.) What is the significance of this case? (4.5.g)

b. In what use is πάντες? What is the significance of this use? (6.4.c, 28.1, and 28.2.b)

c. Explain the unusual point of accidence concerning οἴδατε. (23.1)

4. οὐκ ἔγραψα ὑμῖν ὅτι οὐκ οἴδατε τὴν ἀλήθειαν ἀλλ' ὅτι οἴδατε αὐτὴν καὶ ὅτι πᾶν ψεῦδος ἐκ τῆς ἀληθείας οὐκ ἔστιν. (1 John 2:21)

a. What is the function of οὐκ in this sentence? (9.1 and 9.5) Why use the οὐκ form rather than οὐ or μή? (9.1 and 21.1)

b. Why is αὐτὴν translated into English as if neuter, but in reality it is feminine? What is the antecedent of αὐτὴν? What criteria does αὐτὴν meet in association with its antecedent? (9.1, 9.2, and 9.3.a)

c. How is πᾶν ψεῦδος translated in this sentence? What mandates this translation? (28.a.3)

5. τίς ἐστιν ὁ ψεύστης εἰ μὴ ὁ ἀρνούμενος ὅτι Ἰησοῦς οὐκ ἔστιν ὁ Χριστός; οὗτός ἐστιν ὁ ἀντίχριστος, ὁ ἀρνούμενος τὸν πατέρα καὶ τὸν υἱόν. (1 John 2:22)

a. Why does the apparent genitive/ablative singular feminine noun ψεύστης use a nominative singular masculine definite article? (4.3, 5.4.b.2, and 20.1)

b. Note that εἰ μὴ is an idiom that is translated "except." (See 21.1 of the workbook.)

c. Why must the verb of being ἔστιν be present in the phrase οὗτός ἐστιν ὁ ἀντίχριστος, in order to obtain the predicate use in the translation of this phrase? (6.4.b, 10.1, 10.2.a, and 10.3.b)

6. πᾶς ὁ ἀρνούμενος τὸν υἱὸν οὐδὲ τὸν πατέρα ἔχει, ὁ ὁμολογῶν τὸν υἱὸν καὶ τὸν πατέρα ἔχει. (1 John 2:23)

a. How is the participle ἀρνούμενος used in this sentence? What is the significance of this use? (20.7.b.2 and 29.1)

b. What is the function of οὐδὲ in this sentence? (13.1 and 13.3.a)

c. Locate πατέρα. (18.1 and 18.3)

PART OF SPEECH: FUNCTION IN THE SENTENCE:

CASE: GENDER: DECLENSION:

NUMBER: LEXICAL FORM:

7. ὑμεῖς ὃ ἠκούσατε ἀπ᾽ ἀρχῆς, ἐν ὑμῖν μενέτω. ἐὰν ἐν ὑμῖν μείνῃ ὃ ἀπ᾽ ἀρχῆς ἠκούσατε, καὶ ὑμεῖς ἐν τῷ υἱῷ καὶ ἐν τῷ πατρὶ μενεῖτε. (1 John 2:24)

a. Distinguish the reality or potentiality of the imperative mood verb μενέτω and the subjunctive mood verb μείνῃ. (24.2 and 25.3)

b. Parse μενεῖτε. (7.1 and 24.2)

PART OF SPEECH: TENSE: PERSON:

SUBJECT: VOICE: NUMBER:

STEM: MOOD: LEXICAL FORM:

8. καὶ αὕτη ἐστὶν ἡ ἐπαγγελία ἣν αὐτὸς ἐπηγγείλατο ἡμῖν, τὴν ζωὴν τὴν αἰώνιον. (1 John 2:25)

a. According to rules of Greek syntax, is αὕτη or ἐπαγγελία the subject of ἐστὶν? On what do you base your answer? (7.5 and 9.4)

b. Is αὕτη a nominative singular feminine personal pronoun or a nominative singular feminine demonstrative pronoun? How can you be sure? (7.5, 10.1, and 10.2.a)

c. Is ἦν an imperfect form of εἰμί or an accusative singular feminine relative pronoun? How can you be sure? (12.3.d and 27.3.a)

9. ταῦτα ἔγραψα ὑμῖν περὶ τῶν πλανώντων ὑμᾶς. (1 John 2:26)

a. Why does the stem consonant (φ) of γράφω change to (ψ) in ἔγραψα? (3.1, 14.3.b.2, and 15.2)

b. How is περὶ translated in this sentence? On what do you base your answer? (7.5, 8.1, and 8.4)

c. Dissect and parse πλανώντων. (20.2 and 27.1)

PART OF SPEECH: TENSE: CASE:

STEM: VOICE: NUMBER:

LEXICAL FORM: VERBAL FORM: GENDER:

CONNECTING VOWEL: PART. SIGN: ENDING:

10. καὶ ὑμεῖς τὸ χρῖσμα ὃ ἐλάβετε ἀπ᾽ αὐτοῦ, μένει ἐν ὑμῖν καὶ οὐ χρείαν ἔχετε ἵνα τις διδάσκῃ ὑμᾶς, ἀλλ᾽ ὡς τὸ αὐτοῦ χρῖσμα διδάσκει ὑμᾶς περὶ πάντων καὶ ἀληθές ἐστιν καὶ οὐκ ἔστιν ψεῦδος, καὶ καθὼς ἐδίδαξεν ὑμᾶς, μένετε ἐν αὐτῷ. (1 John 2:27)

a. Is this verse an example of a simple, a compound, or a complex sentence? Explain. (7.4.d)

b. What kind of clause does ἵνα introduce? What is the significance of this kind of clause? (13.3.a)

c. Is πάντων a positive, a comparative, or a superlative adjective? What is the significance of this type of adjective? (28.1 and 28.3)

d. Parse ἐδίδαξεν. (3.1, 15.1, and 15.2)

PART OF SPEECH: TENSE: PERSON:

SUBJECT: VOICE: NUMBER:

STEM: MOOD: LEXICAL FORM:

LESSON 30: The Article

30.1 Supplemental vocabulary:

ὅμοιος, -α, -ον - like, similar, resembling (adj.)

30.2.a The Greek definite article (ὁ, ἡ, τό), in its origin, was probably a(n) _____ _____ and often retains this usage in the New Testament.

30.2.b Greek does not have an indefinite article. Occasionally the _____ _____ τις, τι appears instead of an indefinite article.

30.2.c List the three purposes of the definite article.

a.   c.

b.

30.2.d When the definite article is present, it emphasizes _____; and when it is absent, the emphasis is usually _____ and not specificity.

30.2.e When the divine _____ is intended, a writer will use ὁ θεός; when the divine _____ or _____ of God is meant, θεός is used.

30.3.a Review the ordinary uses of the definite article.

30.3.b Sometimes the definite article has the force of a(n) _____ _____. (See also 30.2.a above.)

30.4.a When two nouns are joined by the conjunction καί, if both nouns have a definite article, they refer to _____ _____.

30.4.b When two nouns are joined by the conjunction καί, if the first of the two nouns has the definite article and the second does not, the two are _____ _____.

30.4.c Review the additional specific uses of the definite article.

30.4.d The article helps determine the _____ and the _____ with substantives joined by εἰμί.

30.4.d.1 In clauses or sentences with substantives joined by εἰμί, if only one of the substantives has the definite article, the substantive with the definite article is the _____ and the other substantive is the _____.

30.4.d.2 If both substantives have a definite article, they are interchangeable as to _____ and _____.

30.5.a Greek writers usually included the definite article when they wanted to _____ and _____, and did not include the definite article when the emphasis was _____ and _____.

30.5.b True/False: In no case is the meaning of a word so definite that the definite article is not included.

30.5.c Whenever the definite article is present the object is _____; and when the definite article is absent, the object may be _____ or _____.

30.6 EXERCISES:

1. Καὶ νῦν, τεκνία, μένετε ἐν αὐτῷ, ἵνα ἐὰν φανερωθῇ σχῶμεν (2nd aor. of ἔχω) παρρησίαν καὶ μὴ αἰσχυνθῶμεν ἀπ' αὐτοῦ ἐν τῇ παρουσίᾳ αὐτοῦ. (1 John 2:28)

  a. Is μένετε a second person plural present active indicative or a second person plural present active imperative verb? How can you be sure? (3.3, 7.1, 25.2, and 25.4)

  b. What mood is ἵνα usually used with? (24.1) What kind of clause does ἵνα introduce? (13.3.a) Explain the significance of this type of clause. (13.3.a)

  c. What elements identify αἰσχυνθῶμεν as a subjunctive mood verb? (24.1 and 24.4.b.1)

2. ἐὰν εἰδῆτε ὅτι δίκαιός ἐστιν, γινώσκετε ὅτι καὶ πᾶς ὁ ποιῶν τὴν δικαιοσύνην ἐξ αὐτοῦ γεγέννηται. (1 John 2:29)

a. Is ὅτι a coordinating or a subordinating conjunction? What is the significance of this conjunction? (10.1 and 13.3.a)

b. Is the noun δικαιοσύνην definite or indefinite? How can you be sure? (30.3 and 30.5)

3. ἴδετε ποταπὴν ἀγάπην δέδωκεν ἡμῖν ὁ πατήρ, ἵνα τέκνα θεοῦ κληθῶμεν, καὶ ἐσμέν. διὰ τοῦτο ὁ κόσμος οὐ γινώσκει ἡμᾶς, ὅτι οὐκ ἔγνω (2nd. aor. of γινώσκω) αὐτόν. (1 John 3:1)

a. In what use is the adjective ποταπὴν in the above sentence? What is the significance of these use in these sentences? (See 6.3 and 6.4.a of the textbook and 30.1 of the workbook.) How can you be sure since the definite article is not present? (7.5)

b. Is θεοῦ definite or indefinite? Why is the presence of the definite article not necessary? (4.3, 7.1, and 30.5)

c. Is τοῦτο a nominative or an accusative singular neuter demonstrative pronoun? How can you be sure? (7.5, 8.1, 8.4, 10.1, and 10.2.a)

4. Ἀγαπητοί, νῦν τέκνα θεοῦ ἐσμεν, καὶ οὔπω ἐφανερώθη τί ἐσόμεθα. οἴδαμεν ὅτι ἐὰν φανερωθῇ, ὅμοιοι αὐτῷ ἐσόμεθα, ὅτι ὀψόμεθα (fut. of ὁράω) αὐτὸν καθώς ἐστιν. (1 John 3:2)

a. Explain the unusual point of accidence concerning οἴδαμεν. (23.1)

b. What use is the adjective ὅμοιοι in? What is the significance of this use? (See 6.3 and 6.4.c of the textbook and 30.1 of the workbook.) What is the use of ὅμοιοι in relation to ἐσόμεθα? (9.4)

c. Parse ἐσόμεθα. (14.2 and 26.1.2)

PART OF SPEECH: TENSE: PERSON:

SUBJECT: VOICE: NUMBER:

STEM: MOOD: LEXICAL FORM:

5. καὶ πᾶς ὁ ἔχων τὴν ἐλπίδα ταύτην ἐπ' αὐτῷ ἁγνίζει ἑαυτόν, καθὼς ἐκεῖνος ἁγνός ἐστιν. (1 John 3:3)

  a. What is the significance of καὶ in relation to the previous verse? (13.3.a)

  b. Is πᾶς a regular, a comparative, or a superlative adjective? What is the significance of this type of adjective? (28.1 and 28.3)

  c. In the phrase ἐκεῖνος ἁγνός ἐστιν, how are you able to determine the subject and predicate nominative of ἐστιν? (7.5) What is missing that usually aids in the identification of the subject and compliment? (9.4 and 30.4)

6. Πᾶς ὁ ποιῶν τὴν ἁμαρτίαν καὶ τὴν ἀνομίαν ποιεῖ, καὶ ἡ ἁμαρτία ἐστὶν ἡ ἀνομία. (1 John 3:4)

  a. Is ποιῶν an verbal or adjectival participle? (20.7.b) What is the significance of the use of this participle? (20.7.b.2)

  b. How can you distinguish between a third singular present active indicative regular -ω conjugation verb and a third singular present active indicative contract verb? (3.3, 26.4.c, and 26.5)

c. What is the significance of the presence of the definite article with both nouns in the phrase ἡ ἁμαρτία ἐστὶν ἡ ἀνομία? (9.4 and 30.4)

7. καὶ οἴδατε ὅτι ἐκεῖνος ἐφανερώθη, ἵνα τὰς ἁμαρτίας ἄρῃ (aor. subj. of αἴρω), καὶ ἁμαρτία ἐν αὐτῷ οὐκ ἔστιν. (1 John 3:5)

a. State the reasons why ἐκεῖνος cannot be the subject of οἴδατε. (3.2.d and e, 7.5, 10.1, 10.2.b, and 23.2)

b. What clues indicate that ἐφανερώθη is a first aorist passive indicative verb? (15.2 and 17.2)

8. πᾶς ὁ ἐν αὐτῷ μένων οὐχ ἁμαρτάνει· πᾶς ὁ ἁμαρτάνων οὐχ ἑώρακεν (perf. of ὁράω) αὐτὸν οὐδὲ ἔγνωκεν (perf. of γινώσκω) αὐτόν. (1 John 3:6)

a. How is πᾶς used in this sentence? (28.1 and 28.2.a.4) In what use is πᾶς in the phrase πᾶς ὁ ἐν αὐτῷ μένων? What is the significance of this use? (6.4.b)

b. What part of speech is οὐδὲ? Explain the significance of the use of οὐδὲ in this sentence. (13.3.d)

c. Dissect and parse ἔγνωκεν. (3.1, 23.1, and 23.2)

PART OF SPEECH: REDUPLICATION: STEM:

TENSE: PERSON: TENSE SIGN:

VOICE: NUMBER: ENDING:

MOOD: LEXICAL FORM: SUBJECT:

9. Τεκνία, μηδεὶς πλανάτω ὑμᾶς· ὁ ποιῶν τὴν δικαιοσύνην δίκαιός ἐστιν, καθὼς ἐκεῖνος δίκαιός ἐστιν· (1 John 3:7)

  a. Locate Τεκνία. (4.5.h, 4.8.b, 7.5, and 9.1)

PART OF SPEECH: FUNCTION IN THE SENTENCE:

CASE: GENDER: DECLENSION:

NUMBER: LEXICAL FORM:

  b. With what mood is μηδεὶς not usually used with? (27.1) Explain the formation of μηδεὶς. (27.3.f)

  c. What is unusual concerning the number of the subject of πλανάτω in comparison of this mood in Greek and the normal usage of this mood in English? (25.3) What other mood function does the translation of this verb resemble? (24.4.c.1)

10. ὁ ποιῶν τὴν ἁμαρτίαν ἐκ τοῦ διαβόλου ἐστίν, ὅτι ἀπ᾽ ἀρχῆς ὁ διάβολος ἁμαρτάνει, εἰς τοῦτο ἐφανερώθη ὁ υἱός τοῦ θεοῦ, ἵνα λύσῃ τὰ ἔργα τοῦ διαβόλου. (1 John 3:8)

  a. Is ὁ a nominative singular masculine definite article or a nominative/accusative singular neuter relative pronoun? How can you be sure? (4.3 and 27.3.a)

  b. Is the first use of διαβόλου genitive or ablative singular? (4.5.c, 4.8.a, and 30.1) How does ἐκ help determine the case of διαβόλου in this sentence? (8.1 and 8.4)

  c. Why is the definite article translated in the phrase ὅτι ἀπ᾽ ἀρχῆς and there is no definite article present? (30.5)

11. Πᾶς ὁ γεγεννημένος ἐκ τοῦ θεοῦ ἁμαρτίαν οὐ ποιεῖ, ὅτι σπέρμα αὐτοῦ ἐν αὐτῷ μένει, καὶ οὐ δύναται ἁμαρτάνειν, ὅτι ἐκ τοῦ θεοῦ γεγέννηται. (1 John 3:9)

a. What would cause you to suspect that ποιεῖ is not a third singular present active indicative regular -ω conjugation verb? (3.3.a, 26.1, 26.3, and 26.5)

b. Is ἁμαρτάνειν a verb form, a noun, or an adjective? Explain. (3.3, 11.1, and 31.2)

c. Why is γεγέννηται translated as if it were a perfect active and it appears as perfect middle in form? Explain. (11.4.d and 23.2)

12. ἐν τούτῳ φανερά ἐστιν τὰ τέκνα τοῦ θεοῦ καὶ τὰ τέκνα τοῦ διαβόλου· πᾶς ὁ μὴ ποιῶν δικαιοσύνην οὐκ ἔστιν ἐκ τοῦ θεοῦ, καὶ ὁ μὴ ἀγαπῶν τὸν ἀδελφὸν αὐτοῦ. (1 John 3:10)

a. Is τούτῳ dative, locative, or instrumental? (4.5.e, 8.1, 10.1, and 10.2.a) How can you be sure? (7.5 and 8.4)

b. The two occurrences of the plural τέκνα are subjects of ἐστιν (a third singular verb). Explain this phenomenon. (9.4 and 10.4 of the textbook and 10.4 of the workbook)

c. Why is it appropriate to negate ποιῶν and ἀγαπῶν with μὴ rather than οὐ or οὐκ? (9.1 and 21.1)

LESSON 31: The Infinitive

31.1 Supplemental vocabulary:

Κάϊν, ὁ - Cain

31.2.a In Greek the infinitive is a _____ _____, whereas the participle is a _____ _____. In English the infinitive is expressed with _____ preceding the verb.

31.2.b The Greek infinitive has aspects of both a _____ and _____ and functions both ways.

31.2.c The Greek infinitive has _____ and _____ like a verb, but not _____ and _____.

31.2.d The infinitive is usually classified with _____; however, it probably originated as a(n) _____ becoming fixed, often in the _____ case.

31.2.e Distinguish between finite and non-finite verbs.

31.3.a What four tenses does the infinitive appear in?

1.   3.

3.   4.

31.3.b The four tenses in which the infinitive appears are built on their given tense stem with the exception of the aorist passive, which adds _____ to the augmented present stem and the future passive, which adds _____ to the present stem.

31.3.c Why are the endings of the infinitive predictable?

31.4.1 Tense in the infinitive has to do primarily with _____ of action rather than _____ of action.

31.4.2 What kinds of action are expressed by the infinitive, and what tenses are associated with these kinds of action?

31.4.3 When does time come into consideration with the infinitive?

31.4.a.1 Review the characteristics of the infinitive as a verb.

31.4.a.2 Occasionally, the infinitive is used as a finite verb with a subject accusative and may be used _____.

31.4.b.1 Review the characteristics of the infinitive as a noun.

31.4.b.2 The article will usually accompany the infinitive when it is combined with a _____.

31.4.b.3 The presence of the definite article stands as evidence of the infinitive as a _____.

31.5 EXERCISES:

1. Ὅτι αὕτη ἐστὶν ἡ ἀγγελία ἥν ἠκούσατε ἀπ' ἀρχῆς, ἵνα ἀγαπῶμεν ἀλλήλους (1 John 3:11).

a. Why is the relative pronoun ἥν, not be the subject of ἠκούσατε? (3.2.d and e, 7.5, 9.3.b, 15.1, 15.2, 27.1, and 27.3.a)

b. What use of the subjunctive is ἀγαπῶμεν? What is the significance of this use? (24.4.c.5 and 28.1)

c. What kind of pronoun is ἀλλήλους, and what is the significance of this pronoun? (27.1 and 27.3.d)

2. οὐ καθὼς Κάϊν (Cain) ἐκ τοῦ πονηροῦ ἦν καὶ ἔσφαξεν τὸν ἀδελφὸν αὐτοῦ· καὶ χάριν τίνος ἔσφαξεν αὐτόν; ὅτι τὰ ἔργα αὐτοῦ πονηρὰ ἦν τὰ δὲ τοῦ ἀδελφοῦ αὐτοῦ δίκαια. (1 John 3:12)

    a. Explain the significance of the ¨ over the ι in the word Κάϊν. (2.5)

    b. What type of aorist is ἔσφαξεν? What is the significance of this type of aorist? (15.3.a)

    c. What is the use of the definite article τὰ in the phrase τὰ δὲ τοῦ ἀδελφοῦ αὐτοῦ δίκαια? Explain the significance of this use. (30.3) What word is implied by this use of the definite article? (4.8.b and 10.1)

3. [καὶ] μὴ θαυμάζετε, ἀδελφοί, εἰ μισεῖ ὑμᾶς ὁ κόσμος. (1 John 3:13)

    a. How can you be sure that θαυμάζετε is an imperative mood verb rather than an indicative mood verb in this sentence? Why is this a problem? (25.4) How is the imperative mood verb θαυμάζετε used in this sentence? (25.3.2)

    b. How can you be sure that μισεῖ is indicative in mood? (28.1, 26.5, and 28.1) Explain the unusual accent of μισεῖ. (26.4.c.1)

    c. Is the noun κόσμος definite or indefinite? How can you be sure? (30.3 and 5)

4. ἡμεῖς οἴδαμεν ὅτι μεταβεβήκαμεν ἐκ τοῦ θανάτου εἰς τὴν ζωήν, ὅτι ἀγαπῶμεν τοὺς ἀδελφούς· ὁ μὴ ἀγαπῶν μένει ἐν τῷ θανάτῳ. (1 John 3:14)

a. Is the presence of ἡμεῖς necessary in this sentence? Why or why not? What is the significance of ἡμεῖς in this sentence? (9.1, 9.2 and 9.3.b)

b. Dissect and parse μεταβεβήκαμεν. (3.1 and 23.2)

PART OF SPEECH: REDUPLICATION: STEM:

TENSE: PERSON: TENSE SIGN:

VOICE: NUMBER: ENDING:

MOOD: LEXICAL FORM: SUBJECT:

c. Is ἀγαπῶμεν present active indicative or subjunctive? How can you be sure? (13.3.a, 24.3.b.1, 24.3.c.1, and 28.1)

5. πᾶς ὁ μισῶν τὸν ἀδελφὸν αὐτοῦ ἀνθρωποκτόνος ἐστίν, καὶ οἴδατε ὅτι πᾶς ἀνθρωποκτόνος οὐκ ἔχει ζωὴν αἰώιον ἐν αὐτῷ μένουσαν. (1 John 3:15)

a. How is πᾶς properly translated in this sentence? Why? (28.1 and 28.2.a.4)

b. Why is οὐκ used to negate ἔχει rather than οὐ? (9.1) Why not use μή to negate ἔχει? (21.1)

c. Explain how αἰώιον modifies ζωὴν and αἰώιον appears as nominative singular masculine and ζωὴν appears as nominative singular feminine. (5.4.a.3, 7.1, and 21.1)

This adjectival form can be located as either accusative singular masculine or accusative singular feminine.

6. ἐν τούτῳ ἐγνώκαμεν τὴν ἀγάπην, ὅτι ἐκεῖνος ὑπὲρ ἡμῶν τὴν ψυχὴν αὐτοῦ ἔθηκεν· καὶ ἡμεῖς ὀφείλομεν ὑπὲρ τῶν ἀδελφῶν τὰς ψυχὰς θεῖναι. (1 John 3:16)

a. Explain why the definite article τὴν is not translated in the phrase τὴν ἀγάπην. (30.3) What is the significance of the presence of τὴν in the phrase τὴν ἀγάπην? (30.2)

b. Is ἔθηκεν an -ω conjugation verb or a -μι conjugation verb? (29.1) How can you identify ἔθηκεν as a first aorist verb of this conjugation? (29.2.d)

c. Is θεῖναι an infinitive used as a verb or a noun? What is the significance of this use? (29.1 and 31.4.a)

7. ὃς δ' ἂν ἔχῃ τὸν βίον τοῦ κόσμου καὶ θεωρῇ τὸν ἀδελφὸν αὐτοῦ χρείαν ἔχοντα καὶ κλείσῃ τὰ σπλάγχνα αὐτοῦ ἀπ' αὐτοῦ, πῶς ἡ ἀγάπη τοῦ θεοῦ μένει ἐν αὐτῷ; (1 John 3:17)

a. Dissect and parse ἔχοντα. (2.1 and 20.2)

PART OF SPEECH:	TENSE:	CASE:
STEM:	VOICE:	NUMBER:
LEXICAL FORM:	VERBAL FORM:	GENDER:
CONNECTING VOWEL:	PART. SIGN:	ENDING:

b. What is the significance of the mood of κλείσῃ? (24.4.a)

c. What part of speech is πῶς? (20.1, 28.4, and 28.5) What idea does this word express? (28.4)

8. Τεκνία, μὴ ἀγαπῶμεν λόγῳ μηδὲ τῇ γλώσσῃ ἀλλὰ ἐν ἔργῳ καὶ ἀληθείᾳ. (1 John 3:18)

a. What use of the subjunctive is ἀγαπῶμεν? What is the significance of this use? (24.4.c.1)

b. What type of conjunction is ἀλλὰ? What is the significance of this type of conjunction? (13.3.a)

c. How can you determine the gender of ἔργῳ since it could be either masculine or neuter? (4.6, 4.8.b, and 10.1) How would the definite article help in identifying the gender of ἔργῳ? (4.3 and 4.4)

The Greek Alphabet and its Pronunciation:

Capital Letters	Small Letters	Letter Name	Erasmian Pronunciation	Modern Pronunciation
A	α	Alpha	**a** as in f<u>a</u>ther (long) **a** as in c<u>a</u>t (short)	**ah**
B	β	Beta	**b** as in <u>b</u>all	**v**
Γ	γ	Gamma	**g** as in <u>g</u>ift	**gh**, but **y** as in <u>y</u>et preceding "eh" and "ee" sounds
Δ	δ	Delta	**d** as in <u>d</u>ebt	soft **th** as in "the"
E	ε	Epsilon	**e** as in m<u>e</u>t	**eh**
Z	ζ	Zeta	**dz** as in <u>z</u>ion	**z**
H	η	Eta	**e** as in ob<u>e</u>y	**ee**
Θ	θ	Theta	**th** as in <u>th</u>eme	hard **th** as in "think"
I	ι	Iota	**i** as in magaz<u>i</u>ne (long i) **i** as in p<u>i</u>t (short)	**ee**
K	κ	Kappa	**k** as in <u>k</u>it	**k**
Λ	λ	Lambda	**l** as in <u>l</u>ong	**l**
M	μ	Mu	**m** as in <u>m</u>an	**m**
N	ν	Nu	**n** as in <u>n</u>o	**n**
Ξ	ξ	Xi	**x** as in rela<u>x</u>	**x**
O	ο	Omicron	**o** as in <u>o</u>melet	**oh**
Π	π	Pi	**p** as in <u>p</u>ay	**p**
P	ρ	Rho	**r** as in <u>r</u>ing	**r**
Σ	σ (ς)	Sigma	**s** as in <u>s</u>ing	**s**
T	τ	Tau	**t** as in <u>t</u>ale	**t**
Υ	υ	Upsilon	**u** as in t<u>u</u>be	**ee** except in diphthongs
Φ	φ	Phi	**ph** as in <u>ph</u>onetics	**ph**
X	χ	Chi	**ch** as in <u>ch</u>emical	**kh**
Ψ	ψ	Psi	**ps** as in ta<u>ps</u>	**ps**
Ω	ω	Omega	**o** as in t<u>o</u>ne	**oh**

Diphthongs

αι	**ai** in <u>ai</u>sle	**eh** as in "bet"
ει	**ei** in h<u>ei</u>ght (long a sound)	**ee** as in "bee"
οι	**oi** in <u>oi</u>l	**ee** as in "bee"
αυ	**au** in kr<u>au</u>t	**ahu** preceding vowels and β, γ, δ, ζ, λ, μ, ν, ρ, and σ; otherwise "auf"
ευ	**eu** in f<u>eu</u>d	**ehv** preceding vowels and β, γ, δ, ζ, λ, μ, ν, ρ, and σ; otherwise "euf"
ου	**ou** in gr<u>ou</u>p	**oo** sound oo as in "boo"
υι	**wee** in s<u>ui</u>te	**ee** + "y" as in "yet"

Improper Diphthongs

ηυ	**eu** in f<u>eu</u>d	**eehv** unless this diphhong precedes θ, κ, ξ, π, σ, τ, φ, χ, ορ ψ. Τη∈ν ιτ ισ pronounced "if."
ωυ	**ou**	**ou** as in soup

Double Consonants

γγ	**ng** as in a<u>ng</u>el	**ng** as in a<u>ng</u>el
γκ	**ng** as in a<u>ng</u>el	**ngk** as in <u>ink</u>
γχ	**ng** as in a<u>ng</u>el	**ngkh** as in a<u>nch</u>or
μπ	**mp** as in sa<u>mp</u>le	**b** as in boy
ντ	**nt** as in sile<u>nt</u>	**d** as in dog
τζ	**tz** as in sa<u>tz</u>	**dz** this is used frequently in modern Greek to transliterate the English "j" and soft "g."

Modern Greek has no rough breathing; however, the symbol for it has been been retained.

The rules of accent are not affected by whether one uses Erasmian or Modern pronunciation. There is no difference between the pronunciation of an acute/grave or a circumflex accent.

Appendix B

The purpose of this answer key is to assist the student in the translation of the exercises of Sawyer. The student should attempt translating each of the sentences on his own and then, use this key to check accuracy in the translation. When scriptures are used in the exercises, consult the NIV in order to check the accuracy of your translation. (Many of these scriptures in the exercises are only partial verses.)

LESSON 1

1.6.d

1. Ioannes 2. Petros 3. Philippos 4. Gabriel 5. Paulos 6. Timotheos 7. Titos 8. Iakobos

LESSON 2

2.a

lu-eis, lo-ou-si(n), lam-ba-no-min, phe-rō, tau-ta, er-cho-me-tha, tha-na-tos, dō-ron, hi-e-rou, ei-rē-nē, hē-me-rōn, hui-os, ē-ga-gon, an-ge-li-a, ha-gi-os, ka-tha-ri-zō, poi-ou-men, pseu-do-mai

2.b

ἄγω	ἄ-γω	a-gō
ἀκούω	ἀ-κού-ω	a-kou-ō
βλέπω	βλέ-πω	ble-pō
ἔχω	ἔ-χω	e-chō
λύω	λύ-ω	lu-ō
ἄγγελος	ἄγ-γε-λος	an-ge-los
ἀδελφός	ἀ-δελ-φός	a-del-phos
δοῦλος	δοῦ-λος	dou-los
καρπός	καρ-πός	karpos
λογός	λο-γός	lo-gos

LESSON 3

3.a

1. he/she/it leads (is leading), he/she/it hears (is hearing), he/she/it sees (is seeing), he/she/it has

(is having).* 2. we are raising up, we know, we are writing, we take/receive. 3. they see, they are taking/are receiving, they are saying/are speaking, they send. 4. you (sg.) bear/bring, you (pl.) are bearing/are bringing, we are leading, they hear. 5. he/she/it is writing, he/she/it knows, they are teaching, you (sg.) are saying/are speaking, you (pl.) wish/will.

*The present active indicative verb λύω is correctly translated "I loose" or "I am loosing." The major difference between these two translations is that the latter emphasizes continuation. The alternate verb translation of the present active indicative and present middle-deponent verb forms is possible throughout these exercises. In some cases the alternate translation will not make sense due to context. From this point on only one of the translations of the verb will be offered in this translation key; however, the alternate translation may be appropriate.

3.b

1. present active indicative second singular of γινώσκω: **you know.** 2. present active indicative first plural of ἔχω: **we have.** 3. present active indicative third plural of ἄγω: **they are leading.** 4. present active indicative third singular of πέμπω: **he/she/it sends.** 5. present active indicative third singular of ἐγείρω: **he/she/it raises up.** 6. present active indicative first plural of ἀκούω: **we hear.** 7. present active indicative second plural of ἔχω: **you have.** 8. present active indicative third plural of φέρω: **they are bearing/bringing.** 9. present active indicative first singular of ἀκούω: **I hear.** 10. present active indicative second singular of διδάσκω: **you are teaching.**

LESSON 4

1. The man knows the law. 2. The servant/slave is bearing/is bringing a gift. 3. The apostle is saying/is speaking a word. 4. You (sg.) have the fruit. 5. The brothers are hearing the words of the angel. 6. You (pl.) are sending gifts to the temple. 7. We see the houses of the brothers. 8. The sons of the men are leading the servants/slaves. 9. I am receiving gifts of fruit and bread. (The English word "fruit" can be either singular or plural. The use in this sentence is plural.) 10. We are writing to the brothers. 11. I see the Lord in the house. 12. The apostles know the law and are teaching the men. 13. The men see the apostles in the temple and in the house. 14. The angel is speaking words of death to the men and to the sons. 15. The crowd wishes to see the Lord. 16. The sons are bringing stones to the house.

LESSON 5

1. The apostle is teaching a parable to the men. 2. The disciple sees the prophet in the church. 3. The sons of the men know love and truth and the scriptures. 4. (1 Corinthians 13:1) 5. The prophet is teaching peace and truth. 6. The disciple knows sin and says words of the kingdom. 7. The apostle writes from the house to the church. 8. The sons know the commandment and are saying a parable in the house. 9. They wish to speak the truth of the commandment. 10. The

angel sees the Lord and knows the day of peace. 11. You (pl.) hear the teaching/doctrine of the disciple and you (pl.) know the glory of the kingdom. 12. The prophets are saying words of truth to the crowds of men. 13. You (sg.) are leading the sons and are saying a parable from the Scriptures. 14. The disciples of the prophets know the commandments of the Lord. 15. The son of man has the authority to forgive sins. (Mark 2:10) 16. The Lord is teaching the church by love.

LESSON 6

1. The beloved disciple hears the good words. 2. She is leading the only son into the small house. 3. (Revelation 4:8) 4. Sin (is) bad and the kingdom (is) good. 5. We see the bad fruit and the good bread. 6. (1 John 2:7) 7. The prophets are saying new words of truth to the faithful. 8. The apostle knows the righteous (men) and the righteous (women). 9. (Ephesians 5:16) 10. God is raising the dead in the last days. 11. (1 Corinthians 10:13) 12. The son of man has righteousness to bear the truth to the men. 13. The brother (is) good and he teaches the faithful ones (men, people) in the church. 14. The righteous disciple writes another parable to the whole church. 15. The other man has the only good son. 16. The teaching (is) faithful and the law (is) righteous. 17. (1 Corinthians 14:25) 18. The bad men are speaking another gospel.

LESSON 7

1. The brothers are first and the servants are last. 2. We know the parables of the kingdom and the teachings of the churches. 3. The disciples are writing scriptures of love, peace, and truth to the men. 4. (1 Corinthians 11:3) 5. He is destroying churches with evil words. 6. The prophets are leading the men, and he is about to speak words of the kingdom of God. 7. (Romans 14:17) 8. They are receiving bread and fruits and are bringing gifts to the crowds. 9. God is sending apostles to the Jews and He is judging the whole world. 10. (John 14:6) 11. Men are destroying the good churches and the new houses. 12. He is teaching the scriptures to the people and they are finding the truth. (Note that the antecedent of the implied subject of εὑρίσκει is the nominative singular form of the dative singular noun λαῷ.) 13. We gather together to baptize in the church. 14. The elders are leading the sinners to the truth. 15. The Lord sends the disciples to the world to speak to the people. 16. The people are gathering/gather together to rejoice in the temple. 17. (1 John 2:8) 18. (1 John 4:16)

LESSON 8

1. The apostle is teaching in the church. 2. The disciple says a parable about/concerning the kingdom. 3. They are bringing bread with fruits out of the house and to the men. (The English word "fruit" can be either singular or plural. The use in this sentence is plural.) 4. (1 Corinthians, 15:3) 5. We are receiving the good teachings from the faithful brother. 6. (Romans 5:1) 7. We know the truth through the writings of the disciples. 8. The brother sends the disciples out of the houses and into the church. 9. The Lord says a parable by words of truth of love. 10.

(Matthew 4:4) 11. The faithful prophets are leading the righteous disciples of the Lord to the temple. 12. The man says a good word to the disciple and he is leading the sons into the house. 13. (Mark 2:28) 14. We are taking/are receiving good fruit instead of bad fruit. 15. From the temple, through the house, to the church, the man is leading the sons. 16. (1 John 3:8) 17. We hear words of love from the faithful messenger. 18. He is speaking the truth in love and is leading the sons into the kingdom of peace. 19. (Matthew 10:24) 20. Christ is bringing love from God to the sons of men.

LESSON 9

1. Your disciples are teaching the church and are leading their brothers to it. 2. (James 5:14) 3. I teach my sons and we are glorifying God. 4. Through you God leads the children into his kingdom and through them the others. 5. (3 John 1) 6. I (with emphasis) am a servant, but you are a disciple. 7. (1 Corinthians 1:12) 8. You (pl.) are prophets of God and messengers of love. 9. The Lord is faithful, but the crowds are evil. 10. My brother is going up to the house and I am teaching him. 11. (Mark 8:29) 12. We know the way, and we are leading you into the church. 13. Jesus said to them, I (with emphasis) am the fruit of life. (John 6:35) 14. (Matthew 16:18) 15. My brothers are in the crowd and they are eating bread. 16. The disciples of the Lord are leading their children into his kingdom. 17. (Romans 8:16) 18. He himself is bringing my gifts and his gifts to the temple. 19. (John 1:20) 20. (John 5:24)

LESSON 10

1. (John 10:3) 2. He sins in his heart and does not know joy. 3. We hear this parable concerning the church. 4. We are leading these sinners and those children into the same place . 5. This man hears the good news/gospel of his Lord and is proclaiming it to the people. 6. This is a man of the world, but that is a man of the kingdom of Christ. 7. The Lord himself is saying words of joy and I myself am receiving them into my heart. 8. Those messengers are the disciples of the same teacher and they are preaching concerning the children. 9. (John 16:30) 10. Christ is Lord of the world and he brings love and joy and peace to it. 11. (Matthew 3:17) 12. (Matthew 7:12) 13. You are sinners, and your brother opens the way of joy and peace to you. 14. He himself is going up to the temple because he has sin in his heart. 15. That (man) knows peace and joy, but this (man) knows sin because he does not hear the gospel of God. 16. (Ephesians 5:23) 17. (Galatians 3:10) 18. He is throwing his clothing on the stone. 19. (2 John 6) 20. (Romans 6:14)

LESSON 11

1. (Matthew 12:45) 2. The truth is being taught by the words of the apostle. 3. The faithful brother is being saved through the disciple of the Lord. 4. (Romans 10:10) 5. The son of God proclaims love and truth. 6. They began to throw stones at the sinners. 7. A voice is being heard in the desert and a way is being seen into heaven. 8. (Luke 8:13) 9. The good prophet is going

away from the house. 10. God knows the hearts of the men and he is sending words of life. 11. (1 Corinthians 15:29) 12. (John 13:38) 13. The crowds hear the good (things) of the kingdom of God and are being saved from the world. 14. (1 Corinthians 16:4) 15. The disciples are teaching one another the word of truth. 16. She judges herself by the parable of the prophet. 17. A parable of the kingdom of heaven is being taught by the faithful apostle. 18. The teacher goes to the people in the house. 19. Men of the world glorify one another: righteous men glorify God. 20. (1 Corinthians 15:1-2)

LESSON 12

The translation of μὲν . . . δὲ is optional and does not affect the meaning of the sentence. The translation of μὲν only emphasizes transition. For the sake of illustration, μὲν will be translated in brackets in these exercises.

1. Then we were hearing his voice, but now we no longer hear it. 2. (On the one hand) those sinners remain in darkness, but these (sinners) are going into the kingdom of God. 3. (Mark 14:49) 4. In those days the Lord was healing the crowds and was saving them from their sins. 5. Evil men were preparing their hearts because they were hearing the Scriptures and were believing them. 6. (John 2:25) 7. Because of the love of God we are entering into the kingdom of God, and we are receiving life with His Son. 8. (Acts 3:1) 9. When you (pl.) were evil, you (pl.) did not know Christ. 10. (Matthew 2:11) 11. Then the Lord was teaching us, but now we are teaching the church. 12. (1 Corinthians 11:18) 13. The evil men were killing the prophets and they remain in darkness. 14. (John 1:10) 15. (Mark 1:4) 16. They are still in their sins because they do not enter into the kingdom of God. 17. (John 4:2) 18. The apostles were preparing their hearts and were proclaiming the gospel to the people. 19. (1 Corinthians 10:26) 20. (Galatians 6:16)

LESSON 13

1. (Matthew 24:1) 2. Both the words and the teachings of the prophets were being heard by the sinners. 3. In those days we were neither being taught by him nor were we teaching the others. 4. (Mark 1:5) 5. Good gifts were being brought to the good brothers. 6. They see the Lord in His glory, but they were being taught by Him even in the bad days. 7. (Mark 2:13) 8. The disciples were going down to the sea and we were entering into the boat with the Lord. 9. (John 12:39) 10. Jesus was casting the demons out of the sinners and He was cleansing them from their sins. 11. (Mark 3:7) 12. Because of the word of the Lord the demons went out of the sinners. 13. Neither were you (pl.) receiving the truth from us nor were you (pl.) saying it to others. 14. (Mark 1:12) 15. They know the books of the men, but they also know the scriptures of God. 16. (Romans 14:8) 17. (Matthew 3:6) 18. (Matthew 21:25) 19. (1 Corinthians 3:2) 20. (Mark 1:23)

LESSON 14

1. Christ will lead His disciples into the way of love. 2. In that day the Messiah will come with His angels. 3. (2 Corinthians 13:11) 4. (On the one hand) you (pl.) were dead in your sins, but you will become sons of God. 5. Then they will know that He (with emphasis) is the Lord. 6. You (pl.) will receive both the gifts and the houses. 7. (John 5:25) 8. (Matthew 13:41) 9. Not even will I know these things. 10. The bad days will come. 11. (Matthew 1:21) 12. The disciples will hear the voice of their Lord and they will lead their children to Him. 13. (John 16:14) 14. We will be with him in his kingdom. 15. You (sg.) are evil, but you (sg.) will be good. 16. (Luke 17:21) 17. They will lead the sinners and the children into the same church. 18. The voice of the prophet will prepare a way in the hearts of men. 19. (Romans 8:13) 20. He will go down into the places of sins and he will persuade men to go down with him.

LESSON 15

1. The disciple loosed his boat. 2. We sent the children out of the house. 3. (John 18:20) 4. The disciples glorified God and His son. 5. (Matthew 27:20) 6. Because of your words we saw the evil way of the world. 7. You preached the gospel and your (sg.) sons heard it and believed. 8. (Matthew 15:31) 9. He wrote a parable and sent it to the church. 10. (Matthew 4:17) 11. (John 14:3) 12. I (with emphasis) taught you (pl.), but you (pl.) did not receive me into your (pl.) house. 13. (Mark 9:17) 14. You (pl.) heard those commandments in the temple, but you (pl.) hear others in the church. 15. (Matthew 27:42) 16. We preached/proclaimed the gospel/good news to them and we baptized their sons. 17. You (pl.) heard the same parables and believed the same Christ. 18. (Acts 11:1) 19. These good women glorified God because He healed their brothers and saved their sons. 20. (Acts 8:35)

LESSON 16

1. He received the gospel from Christ, and he is proclaiming it in the world. 2. (John 1:14) 3. Christ cast the demons out of the people and he healed them. 4. We both saw the Lord and heard His words. 5. (Colossians 1:18) 6. The apostles saw the son of God, for he himself became a man and remained in the world. 7. (Matthew 22:1) 8. You (pl.) said these things to us in the temple, but (you said) those things (to us) in the house. 9. (Luke 17:16) 10. You (sg.) neither entered into the church, nor did you (sg.) say words of love to the children. 11. The faithful (women) left the temple, and went down into their houses. 12. (1 Peter 2:21) 13. The man led the children to the Lord because he had the love of God in his heart. 14. (John 1:11) 15. The righteous (men, people) ate bread in the desert and they glorified God. 16. (Romans 5:8) 17. (John 17:25) 18. The sinners had houses, but they left them because the voice of the Lord was heard in the church. 19. (John 16:4) 20. The children said bad words because they heard them from the evil men.

LESSON 17

1. (John 12:30) 2. In that day the dead will be raised by the word of God. 3. These things were written in the Scriptures. 4. These sinners were gathered into the house of the prophet. 5. (Mark 16:6) 6. Now (on the one hand the teachers are being sent, but then both the apostles and the disciples were sent. 7. Through the love of Christ the sinners were saved and (they) became disciples of the Lord. 8. (John 3:10) 9. We went into another place, for those (people) did not receive us. 10. The gospel was preached in those days, and it will be preached even now. 11. (John 13:31) 12. The voice was heard and the apostle was sent into the world. 13. 1 Timothy 1:15) 14. You (sg.) entered into the church of the Lord and were baptized. 15. In those days the word of peace was heard. 16. (1 Timothy 1:11) 17. The evil (men) were saved because they were taught the way of Christ. 18. (Revelation 20:12) 19. You (sg.) became a disciple of the Lord because his love was known to you (sg.). 20. Revelation 20:10)

LESSON 18

1. We do not have hope because we do not know the Lord. 2. (1 Corinthians 7:4) 3. The faithful disciples preached the gospel by the night and by the day. 4. (Revelation 1:17) 5. (2 Corinthians 5:16) 6. (John 13:30) 7. (John 1:17) 8. This is the message of the truth: God is good and his sons remain in him for ever and for ever. 9. (John 1:1) 10. The Lord is teaching that God is the Father of good men. 11. (John 2:1) 12. God is the ruler of His kingdom. 13. (John 12:34) 14. (Titus 1:4) 15. (John 8:35) 16. (1 Corinthians 11:12) 17. Through the death of the son we see the love of the Father. 18. (John 11:32) 19. The message of the church bears love, truth, grace, and hope. 20. (Hebrews 1:10)

LESSON 19

1. (John 3:1-2) 2. The disciples of the Lord ate bread and fish and wheat in the city. 3. Christ preached the gospel to the crowds, and the chief priests were sending (their) servants to hear him. 4. (Matthew 3:11) 5. God has the power to judge in the world and in heaven. 6. The priests know the law, but they do not remain in the will of God. 7. (Mark 9:29) 8. (Matthew 26:26) 9. We know both the will and the love of God. 10. (Luke 1:33) 11. We have hope of life in the name of the Holy Spirit. 12. 1 John 1:7) 13. The evil (people) remain in the darkness of sin, but the faithful (people) hear the words of the Lord and are becoming good disciples. 14. (1 Corinthians 13:11) 15. (Luke 10:24) 16. You (pl.) will receive power from God and you (pl.) will be his disciples. 17. (Ephesians 2:8) 18. (Mark 11:27) 19. (Galatians 1:3) 20. (2 Peter 2:18)

LESSON 20

1. (Luke 24:26) 2. (I/they) said these things to the ones who were entering into the boat. 3. While he was entering into the church he was saying the parable to you. 4. (Matthew 16:23) 5.

The churches which are being destroyed by the evil ruler are being glorified by the Lord. 6. The ones who are receiving the grace of God are being saved. 7. (1 John 2:1) 8. We are teaching the things which are written in the book of life. 9. This is the Lord who saves you (pl.) and who cleanses you (pl.) from your (pl.) sins. 10. (John 1:4) 11. The one who says that he has fellowship with God but remains in the darkness of sin is a liar. 12. (1 John 1:5) 13. They were in the house which was being destroyed. 14. With his eyes the apostle saw the hands of the Lord after the resurrection. 15. (John 8:44) 16. They who are sons of God ought to remain in His word. 17. We saw the apostle while he was in the church. 18. (Acts 13:48) 19. The evil men lie until that day when the Lord comes. 20. (Luke 1:34)

LESSON 21

1. When he went out of the house he said these things. 2. The (women) who received the apostles who were being persecuted are faithful. 3. He who had not seen the Lord did not believe in him. 4. While the Lord was still on the road he said these (things) to those who had come out of the house and were walking with him to the church. 5. We preach concerning the one who saved us and cleansed us from our sins. 6. (John 6:50) 7. After the disciples had gathered together they glorified the name of the eternal God. 8. (1 Thessalonians 5:5) 9. These are the ones who preached the gospel of love of love, but those are the ones who persecuted the ones who were believing it. 10. After they had not received a sign from Jesus, the crowds went into the city. 11. (John 3:5) 12. (Romans 10:8) 13. (Mark 12:35) 14. (2 Corinthians 8:21) 15. (Revelation 21:2) 16. (John 6:3) 17. (Ephesians 3:1) 18. (Luke 3:8) 19. (Luke 4:38) 20. (Ephesians 4:27)

LESSON 22

1. (1 Thessalonians 5:1) 2. After the disciples had entered into the boat, the Lord went out to the mountain. 3. (Matthew 28:19) 4. Jesus came and taught in (the) middle of the crowds. 5. (Matthew 17:4) 6. This is the salvation which was preached in the world by the ones who saw Jesus. 7. (John 5:24) 8. After the Holy Spirit had come upon them they received power. 9. (Matthew 5:3) 10. When he said these things while they were looking he was taken up from their eyes into heaven. 11. (Matthew 17:14) 12. Blessed is the one who saw the salvation of God in the midst of His people. 13. (Matthew 5:8) 14. (Acts 3:1) 15. (John 5:18) 16. (Mark 3:1) 17. (Luke 2:29) 18. (1 Corinthians 16:19) 19. ((Ephesians 2:3) 20. While he said these things, they saw the truth of the love of God.

LESSON 23

1. (1 Corinthians 15:16) 2. (John 6:17) 3. (Luke 24:46) 4. (John 11:27) 5. We have heard the truth and we have known that he is from God. 6. (John 5:43) 7. You (pl.) have become children of God. 8. (Mark 1:14-15) 9. Jesus said these things to the (ones) who had believed on him. 10. (Mark 13:32) 11. The disciples who have been baptized are in the church. 12. (1 John 4:3) 13.

(Matthew 4:4) 14. The ones who have come out of the darkness into the light have known that God is love. 15. (2 Corinthians 11:7) 16. (Revelation 19:16) 17. (1 Thessalonians 1:8) 18. (Matthew 22:29) 19. (Matthew 16:19) 20. (Ephesians 2:5)

LESSON 24

1. (2 Thessalonians 3:1) 2. (James 2:17) 3. (John 11:16) 4. (Matthew 5:20) 5. (1 John 1:6) 6. (Mark 4:26) 7. (John 14:3) 8. The ones who do not believe the gospel will by no means be saved by its power. 9. (Matthew 5:17) 10. If you (sg.) preached the gospel, the sinners believed. 11. (1 John 3:23) 12. Let us go into the church in order that we might hear the word of God which was being preached. 13. (John 8:42) 14. (1 John 5:13) 15. (1 Corinthians 12:13) 16. (Hebrews 13:12) 17. (Romans 10:4) 18. (1 Corinthians 10:21) 19. (John 8:21) 20. (1 John 5:11)

LESSON 25

1. (Mark 4:9) 2. (Luke 1:20) 3. (Matthew 3:17) 4. (Galatians 1:8) 5. Drink the water of life and eat the bread of life. 6. (John 17:19) 7. If the man believes in Christ, let him be baptized. 8. (Galatians 6:7) 9. (Matthew 16:16) 10. (John 3:22) 11. (Roman 14:3) 12. (John 20:27) 13. (John 6:53) 14. (Luke 16:29) 15. (Matthew 10:7) 16. (Mark 11:22) 17. (2 Timothy 2:8) 18. (Luke 12:20) 19. (Jude 14) 20. (Philemon 6)

LESSON 26

26.a

1. (Luke 6:46) 2. (John 7:1) 3. (John 5:25) 4. (Revelation 9:6)

26.b

1 John 1:1-7

LESSON 27

1 John 1:8-2:6

LESSON 28

1 John 2:7-17

LESSON 29

1 John 2:18-27

LESSON 30

1 John 2:28-3:10

LESSON 31

1 John 3:11-18

Selected Bibliography

Aland, Kurt, and Barbara Aland. *The Text of the New Testament: An Introduction to the Theory and Practice of Modern Textual Criticism*. Translated by Erroll F. Rhodes. Grand Rapids: Eerdmans, 1987.

_____, Johannes Karavidopoulos, Carlos M. Martini, and Bruce Metzger, eds. *The Greek New Testament*. 4th ed. London: United Bible Society, 1993.

Bauer, Walter. *A Greek-English Lexicon of the New Testament and Other Early Christian Literature*. Translated and edited by W.F. Arndt and F.W. Gingrich. Chicago: University of Chicago Press, 1957.

Blass, Friedrich W., and A. Debrunner. *A Greek Grammar of the New Testament and Other Early Christian Literature: A Translation and Revision of the Ninth-Tenth German Edition Incorporating Supplementary Notes of A. Debrunner*. Translated by Robert W. Funk. Chicago: University of Chicago Press, 1961.

Brooks, James A., and Carlton L. Winbery. *Syntax of New Testament Greek*. Washington, D.C.: University Press of America, 1979.

Chamberlain, William Douglas. *An Exegetical Grammar of the Greek New Testament*. Grand Rapids: Baker 1987.

Dana, H. E., and Julius Mantey. *A Manual Grammar of the Greek New Testament*. New York: Macmillen, 1957.

Davies, William. *Beginner's Grammar of the Greek New Testament*. New York: Harper & Row, 1923.

Easley, Kendell H. *User Friendly Greek: A Common Sense Approach to the Greek New Testament*. Nashville: Broadman & Holman, 1994.

Fee, Gordon D. *New Testament Exegesis: A Handbook for Students and Pastors*. Philadelphia: Westminster, 1993.

Kittel, Gerhard, et al., ed. *Theological Dictionary of the New Testament*. 10 vols. Translated by Geoffrey W. Bromiley. Grand Rapids: Eerdmans, 1974.

Liddell, H. G., and Scott. *An Intermediate Greek-English Lexicon: Founded Upon the Seventh Edition of Liddell and Scott's Greek English Lexicon*. Oxford: Clarendon, 1987.

Louw, Johannes P., and Eugene Nida, eds. *Greek-English Lexicon of the New Testament Based on Semantic Domains*. 2 vols. 2d ed. New York: United Bible Societies, 1989.

Machen, J. Gresham. *New Testament Greek for Beginners*. New York: Macmillan, 1959.

Metzger, Bruce M. *Lexical Aids For Students of New Testament Greek*. Princeton, NJ: Theological Book Agency, 1989.

_____. *The Text of the New Testament: Its Transmission, Corruption, and Restoration*. New York and Oxford: Oxford, 1968.

Moulton, Harold K. *The Analytical Greek Lexicon, Revised*. Grand Rapids: Zondervan, 1980.

Robertson, A. T. *A Grammar of the Greek New Testament in Light of Historical Research*. New York: Hodder and Stoughton, 1915.

_____, and W. Hersey Davis. *A New Short Grammar of the New Testament*. 10th ed. Grand Rapids: Baker, 1982.

Soulen, Richard N. *Handbook of Biblical Criticism*. John Knox, 1978.

Summers, Ray. *Essentials of New Testament Greek*. Nashville, TN: Broadman, 1950.

_____, and Thomas Sawyer. *Essentials of New Testament Greek, Revised*. Nashville: Broadman & Holman, 1995.

Thayer, Joseph H. *Thayer's Greek-English Lexicon of the New Testament*. Grand Rapids: Baker, 1977.